Between the idea
And the reality
Between the motion
And the act
Falls the Shadow

—*T. S. ELIOT*
"The Hollow Men" (1925)

surrealist prints

surrealist prints

Edited by Gilbert Kaplan

Essays

Timothy Baum, Riva Castleman, and Robert Rainwater

Distributed by Harry N. Abrams, Inc.

New York

Published in 1997 by Atlantis

Distributed in 1997 by Harry N. Abrams, Inc., New York, A Times Mirror Company

"Collecting Surrealism in America," by Riva Castleman; "Au rendez-vous des amis: Surrealist Books and the Beginning of Surrealist Printmaking," by Robert Rainwater; "The Surrealist as Printmaker," by Timothy Baum (copyright © 1996 by Timothy Baum and the Regents of the University of California); the Plates; the Checklist; and the Bibliography in this book were originally published by the Grunwald Center for the Graphic Arts (copyright © 1996 by the Regents of the University of California) as part of the catalogue for the exhibition entitled *Visionary States: Surrealist Prints from the Gilbert Kaplan Collection*, held at UCLA at the Armand Hammer Museum of Art and Cultural Center, Los Angeles, from September 17, 1996, to January 5, 1997.

Printed and bound in the United States of America by the Stinehour Press, Lunenburg, Vermont.

Library of Congress Cataloging-in-Publication Data
Surrealist prints/edited by Gilbert Kaplan.
p. cm.
Catalog of an exhibition held at UCLA at the Armand Hammer Museum of Art and Cultural Center, Los Angeles, Sept. 17, 1996–Jan. 5, 1997.
Rev. ed. of: Visionary states. 1996
ISBN 0-8109-6339-6 (Abrams: clothbound)
1. Surrealism—Europe—Exhibitions. 2. Prints—European--Exhibitions. 3. Prints—20th century—Europe—Exhibitions. 4. Kaplan, Gilbert E.—Art collections—Exhibitions. 5. Prints--Private collections—United States—Exhibitions. I. Kaplan, Gilbert E. II. UCLA at the Armand Hammer Museum of Art and Cultural Center. III. Visionary states.
N625.6.S8S87 1997
769.94'074'79494—dc21 96-52626

Cover: Joan Miró, Untitled (from Cahiers d'Art), 1934

Contents

THE VISIONARY STATES
OF SURREALIST PRINTS

Introduction

SURREALISM WAS LAUNCHED in Paris in 1924 as a kind of shock treatment for the art world, with a goal of nothing less than "the transformation of culture and society." By presenting ordinary subjects in extraordinary settings, the surrealists stretched the imagination and revealed just how blurry the line between the real and the unreal can be. Since then, surrealism has never lost its appeal. Many of its greatest exponents—such as Salvador Dalí, René Magritte, and Joan Miró—are among the most popular artists of this century, but they are known primarily through their paintings. This book, the first-ever survey of surrealist prints, introduces remarkable images by these and twenty other artists.

Except for a few examples, all the prints reproduced here are drawn from my own collection (this book was originally conceived as a catalogue for an exhibition of that collection). This is not a limitation, as it would be for a book about paintings, where each work is unique. No single collection of paintings can include practically all the important works of a single artist or art movement. In the case of surrealist prints, however, which were produced in multiple copies, with patience—and luck—this can be accomplished.

Printmaking by the surrealists has had a rich history of more than seventy years, and three members of the group are still alive today: Leonora Carrington, Roberto Sebastián Matta Echaurren, and Dorothea Tanning. The twenty-three artists represented in this volume were born in thirteen different countries (five in France, followed by Spain with four). Five are women. Some, such as Ernst and Dalí, undertook the challenge of printmaking in their twenties, while others—Magritte and fellow Belgian Paul Delvaux—made their first prints after they had turned sixty. Dalí, Miró, and Yves Tanguy were among the most gifted printmakers of their time. Dalí was certainly the most prolific, creating almost one thousand separate editions.

The field of surrealist prints has been largely undocumented until now, as Riva Castleman points out in these pages. Timothy Baum's essay provides an illuminating history of the printmaking activities of each of the surrealists. Many of the outstanding surrealist prints were created as book illustrations, and Robert Rainwater surveys the relationships between surrealist artists and the writers and poets of the era.

The surrealists may not have achieved their ultimate goal of transforming culture and society, but the haunting images of these prints, many of which shocked the art world earlier in this century, remain fresh today and continue to challenge our senses.

GILBERT KAPLAN

Acknowledgments

THIS BOOK WAS ORIGINALLY CONCEIVED as a catalogue for an exhibition of my collection of surrealist prints at UCLA at the Armand Hammer Museum of Art and Cultural Center in Los Angeles. While as editor I take responsibility for the choice of the prints reproduced here, all other aspects of the book—including the selection of authors, topics, and designer—have been a true collaboration with Cynthia Burlingham, associate director and senior curator of UCLA's Grunwald Center for the Graphic Arts. I want to express my gratitude to her; to David Rodes, the center's director; and to Karen Mayers, assistant curator, whose research enriched this publication. I am also grateful to the Grunwald Center staff, including Claudine Dixon, Anne Bennett, Lynne Blaikie, Maureen McGee, Cindi Dale, Mitchell Browning, Patricia Capps, Paula Berry, Amy Weinstein, Marpessa Dawn Outlaw, and Stephanie Rieke.

I would also like to acknowledge the contributions of Susan Silton, for her elegant design; Karen Jacobson, who served as a superb copy editor; and my colleague Jean Ann Golding, who assisted in many aspects of the preparation of this book.

I am grateful to Deborah Wye, chief curator of the Department of Prints and Illustrated Books at the Museum of Modern Art in New York, and to her predecessor, Riva Castleman, for their counsel and to Timothy Baum, from whom I first learned about the special world of surrealist prints.

G.K.

Collecting Surrealism in America

RIVA CASTLEMAN

SINCE THEY WERE FIRST put into groups of various kinds and pasted into albums, prints have been kept as collections. Prints are essentially records of religious, political, scientific, and aesthetic information. A wide variety of attitudes and intentions have informed print collectors' choices of what to acquire; some of the more extreme examples include emotional or clinical interests in subject matter and obsessive ambitions to assemble the "complete works" of single artists. Over the centuries famous treasuries of prints by the most important artists have been gathered; they form the backbone of the great institutional holdings of Europe and the United States. In the last hundred years, as prints have been treated more as art objects than as documents, they have been assembled into collections that emulate in smaller format those of paintings. Because prints are multiples, it is possible for their collectors to amass examples of postimpressionism, German expressionism, cubism, and surrealism of a breadth and quality that would be unattainable for any private collector of paintings.

The German expressionists, who emerged at the beginning of the twentieth century, regarded their prints and paintings as interdependent creations. The great collections made of their work during the first third of this century, many of which were to be dispersed by the Nazis, often emphasized prints. A few German refugees were able to bring their collections to America, and after World

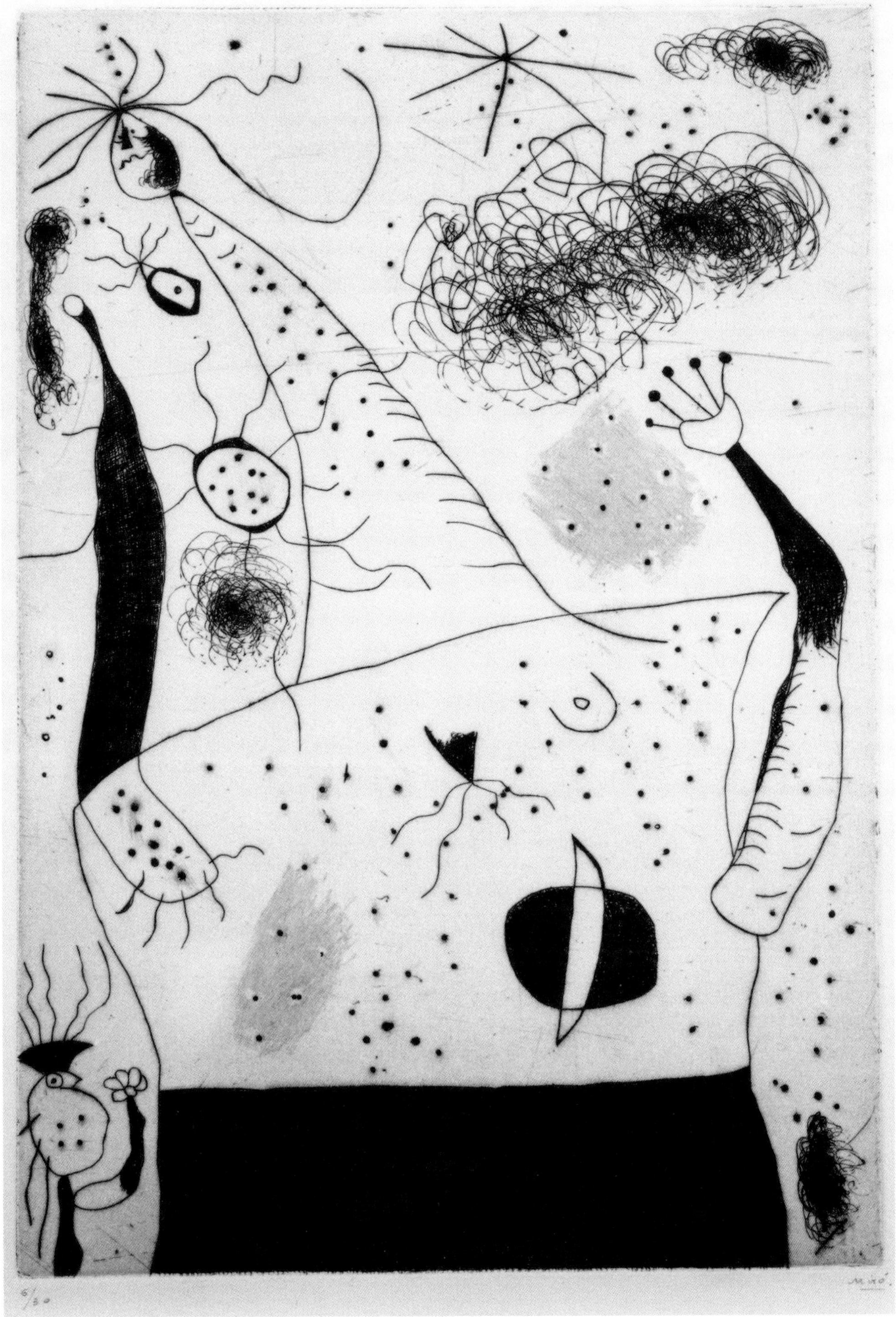

● *Fig. 1*
Joan Miró, *La Géante* (The giantess), 1938 (cat. no. 89).

War II museum exhibitions revealed to the American public the impact of the expressionist idiom in prints. This was the case with other movements as well. The one other group of artists whose unique and multiple works were similarly inextricably bound together were the surrealists, who came a generation later. Given the movement's literary inclination, it was inevitable that surrealist images were often inspired by writing and often found their place in books. Early collections of surrealism, like those of German expressionism, generally included all mediums.

The collecting of surrealism in America prior to World War II was spurred by the presence during World War I and, sporadically, the 1920s of Marcel Duchamp, whose Dada works were essential parts of surrealism's foundation. Under his guidance Katherine S. Dreier in New York and Louise and Walter C. Arensberg in California amassed his best works as well as those of the surrealists. In 1927 Duchamp introduced Julien Levy to the surrealists in Paris, and soon afterward Levy became the first American to deal in surrealist art. It was he and his Harvard schoolmate A. Everett "Chick" Austin, director of the Wadsworth Atheneum in Hartford, who organized the first exhibition of the material in 1931–32, initially at the Wadsworth Atheneum and then at Levy's gallery in New York. Many of the works acquired by James Thrall Soby, who had also contributed to the exhibition, were central loans to succeeding exhibitions, including *Fantastic Art, Dada, Surrealism*, organized by Alfred H. Barr Jr. at the Museum of Modern Art, New York, in 1936. In the meantime other American Duchamp disciples, including Mary Reynolds from Chicago and Peggy Guggenheim from New York, were actively acquiring surrealist works in Europe, which they brought to America in the 1940s.

World War II and its displacement of surrealist artists and writers to the United States further accelerated the collecting of surrealist material—whether unique paintings, sculptures, drawings, and objects or prints and books. After the war a few of the artists remained in the United States, and others continued to visit (Joan Miró worked in New York in 1947, and Salvador Dalí became a landmark to be viewed at the St. Regis Hotel in New York). Acquaintances made by the surrealists in New York were extended by American visits to Europe, particularly in the 1950s. The artists were the subjects of major exhibitions in the United States, enhancing their already well-established fame. While there were important surrealist-associated works in many collections, paintings and objects from the movement were the focus of those assembled during this period by Joseph Shapiro and Edwin Bergman in Chicago and Dominique and John de Menil in Houston.

In the late 1960s and early 1970s several significant collections of surrealist art were begun by another generation, some enthusiastic New Yorkers in their twenties who had been inspired by the Museum of Modern Art's revelatory René Magritte retrospective in 1965–66, followed by the exhibition *Dada, Surrealism, and Their Heritage* in 1968. Up to that time the prints of the surrealists were considered just part of the ephemera of collecting: individual prints ended up in portfolios alongside the books of original poetry and prose. In Paul J. Sachs's seminal book *Modern Prints and Drawings* (1954) surrealism was discussed but was illustrated solely by drawings. Even as late as 1971 in *Prints and People*, the Metropolitan Museum of Art's distinguished curator A. Hyatt Mayor did not even mention surrealism. The 1970s and 1980s, however, were decades when the prolific production of artist's prints was accompanied by widespread corporate and private collecting (very frequently directed by professional consultants) of both new and older works. Representative of the time was Charles Kramer, whose investments included several comprehensive collections, the last of which was a holding of surrealist prints now in Israel.

Of these inspired youngsters, Gilbert Kaplan has continued to collect surrealist works, emphasizing prints over other mediums. When he started to collect, he was entranced by the dreamlike aspects of the imagery, which immediately drew him to the works of Magritte. Without the support of scholarly publications on surrealist prints, Kaplan turned to Timothy Baum, a collector-turned-dealer of Dada and surrealist material, with whom he later collaborated on a catalogue raisonné of Magritte's printed oeuvre. Now, with the publication of this catalogue devoted to a sizable portion of Kaplan's extraordinary collection, the still sparse literature in this field is significantly enriched.

The intriguing prints of the surrealists are filled with haunting imagery that seems suspended in time, often executed with intense delicacy, like the web of a stealthy spider. In the compositions of Dalí, Miró, Yves Tanguy, and many others are found those very qualities that have captured the imaginations of collectors for decades and here await future conquests.

Au rendez-vous des amis: Surrealist Books and the Beginning of Surrealist Printmaking

ROBERT RAINWATER

IN DECEMBER 1922, less than six months after arriving in Paris from Cologne, Max Ernst completed a large painting he entitled *Au rendez-vous des amis* (fig. 2), a group portrait primarily of contemporary artists and poets, posed in a fantastic landscape setting.[1] Among them were three former Dada artists—Jean Arp, Johannes Theodor Baargeld, and Ernst himself—but the majority of those portrayed were from a group of past and present literary dadaists who had frequently contributed to *Littérature*, the major French Dada and proto-surrealist review: René Crevel, Philippe Soupault, Max Morise, Theodor Fraenkel, Paul Eluard, Jean Paulhan, Benjamin Péret, Louis Aragon, and, most conspicuously, André Breton. By their presence in the picture, Giorgio de Chirico and Gala Eluard were also acknowledged, the former as a crucial influence and the latter as the reigning muse. (Less easily explicable were Raphael and Dostoyevsky, on whose right knee Ernst chose to seat himself.) In the painting, which was intended for public exhibition, Ernst not only paid homage to his welcoming colleagues but also documented in a timely roll call the group that would become the founding members of the future surrealist movement. His image also seems extraordinarily prescient because surrealism would be characterized by creative alliances between artists and writers, to an extent unmatched by any other avant-garde movement of the twentieth century.

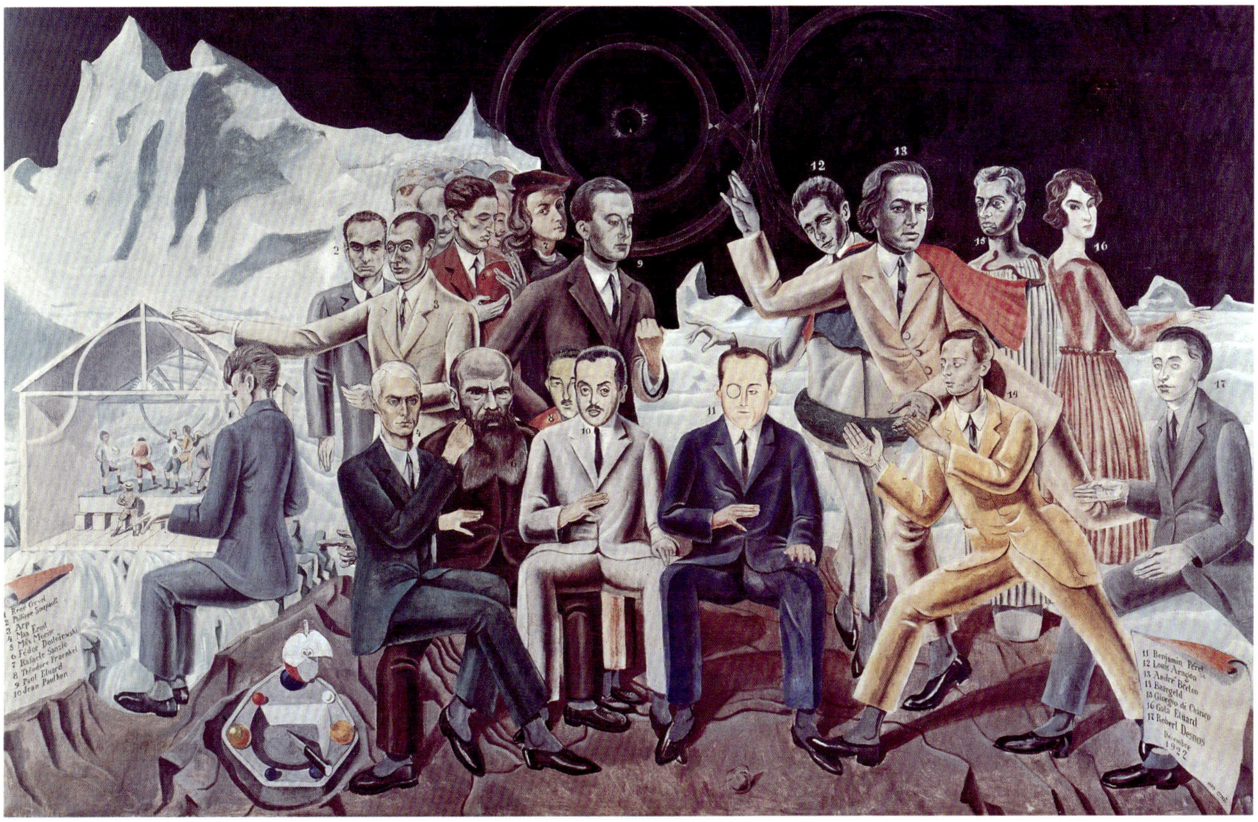

◉ *Fig. 2*
Max Ernst, *Au rendez-vous des amis* (At the rendezvous of the friends), 1922; oil on canvas; 51 x 76 in. Collection P. Bau, Hamburg, Germany.

Following a period of intensive experimentation with automatic writing techniques, the study of Freudian theories, and other joint activities undertaken by the emerging group, on October 15, 1924, Breton, as the forceful progenitor of the collective endeavor, published his first manifesto of surrealism. In it he defined surrealism as "psychic automatism in its pure state" and sanctioned the surrealist movement, whose ultimate goal was the transformation of culture and society.[2] According to Breton's formulation, this revolutionary transformation was first to take place in the mind of each individual through the exercise of hidden inner resources and through the release of potent energies from the irrational subconscious.

With his focus decidedly on literature as surrealism's most important manifestation, Breton initially assigned little importance to painting or to any other visual form of expression. Within a year and a half, however, he had published two articles entitled "Le Surréalisme et la peinture" in the movement's new, official review, *La Révolution surréaliste*, in which he advocated the kind of cursive drawing practiced by André Masson. According to Breton, this method of drawing led to the disclosure of images as a genuine parallel to the use of psychic automatism in writing. Paintings, drawings, and photographs by favored artists and photographers, regularly reproduced in *La Révolution surréaliste* and in other periodicals, serve as evidence of the intensifying associations among artists and writers. And, eager as the founding poets were to promote recognition for surrealism and for themselves, the books they published under the movement's auspices were obviously seen to gain greater significance when created in collaboration with their like-minded painter friends. Within a few years of its founding, surrealism was widely recognized, especially in the popular press, as a movement led by painters, sculptors, and photographers rather than poets.

Whether considered too tradition-bound or, as a collaborative undertaking, too intractable to allow for complete freedom of expression, printmaking was not a major pursuit among most avant-garde artists between the world wars. Most of the painters identified with the early years of surrealism were introduced to printmaking when they were commissioned to provide illustrations for a text or, more exactly, to create prints to accompany a text. Few surrealist prints were made and published as independent works of art during the first two decades of the movement, and because most of those that were produced were for books, they were relatively small in size. Although Ernst and, to a lesser extent, Masson and Joan Miró made prints using techniques that they may have regarded as equivalent to the automatic procedures they followed in the creation of drawings and paintings, technical innovation in itself was not viewed as the significant goal, whereas the exploration of an original vision emphatically was.

As a child Max Ernst displayed a precocious gift for drawing and painting. He contributed twenty-five satirical illustrations to a student publication in 1910 and made his first prints, a series of at least six small linoleum cuts, in 1911–12.[3] Most of the art from his years in the German military during World War I was lost, although a number of pencil sketches have survived. His first illustrated book, *Consolamini*, containing a selection of prewar poems written by his friend Johannes Theodor Kühlemann and reproductions of four expressionist-style ink-and-wash drawings he made in 1918, was published in 1919 in Cologne.[4]

Soon after establishing a local branch of the Dada movement with Baargeld and other artist friends in Cologne, Ernst made his first lithographs in homage to de Chirico for *Fiat modes pereat ars* (1919; see figs. 3, 50–53, cat. nos. 45–49), a portfolio of eight prints originally sponsored by an artists' collective funded by the city of Cologne. He incorporated into these simply executed lithographs elements borrowed from de Chirico—faceless dressmaker's mannequins, sharply receding planes and spaces, and stark shadows—as well as motifs inspired by the work of Francis Picabia, such as pulleys and counterweights linked to improbable instruments and machines. Also in 1919 Ernst made his first intaglio print, an untitled drypoint related in its spare composition, architectural setting, and mannequin-like figure to plates in *Fiat modes*.[5] With these prints he introduced the strikingly unconventional and unsettling qualities that would prevail in the collages and paintings he created over the next several years.

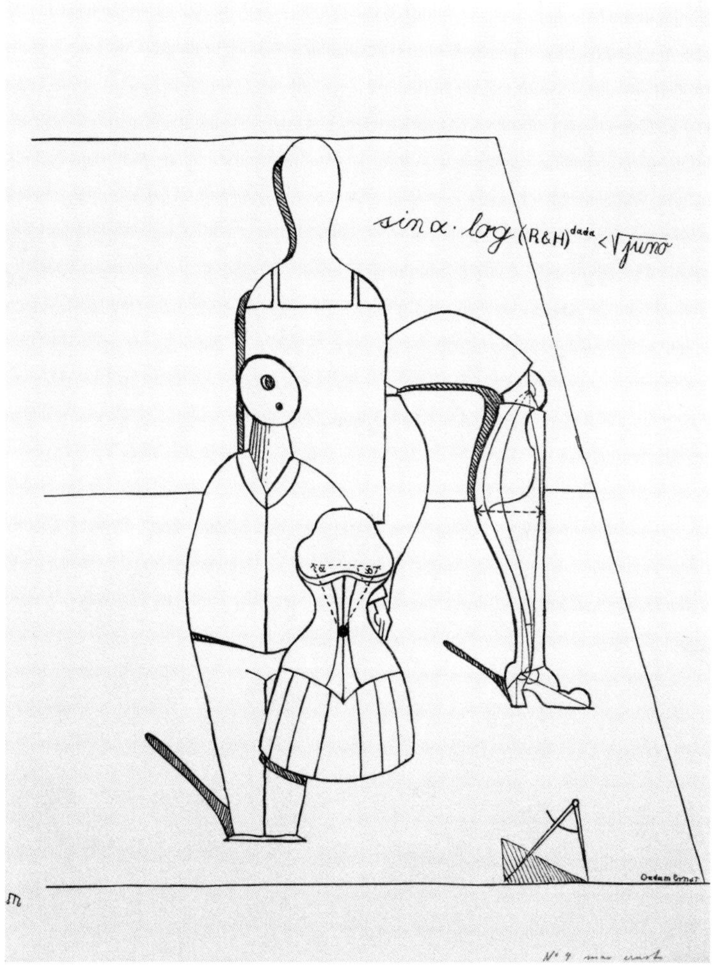

● *Fig. 3*
Max Ernst, Untitled (plate 2 from *Fiat modes pereat ars*), 1919 (cat. no. 45).

For the Spring 1920 issue of their Dada periodical, *Die Schammade*, Ernst and Baargeld solicited work from artists and writers from outside the small Cologne Dada circle. Included in the magazine were contributions from several Dada activists in Paris: Aragon, Breton, Eluard, Picabia, Georges Ribemont-Dessaignes, Soupault, and Tristan Tzara. A year later, in May 1921, at Breton's instigation, Ernst made his entrée as a dadaist in Paris by sending fifty-six collages to the Galerie Au Sans Pareil for a solo show received with great enthusiasm by Breton and the Parisian avant-garde. Although the official launch of sur-

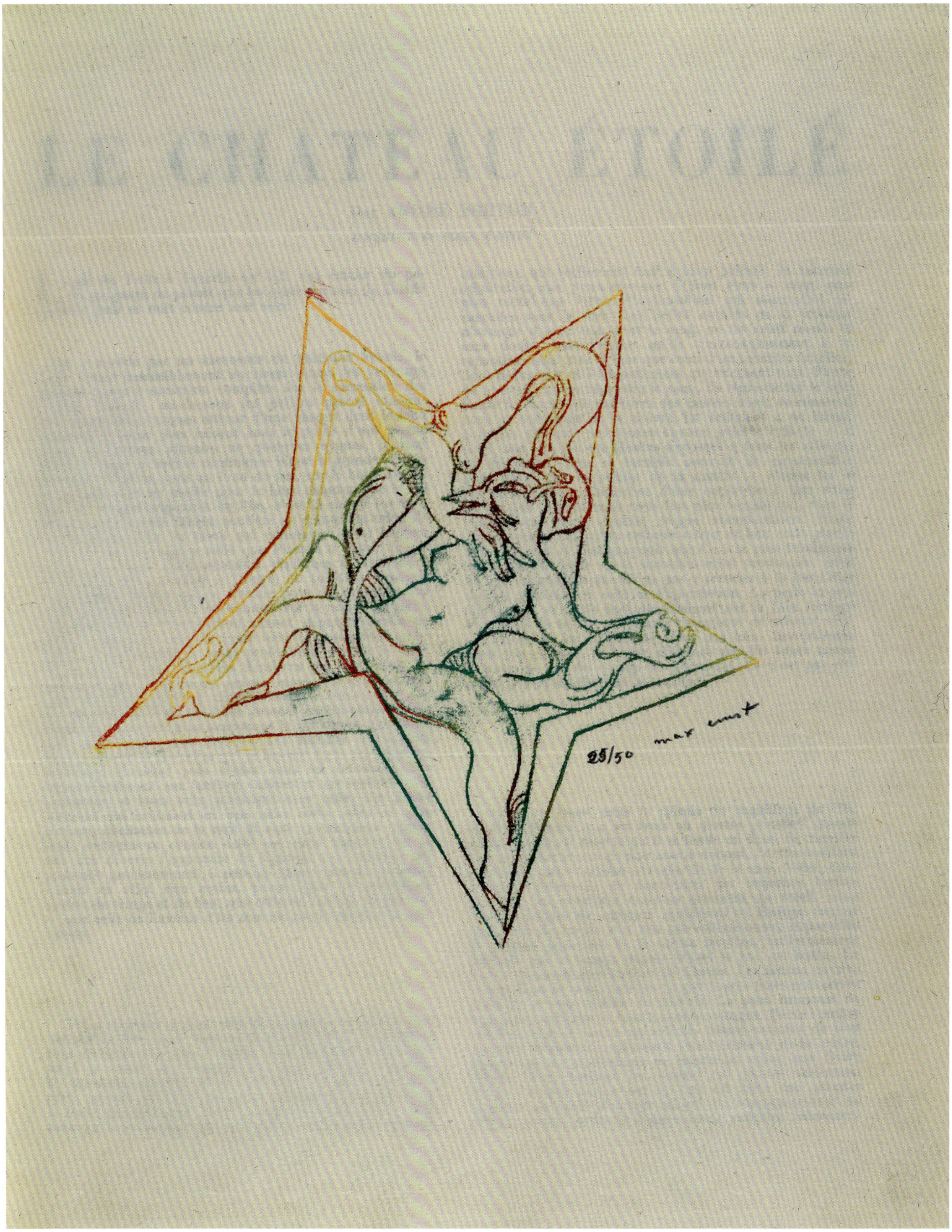
LE CHATEAU ÉTOILÉ
max ernst

realism with the publication of the first manifesto was still some time away, future surrealists came to see in Ernst's art—initially in the collages and overpaintings, then in the collage-derived paintings of c. 1920–23—a visual imagery equivalent to the verbal expression they were seeking in their experimental writing.

The first books to which Ernst contributed proto-surrealist images (essentially surrealist *avant la lettre*) were the two issued in 1922 as the products of two very different collaborations with Paul Eluard. When Eluard, along with his wife, Gala, visited Cologne for a week in the fall of 1921, he selected eleven new collages by Ernst to be reproduced as illustrations in *Répétitions*, a previously planned volume of short poems.[6] Although elements in several of the collages seemingly refer to Eluard's verbal images on the facing pages, the correspondences, almost always tenuous in surrealist art and literature, may have resulted from fortuitous pairings made in the process of choosing collages to match the poems. The second book, *Les Malheurs des immortels*, containing twenty prose poems and reproductions of twenty collages, sprang from a more protracted collaboration that was intimately coordinated from the outset, one in which Ernst eventually contributed all of the illustrations as well as some of the poetry.[7] The original collages for both books were composed of meticulously joined fragments of wood engravings and magazine illustrations, which, when translated into photomechanically printed form, appeared uniform and seamless.

In 1923, a year after he left Cologne for Paris, Ernst made three collage-based intaglios, all apparently printed in very small editions, which would be his last original graphic works until the following decade. Two of the prints were issued separately: *Pays sage I*, a sparsely executed drypoint, and *Pays sage II*, the artist's first etching, partially based on an illustration of a naval mine taken from the popular scientific periodical *La Nature*, a source for many motifs utilized at the time (figs. 5, 54, cat. nos. 50–51). Ernst made the third print, an almost miniature drypoint, as the frontispiece for Péret's *Au 125 du boulevard Saint-Germain*, containing an automatist text and three reproductions of drawings by the author.[8] In the drypoint a nude man—enclosed within a small, fish-lined room—is seen balancing on his left leg, with his left arm extended over his head, in a pose suggestive of a ballet position or an athletic exercise. All visible traces of any originally discrete cut-and-pasted pictorial components have disappeared in the artist's process of transferring the overall collage-based composition to a copper plate for printing.

All of Ernst's prints from the 1930s were made to complement books by his surrealist or former Dada friends or by himself, with the single exception of the mixed-technique intaglio included in *24 Essais* (1935; also known as the *Album de 23 gravures*), with an introductory prose poem by Anatole Jakovski.[9] In

● *Fig. 4 (opposite)*
Max Ernst, Untitled (from *Le Château étoilé*), 1936 (cat. no. 52).

creating even these relatively few prints, Ernst extended his exploration of intaglio techniques, began to use transfer lithography, and adapted his often-employed frottage and grattage processes for making photographically replicated prints and handmade multiple originals.

The five soft-ground etchings Ernst made in 1934 as frontispieces for the sixteen or so deluxe copies of his famous five-volume collage novel, *Une Semaine de bonté*, constituted his most important pre-World War II effort in intaglio printmaking. They represent his synthesis of the semiautomatic image-making procedures of collage and frottage with traditional printmaking techniques, which he developed in master printer Stanley William Hayter's Atelier 17. Hayter acknowledged Ernst's innovative use of the "collage method of assembling different textures on a plate" in soft ground as a brilliant method followed subsequently by many painter-printmakers.[10] Specifically Hayter also described the initial steps of Ernst's technique for making the etching for the first volume of *Une Semaine de bonté*, entitled *Le Lion de Belfort*: "A soft-ground zinc plate which had received the impression of cut-out cardboard forms (toys) was put into very strong acid intended for copper; all the ground was removed by the violent action of the acid and the effect now known as 'open bite' appeared."[11] Ernst identified some of the objects and materials he used to impress shapes into the soft ground, which, when removed, exposed the areas that were then bitten as the zinc plate was immersed in the acid.[12] For *Le Lion de Belfort* he used small, unfolded and flattened cardboard boxes to form the bird-headed creatures and added the cockscomb, the bird's beak, the lion, and the lines in perspective. For the four other prints in the series he used a comb to inscribe waves and rain, various found objects as templates for drawing a monster's form, a plane-tree leaf folded inside a thin sheet of paper, and crinkled tissue paper.

The dramatic change that occurred in Ernst's art after his discovery of frottage in 1925—from the collage-based, illusionist style to a more improvisational, abstract art—was demonstrated the following year in his portfolio *Histoire naturelle*.[13] Containing a Dada prose poem by Arp and thirty-four collotype plates after pencil frottages, the series encompassed Ernst's surrealist interpretation of the creation and evolution of the world. The images were created entirely by rubbing a pencil over paper placed over various textured natural and man-made objects and surfaces. From the time he first began to use it, Ernst considered frottage "the real equivalent of that which is already known by the term *automatic writing*. It is as a spectator that the author assists, indifferent or passionate, at the birth of his work and watches the phases of its development."[14]

In keeping with his predilection for blurring distinctions between reproductive and original works and for distancing himself from purely autographic gestures, Ernst continued to devise ways to adapt frottage as an indirect drawing procedure to other graphic processes. For *Mr. Knife and Miss Fork*, a translated edition of the first chapter of Crevel's 1927 novel *Babylone*, he made nineteen small frottages, which were replicated as negatives for the book by a process related to cliché-verre in collaboration with his friend Man Ray.[15] In 1936, as illustrations for two other books, *Le Château étoilé*, by Breton (fig. 4, cat. no. 52), and *Je sublime*, by Péret, Ernst made multiple, handmade editions of frottages in colors by rubbing crayons over line blocks fabricated after his drawings.[16]

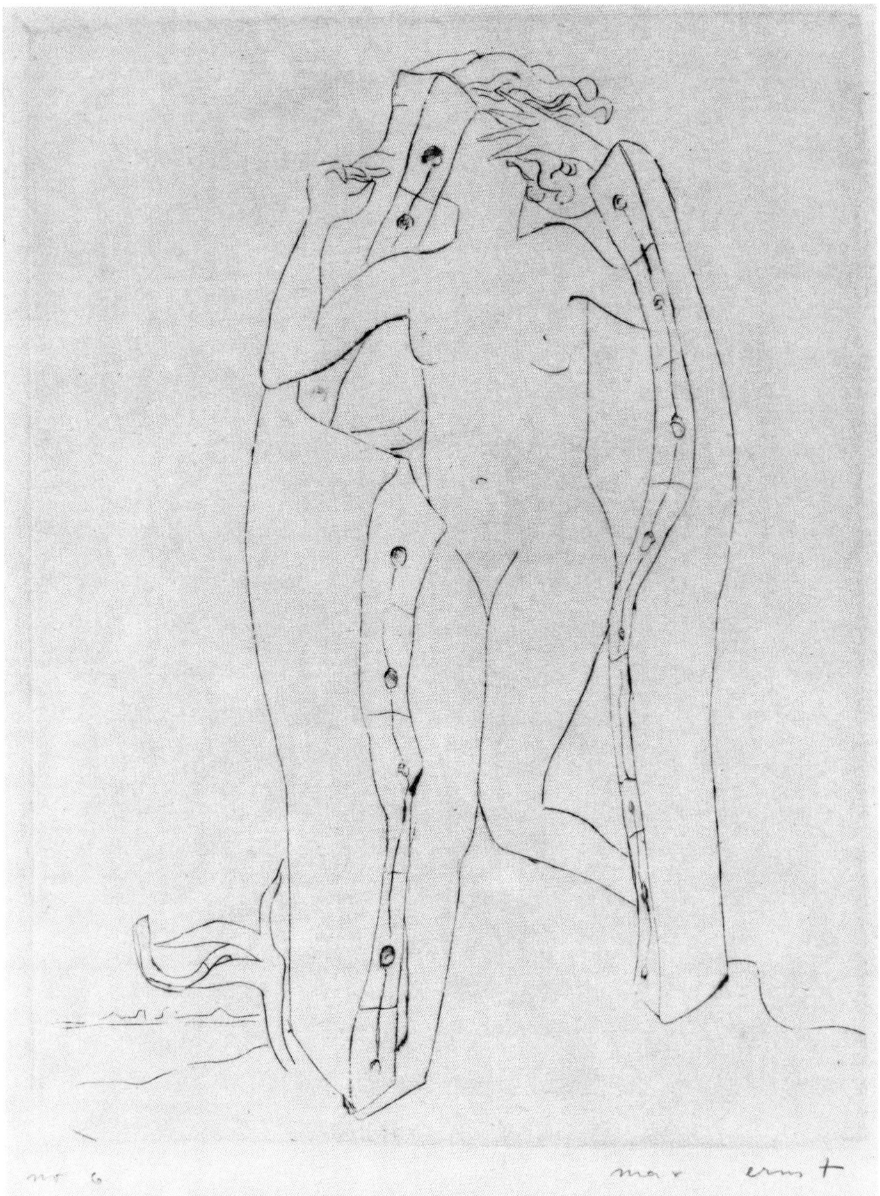

Ernst's return to lithography in 1939 resulted in a breakthrough enabling him to develop his array of characteristic imagery and rich textural effects created in frottage as prints. By adapting the techniques of transfer lithography as the reproducible equivalent of frottage, he made around twelve drawings on paper and transferred them to stones for printing. Four of the lithographs appeared in the first twenty copies of Eluard's *Chanson complète* (1939).[17]

Ernst spent the World War II years in the United States, where his involvement with printmaking was very intermittent. It was only after his return to France in the 1950s that he fully exploited the potentials of intaglio printmaking and of transfer lithography in the large number of prints and books he produced, many with texts by his surrealist colleagues and friends.

By 1923 André Masson was a member of the nascent surrealist circle and an active participant in its members' collective search for methods of tapping into the rich poetic vein of the subconscious. Deeply interested in literature as well as art since his student days, he easily and frequently formed lasting friendships

● *Fig. 5*
Max Ernst, *Pays sage I*, 1923 (cat. no. 50).

with writers. The studio that he established at 45 rue Blomet in Paris in the winter of 1922 served as the meeting place (not unlike Breton's rue Fontaine studio) for a group of artists and writers similarly engaged in intensive literary discussions. Initially included were Georges Limbour and Michel Leiris and, somewhat later, Robert Desnos and Marcel Jouhandeau, all of whom were to collaborate on books with Masson within a few years. Under contract with Daniel-Henry Kahnweiler's Galerie Simon since the summer of 1923, Masson showed regularly in group exhibitions there before his first one-person exhibition of paintings and drawings, early in 1924. Breton expressed his approval by purchasing a painting from the show, by visiting Masson at his studio, and by encouraging him to join the surrealists.

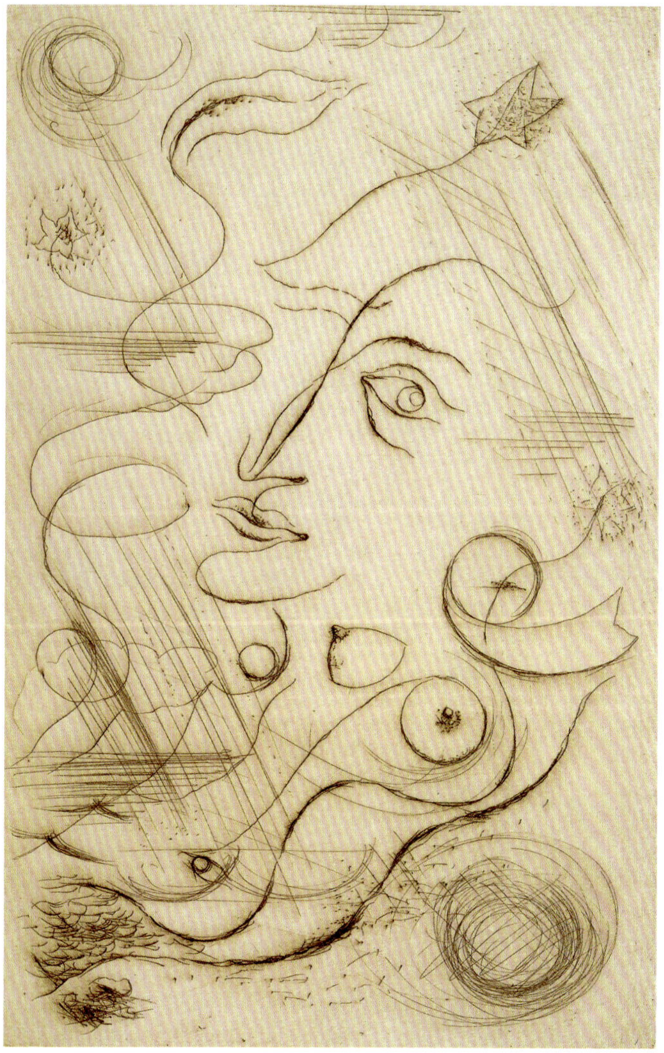

● *Fig. 6*
André Masson, Untitled (from *C'est les bottes de 7 lieues . . .*), 1926 (cat. no. 67).

Kahnweiler, not surprisingly, introduced Masson to the idea of creating a book with original prints soon after their association began. Sharing with Ambroise Vollard the most distinguished history of publishing true *livres de peintre*, Kahnweiler had inaugurated his imprint in 1909 with Guillaume Apollinaire's first book, *L'Enchanteur pourrissant*, accompanied by André Derain's woodcuts. Following with Max Jacob's *Saint Matorel* (1911), which contained Pablo Picasso's first cubist etchings, as well as with subsequent books with prints by Georges Braque, Juan Gris, Fernand Léger, Picasso, and Maurice de Vlaminck, Kahnweiler was often first to sponsor work by advanced poets and painters in printed form.

The young poet Georges Limbour, Masson's friend of two years, who had originally recommended him to Kahnweiler and who had also contributed an introduction to the catalogue of the artist's first show, joined the venture as literary collaborator. Issued in May 1924, *Soleils bas*, a small, thin volume containing the five poems and four etchings with drypoint that they produced, was both Limbour's and Masson's first book.[18] The elegantly restrained format, layout, and title page bearing the monogram HK and Derain's emblematic design of two shells, common to all Kahnweiler editions, remained unchanged. Masson's four prints within this traditional presentation, however, were remarkably fluent not only as first attempts at creating new imagery through the unfamiliar etching technique but also as representing his personal application of a composition-generating procedure analogous to the practice of automatic writing then at the center of surrealist experimentation. Unlike Ernst, who made etched versions of collages assembled from preprinted though apparently unrelated components, Masson may be assumed to have created recognizable motifs in his prints (or in some form of preliminary drawings for them) in much the same way that he did in his paintings and independent drawings at the time. With minimal preconception he moved the etching needle freely over the grounded plate to establish a compositional structure and to reveal the possibilities for images that emerged from the rhythmic flow of the lines during the process of drawing them.

Rather than serving as illustrations, Masson's four prints in *Soleils bas* juxtapose motifs that parallel and sometimes intertwine with imagery from a subconscious state evoked in Limbour's poems. Drypoints with lightly etched lines printed in warm black and brown tones, they present a thematic mixture similar to that found in the artist's paintings and drawings of the middle 1920s. The sun, plant forms, a lighted candlestick, heads, torsos, and birds separate and float within the shallow space allotted by their cubist structures, balanced momentarily by the positioning of geometric fragments and random architectural elements.

Masson chose to use lithography for his next book with Kahnweiler, *Simulacre* (1925), also the first published collection of poetry by Michel Leiris, another close friend, who, according to the painter, composed the poems in his studio.[19] Vaguely magical and less tentative in aspect and detail than the prints for *Soleils bas*, the seven lithographs (including one on the front cover, designed to incorporate the title of the volume) repeat some of the elements found in the previous drypoints for *Soleils bas*, but with more emphasis on heads in profile and classical architectural components. With soft, evenly drafted diagonals and small areas of shading, they also appear more dependent on cubist-derived compositional scaffoldings and on the idealized art of Gris, another close acquaintance of Masson's at the time. In some of the prints, however, pictorial incidents are distributed more evenly over the composition, and the rhyming of forms and doubling of motifs are more pronounced.

Masson returned to etching in the third and fourth of the four books sponsored by Kahnweiler in the 1920s, Robert Desnos's *C'est les bottes de 7 lieues cette phrase "Je me vois"* (1926; figs. 6, 69, 85, cat. nos. 67–69) and Marcel Jouhandeau's *Ximenès Malinjoude* (1927).[20] Larger than Masson's first etchings and lithographs, the four prints for *C'est les bottes* present further, although somewhat more loosely structured, intimate variations of the artist's distinctive automatic drawing style. The compositions appear in flux, only momentarily frozen in their process of creation. Interdependency with Miró may also account for such signlike motifs as a pierced heart, fish heads, and leaf-flowers tenuously connected by looping, whiplash lines. Etched, linear meanderings interspersed with hatchworked patches define the full, upright human figures represented in the six diminutive etchings for Jouhandeau's short novel. These prints are infused with much the same spirit and energy as Masson's beautiful contemporaneous series of figural paintings and drawings, which he created by pouring and manipulating glue, sand, and paint, combined with spontaneously drawn lines.

In an entirely different vein from his work with Kahnweiler, Masson undertook his next book illustrated with prints, *Le Con d'Irène* (1928), written by Louis Aragon, an early surrealist acquaintance.[21] As the first of a proposed series of erotic books to be published by Pascal Pia but issued anonymously, it contained pornographic prose and five extremely explicit line etchings depicting scenes of sexual abandon evocative of de Sade, but with no advance in technical or aesthetic innovation. The second and final book in the series, *Histoire de l'oeil*, written by Breton's aggressive opponent Georges Bataille and illustrated similarly with eight lithographs by Masson, appeared in the same year. In the 1930s Masson continued to contribute prints to books periodically and initiated several projects that were never completed for various reasons. Ten years after it was announced, Masson's final book before the outbreak of war and his last with Kahnweiler, *Glossaire, j'y serre mes gloses* (1939), was published, with sixteen pen lithographs executed in the style of his so-called second surrealist period.[22]

Joan Miró's contributions to printmaking in its traditional fine art techniques, particularly in the form of separate prints, were probably more significant than those of any other major painter associated with surrealism. In Barcelona his boyhood aptitude for painting had been encouraged by formal art training, and even years before arriving in Paris for the first time, in 1920, he had developed a passionate interest in poetry and in literary criticism, which he read in both Catalan and French journals. His earliest known involvement with prints, however, came well after his art had matured.

As with most of the other original surrealists working in the 1920s, Miró's initiation into the printmaking media resulted from relationships with poets or their publishers, who invited him to provide prints as illustrations for their books. Since his studio in the rue Blomet happened to be located adjacent to Masson's, some of Miró's earliest and most enduring acquaintances were with those who gathered there regularly for theoretical discussions, including the poets Paul Eluard, Max Jacob, Michel Leiris, Georges Limbour, and Roland Tual. Although Miró ultimately participated less than others in collective surrealist efforts, in an interview published in 1948, he acknowledged the extraordinary intellectual

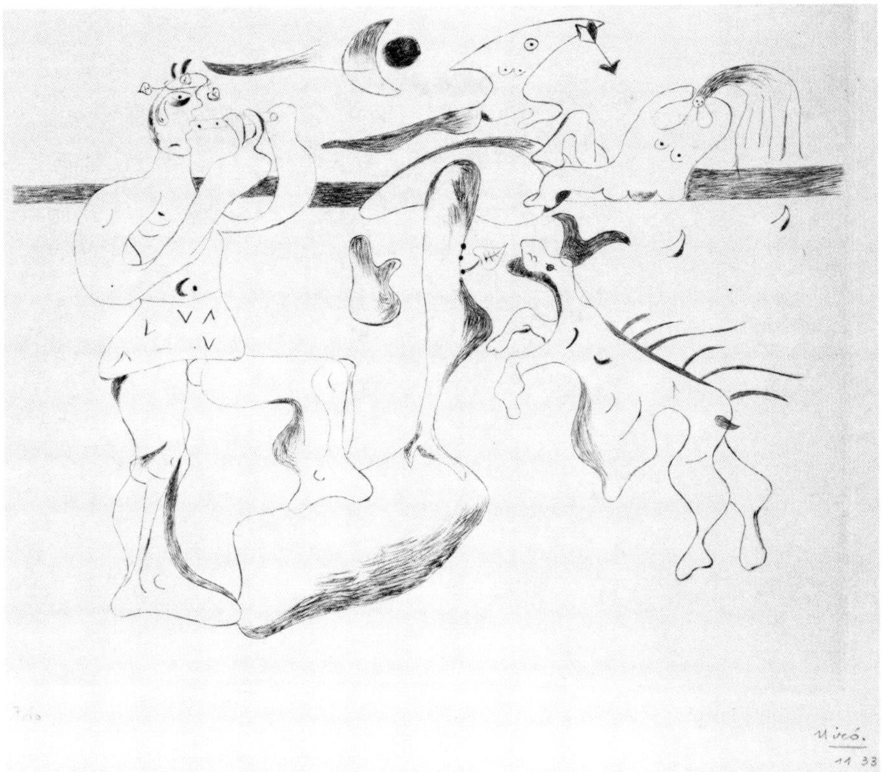

◉ *Fig. 7*
Joan Miró, *Daphnis et Chloé* (Daphne and Chloe), 1933 (cat. no. 79).

stimulation this situation had given him: "The poets Masson introduced me to interested me more than the painters I had met in Paris. I was carried away by the new ideas they brought and especially the poetry they discussed. I gorged myself on it all night long."[23]

Miró began his extraordinarily long and prolific career as a book artist in 1927, when, at Breton's request, he painted eight colorful gouaches to accompany poems by the surrealist leader's protégée Lise Deharme. Published the following year under the name Lise Hirtz, *Il était une petite pie* contained Miró's designs and Deharme's short, handwritten poems, faithfully translated into pochoir prints by the master stencil printer Jean Saudé.[24] Reflecting the symbolic and schematic language Miró had developed by then, the compositions constituted small-scale versions of his picture-poems of c. 1925–27. They included elements as specific as a stylized magpie (referring to the title poem) and a rat, in addition to other familiarly Miróesque, abstracted pictorial motifs incorporating words and numbers.

Miró made his first lithographs in 1930, comprising a small, separate print and four simply drawn crayon lithographs for Tzara's *L'Arbre des voyageurs*.[25] In a letter written in 1931 to the Belgian collector René Gaffé, Miró explained the motivation behind his venture into lithography for the book: "I should tell you that [Tzara] was one of the first to see and like my painting. On my end, I have long considered his poetry to be of great spiritual value and his *Dada* position has always been extremely appealing to me, as *clairvoyance* and as a method of action. . . . If I have done the lithographs in the way I have done them, it was because his poetry—desertlike, with blinding showers of sand—suggested them to me."[26] In 1933, again inspired by literary themes rather than by any great interest in further technical involvement, Miró made his first intaglio prints: three etchings for Georges Hugnet's *Enfances* (see fig. 95, cat. no. 80) and an independent work, *Daphnis et Chloé* (fig. 7, cat. no. 79), both projects published under the auspices of prominent art periodicals, *Cahiers d'art* and the surrealist-oriented *Minotaure*. Perhaps referring only obliquely to Hugnet's text, Miró presents three exaggeratedly biomorphic conceptions of the human figure, more monstrously humorous than childlike, etched with minimally inflected contours and scattered patches of hatching. In *Daphnis et Chloé* he interprets the well-known myth of two young lovers in an almost illustrational manner, with the easily recognizable characters occupying a natural setting suggestive of the seashore.

Before the disruption of war Miró's forthcoming, almost unmatched commitment to exploring the printmaking mediums began seriously in 1938 with a group of more than twenty extraordinary intaglio prints. These etchings, some with the addition of drypoint, were effectively brought about by means of the greatly enhanced technical facility he gained by developing his plates in the studio of the painter-printmaker Louis Marcoussis and then printing them with Hayter at Atelier 17. Although five etchings from this group were made for books or reviews or were to be included in album-portfolios, the major effort now went into the creation of single prints. Among the most confident in revealing latent print qualities as integral sources of invention is the collaborative *Portrait de Miró* (fig. 8, cat. no. 91), a visual metaphor for the two creative modes represented by Marcoussis's sensitive interpretation of his subject's physical appearance and the overlay of Miró's own spontaneous network of automatist lines, motifs, and words. The two basic plates and six variant combinations of the two in *Série noire et rouge* (figs. 101–8, cat. nos. 92–99) were also developed in Marcoussis's studio. They show not only the elaboration of Miró's handling of materials and processes but also his more powerful response to the terror erupting within his native country and the pervading sense of its imminent spread, matched thematically and spiritually by a number of related paintings from the late 1930s.

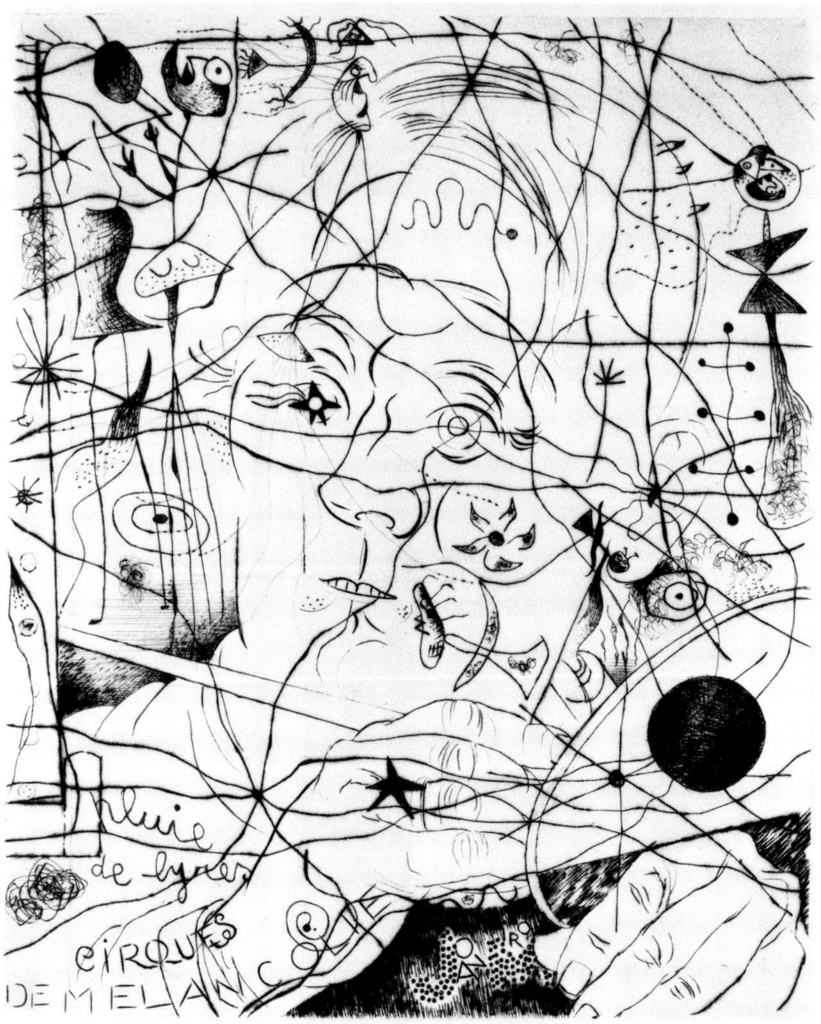

● *Fig. 8*
Joan Miró, *Portrait de Miró* (Portrait of Miró), 1938 (cat. no. 91).

In 1940 Miró resumed working in lithography on the *Barcelona Series*, conceived in response to the Spanish Civil War.[27] Eventually numbering fifty black-and-white prints, the series was not published until 1944, by Miró's longtime friend Joan Prats in Barcelona. Miró's true genius as a book artist is best exemplified in the three masterpieces he produced following World War II in three different techniques with virtually unparalleled effectiveness: *Parler seul* (1948–50), by Tzara, with lithographs; *A toute épreuve* (1950), by Eluard, with woodcuts; and *Le Courtisan grotesque* (1974), by Adrien de Montluc, comte de Cramail, with etchings and aquatints.[28]

By April 1929, when Salvador Dalí arrived in Paris to work with his friend and colleague Luis Buñuel on the film *Un Chien andalou*, he was already an avid devotee of surrealism and was steeped in its dogma. The year before, he had concluded a letter to Federico García Lorca, his more intimate friend, by stating: "Surrealism is *one* of the means of Escape. But it's Escape *itself* that is the important thing."[29] Dalí had been intensely involved with painting from a young age. By fourteen he had begun contributing articles, drawings, and poetry to various periodicals, and in 1924 his first illustrations for a book were published.[30] While enrolled in the art school of the Academia de San Fernando in Madrid, he associated with an intellectually elite group of student writers and artists, including Buñuel and Lorca. Later, while a prime instigator of avant-garde activities in Barcelona, he began exhibiting his paintings professionally and in 1927 inaugurated an extensive series of critical and theoretical writings over a two-year period for the journal *L'Amic de les arts*. He further provided drawings for the surrealist-inspired little magazine, *gallo*, published in Granada by Lorca.

Once in Paris, Dalí was introduced to members of the surrealist group by his fellow Catalan painter Miró. His first solo exhibition there opened in November 1929, accompanied by a catalogue with an introduction by Breton. In his second surrealist manifesto, published on December 15 in the final issue of *La Révolution surréaliste*, Breton expelled Masson and several others from the movement. In revising surrealist principles in the manifesto, Breton demoted the previously indispensable practice of automatism in writing and drawing in favor of a different mode of surrealist painting then coming to the fore, primarily variations on illusionist, interior landscapes recalled from dreams. A significant part of Breton's shift in preference toward an art of the captured image and away from a process such as automatism was attributable to Dalí's recent introduction of a new style in his paintings. Dalí's immediate success in seizing critical and popular attention and in helping to redefine the look of surrealist art propelled him into the center of Breton's fold.

During the following months, Dalí was heavily involved with projects initiated by himself as author and by surrealist writers and their publishers. In

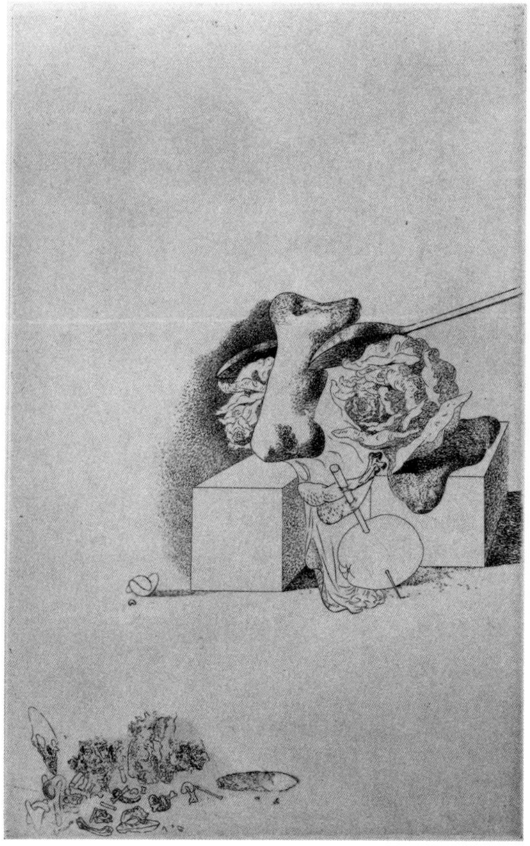

addition to a drawing reproduced as the frontispiece to Breton's expanded edition of his second surrealist manifesto, Dalí also furnished stylistically related drawings to three other books issued in limited editions in 1930: André Breton and Paul Eluard's *L'Immaculée Conception* (fig. 31, cat. no. 19); René Char's *Artine* (fig. 32, cat. no. 20); and *La Femme visible* (fig. 11, cat. no. 21), containing a collection of texts by the painter establishing the basis of his later well-publicized paranoiac-critical method.

Despite considerable experience with reproductive graphic arts processes and formal art training that included instruction by recognized painters as well as printmakers, Dalí is known to have produced only one early original print, *Head of a Young Girl*, an etching in a single recorded impression from 1924.[31] Rather than turning to a traditional autographic medium for the 1930 frontispieces, Dalí utilized heliogravure, a combination photographic and intaglio process, as the means of transforming his pen-and-ink drawings into prints pulled from copper plates. By transferring the drawings photographically to copper plates and apparently reworking them in drypoint with an etching needle or roulette, Dalí and his technically adept collaborators printed the heliogravures so that they would bear features and qualities characteristic of hand-printed etchings or engravings. The three frontispiece drawings were executed in a highly finished, calligraphic style imitative of burin work in Old Master engravings. Virtuoso penmanship in the handling of swelling and tapering hatchings is extravagantly displayed in the densely packed, emphatically modeled forms of metamorphosing, sexually charged figures in the drawing for *La Femme visible*. In the most abstract and effective of the frontispieces, which he created four years later for an edition of Hugnet's *Onan* (fig. 10, cat. no. 24), Dalí spontaneously scratched dozens of clustered drypoint lines and scribbles in a random distribution over the surface of the plate. He described the apparently automatic process in an inscription in the

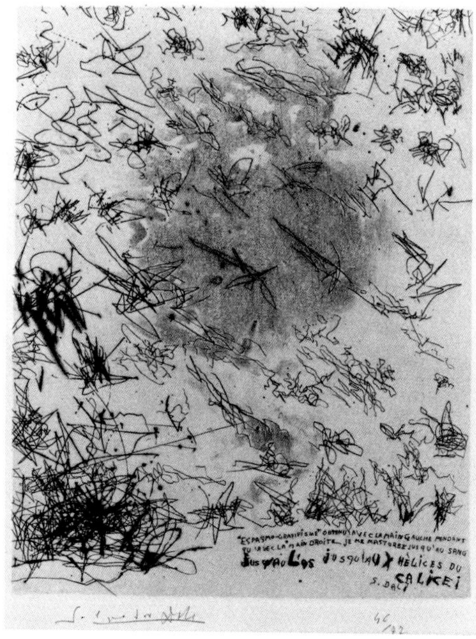

● *Fig. 9*
Salvador Dali, Untitled (from *Les Chants de Maldoror*), 1934 (cat. no. 25).

● *Fig. 10*
Salvador Dali, *Onan*, 1934 (cat. no. 24).

● *Fig. 11 (opposite)*
Salvador Dali, *La Femme visible* (The visible woman), 1930 (cat. no. 21).

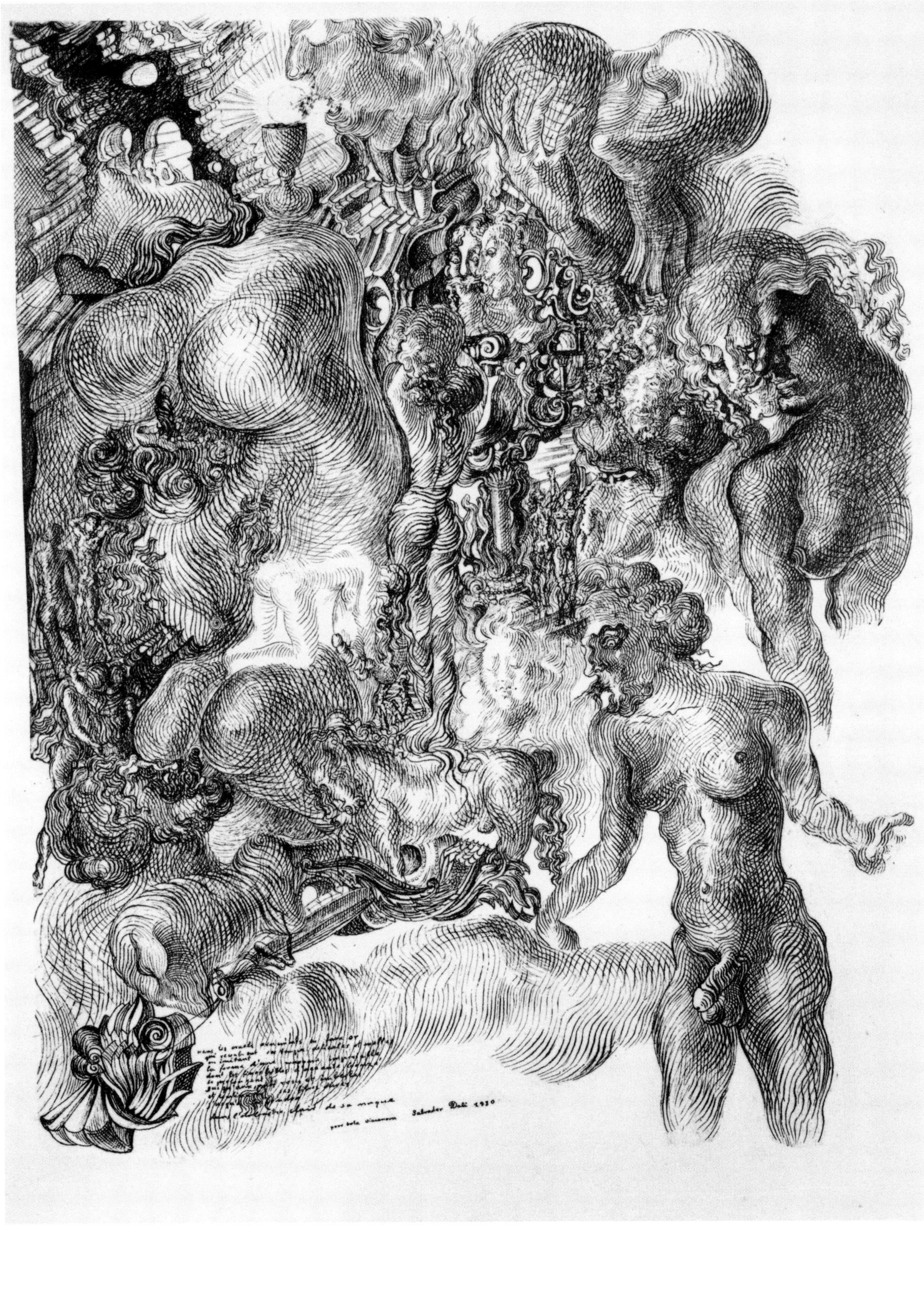
Salvador Dalí 1930

lower right of the plate as "espasmo-grafifisme," obtained while masturbating.

In the same year as *Onan* Dalí, still pursuing printmaking on his own terms, produced what is unquestionably the highest achievement of his career as an artist of the book and as a printmaker: his illustrations for the 1934 Skira edition of *Les Chants de Maldoror* (see figs. 9, 35–37, cat. nos. 25–28). Written by the obscure nineteenth-century author Isidore Ducasse, the self-appointed comte de Lautréamont, who was canonized as their true ancestor by the surrealists, this long narrative prose poem was the one literary work from past or present hailed by the surrealists without exception as a true masterpiece. Innovative in neither structure nor format, the 1934 *livre de peintre* was nevertheless clearly of major importance to Albert Skira, its Swiss publisher, who produced it on a level to rival two of his previous publications, Ovid's *Les Métamorphoses* (1931), with etchings by Picasso, and Stéphane Mallarmé's *Poésies* (1932), with etchings by Matisse, both also acknowledged landmarks of the genre.

Dalí's cycle of forty-two illustrations for *Les Chants de Maldoror* presents what may be read as his parallel visual narrative of dreamscapes symbolic of the darkest recesses of the psyche, recognizable from his paintings of the time but most likely not discoverable in Lautréamont's violently grim, hallucinatory text. Occupying these psychological spaces in Dalí's prints are pulsating organic forms and degenerating body parts, frequently supported by crutches and constructions made of bones. Various adaptations from the peasant figures at prayer in Jean-François Millet's venerable painting *The Angelus* appear in several of the prints, their presence referring to "imminent sexual aggression," according to Dalí's recorded interpretation.[32]

Generally regarded without apology as original etchings by Dalí, as they are described on the book's colophon page, the illustrations for *Les Chants de Maldoror* have recently been demonstrated to be photomechanically derived, at least in part.[33] They are described in the recent and first authoritative catalogue raisonné of the artist's intaglio prints as heliogravures with drypoint. More extensive descriptions of Dalí's working methods have proposed that the images for the prints were first made as celluloid engravings, and impressions of these intermediary prints made with graphite or soot were then photomechanically transferred onto copper plates. An examination of the prints in the book suggests to this writer that although important motifs and significant areas in a number of the prints may have been photomechanically produced at some stage in the process of making the plates, there also appear in the prints considerable amounts of hand-drawn additions and reworkings in etching. By whatever means, the particular vision conveyed in the prints in *Les Chants de Maldoror* is convincing and well recognized as having originated with Dalí.

Allied with surrealism since the mid-1920s, Yves Tanguy treated printmaking as a vital if not ongoing creative pursuit for more than twenty years. Through his close friendship with the poet Jacques Prévert, he met Breton in 1925 and was encouraged to join the surrealist group. One day, while riding a bus on the rue La Boétie, Tanguy glimpsed two of de Chirico's metaphysical paintings in a gallery window, and this chance encounter was decisive both in influencing him to become a painter and in providing inspiration for his art throughout his career. In 1926 Tanguy's work was reproduced in *La Révolution surréaliste*, and in the following year, he had his first solo show at the Galerie Surréaliste, to which Breton contributed a catalogue essay.

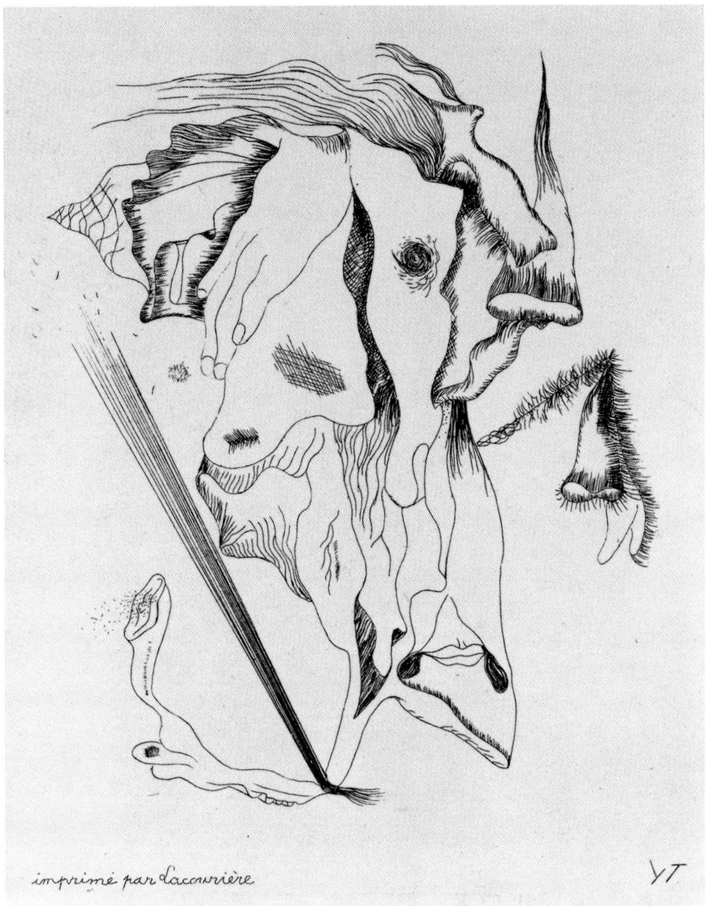

Tanguy's small printmaking oeuvre began almost a decade into surrealism's formative years and—much like those of Ernst, Masson, Miró, and Dalí—was first motivated and largely sustained by connections with surrealist poets. For his earliest book, *Dormir, dormir dans les pierres* (1927), and the first with his sympathetic friend Benjamin Péret, Tanguy supplied drawings for reproduction: an illustrated title page (repeated on the front cover), three full-page drawings (hand-colored in some copies), and several smaller vignettes.[34] In his transitional style—from which all previously abstracted figuration, except for the presence of three severed but gesturing human hands, had been eliminated—the drawings present imaginary, mountainous landscapes as parallel visual environments for Péret's automatist texts.

Having fully developed his precise and illusionistic style by 1932, Tanguy had rid his dreamscape paintings of all obvious references to the natural world, but for his first original print, an etching published that year as the frontispiece to ten copies of Eluard's *La Vie immédiate* (fig. 12, cat. no. 115), he adapted a 1927–28 drawing incorporating a hand and germinating motifs characteristic of its earlier date. Two years later at Atelier 17, while developing the plate for his second print, an etching with aquatint created to accompany *Primele poème* (fig. 129, cat. no. 116), by Tzara, Tanguy established a relationship with Hayter, which was crucial for his serious involvement with the elaboration of printmaking in

◉ *Fig. 12*
Yves Tanguy, Untitled (from *La Vie immédiate*), 1932 (cat. no. 115).

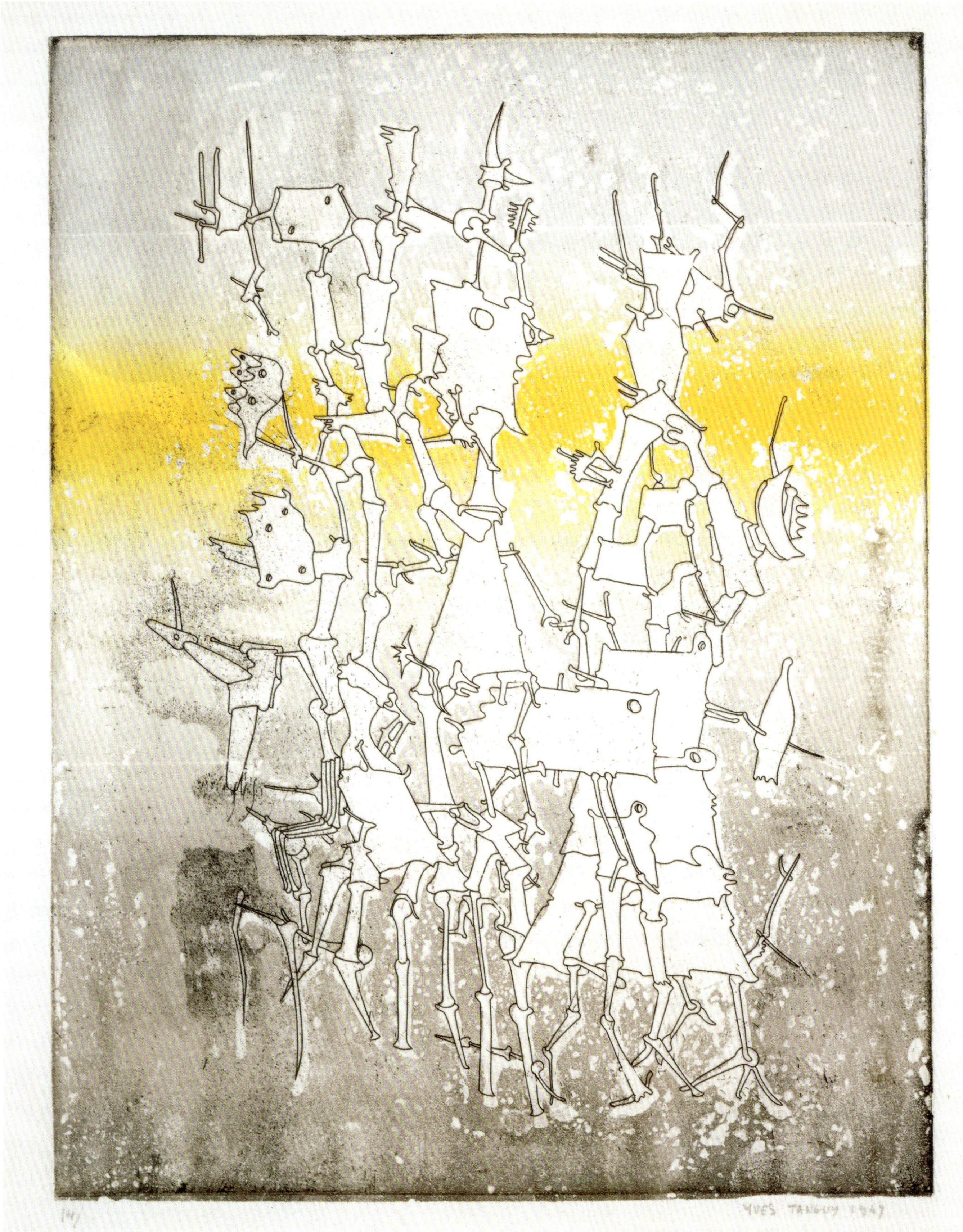
14/
YVES TANGUY 1947

Paris and later in New York. The seven remaining prints Tanguy made before emigrating to the United States in 1939, five of which were for books by surrealist poets or collective portfolios of prints primarily by surrealist artists, were produced in collaboration with Hayter at Atelier 17.

The extreme technical refinement evident in all of Tanguy's prints and his use of innovative processes such as the addition of color monoprinting to etchings—first used in 1947 for his largest single print, *Rhabdomancie* (fig. 13, cat. no. 120), created in collaboration with master printer Fred Becker in Hayter's workshop—went virtually unsurpassed in printmaking by surrealist artists. With each new print until his last, in 1953, Tanguy's meticulously delineated signature forms and structures served as stunning visual metaphors for the accompanying verbal imagery of the surrealist poets.

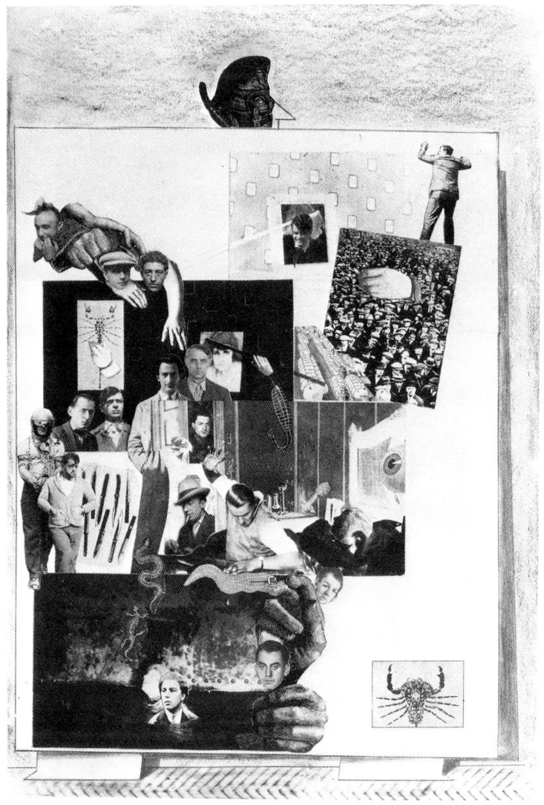

As artists and writers joined and as members of the original group and their factions diverged, the surrealist movement spread to establish an international network. In 1931, after the purges and desertions of the previous two years, Ernst updated the membership list of the principal artists then faithful to surrealism in his collage *Loplop présente les membres du groupe surréaliste* (fig. 14).[35] Reproduced in the December 1931 issue of *Surréalisme au service de la révolution* (with the title *Au rendez-vous des amis*), the collage included photo portraits and candid shots of some of the original participants depicted in his 1922 painting, including Breton and Ernst himself, as well as more recent additions: Char, Buñuel, Dalí, Alberto Giacometti, Man Ray, and Tanguy.

● *Fig. 14*
Max Ernst, *Loplop Introduces Members of the Surrealist Group*, 1931; collage of cut-and-pasted photographs, pencil, and pencil frottage; 19¾ x 13¼ in. The Museum of Modern Art, New York, purchase.

Like that in the earlier painting (but with painters now forming the nucleus), the gathering in Ernst's collage demonstrated surrealism's organization as a literary-artistic enterprise. Its programs, literature, and art were more widely disseminated in illustrated reviews than in any other form, but with poetry remaining a central concern, the movement's collective endeavor was perhaps best represented in the books created jointly by its poets and painters. For several leading surrealist artists, their early and often most original prints, which they contributed to books by their poet friends, established the essential elements of their printmaking and the personal approaches to it that they developed over the following decades.

● *Fig. 13 (opposite)*
Yves Tanguy, *Rhabdomancie*, 1947 (cat. no. 120).

Notes

1. Werner Spies and Sigrid and Günter Metken, *Max Ernst: Oeuvre Katalog*, vol. 2, *Werke, 1906–1925* (Houston: Menil Foundation; Cologne: Dumont Schauberg, 1975), no. 505.
2. André Breton, *Manifestoes of Surrealism*, trans. Richard Seaver and Helen R. Lane (Ann Arbor: University of Michigan Press, 1972), 26.
3. *Aus unserm Leben an der Penne*, 1910; twenty-five pages of drawings reproduced in a student newspaper (Spies and Metken, *Oeuvre Katalog*, vol. 2, nos. 15–39). The linoleum cuts are Spies-Leppien 1–6.
4. *Consolamini: Dichtungen von Johannes Th. Kühlemann* (Cologne: Kairios-Verlag, 1919).
5. Spies-Leppien 8.
6. Paul Eluard, *Répétitions* (Paris: Au Sans Pareil, 1922). For the collages by Ernst reproduced on the cover and as illustrations, see Spies and Metken, *Oeuvre Katalog*, vol. 2, nos. 438–48.
7. Paul Eluard, *Les Malheurs des immortels* (Paris: Librairie Six, 1922); for Ernst's collages, see Spies and Metken, *Oeuvre Katalog*, vol. 2, nos. 471–91. The various sources for the engravings and magazine illustrations Ernst used in making his collages for *Répétitions* and *Les Malheurs des immortels* have been identified by several scholars. For a recent summation of these findings, see William Camfield, "Ernst and the Dadaists of Paris: Vacations in the Tirol and Collaborations with Eluard," in *Max Ernst: Dada and the Dawn of Surrealism* (Munich: Prestel-Verlag; Houston: Menil Collection, 1993), 101–23.
8. On *Pays sage I* and *Pays sage II*, see Werner Spies, "On the Graphic Work," in *Max Ernst: Oeuvre-Katalog: Das graphische Werk*, ed. Werner Spies, comp. Helmut R. Leppien (Houston: Menil Foundation; Cologne: DuMont Schauberg, 1975), vol. 1, x. Benjamin Péret, *Au 125 du boulevard Saint-Germain* (Paris: Collection Littérature, 1923); Spies-Leppien 9.
9. Untitled etching in Anatole Jakovski, *24 Essais* (Paris: G. Orobitz, 1935); Spies-Leppien 12.
10. *Une Semaine de bonté* (Paris: Editions Jeanne Bucher, 1934); Spies-Leppien 15; Stanley William Hayter, *New Ways of Gravure*, 2d ed. (London: Oxford University Press, 1966), 213.
11. Hayter, *New Ways of Gravure*, 97.
12. Spies, "On the Graphic Work," x.
13. *Histoire Naturelle* (Paris: Jeanne Bucher, 1926); see Spies and Metken, *Oeuvre Katalog*, vol. 3, *Werke, 1925–1929*, nos. 790–823.
14. Max Ernst, "History of a Natural History," in *Max Ernst: Beyond Painting and Other Writings by the Artist and His Friends*, ed. Robert Motherwell, trans. Dorothea Tanning (New York: Wittenborn, Schultz, 1948), 8.
15. René Crevel, *Mr. Knife and Miss Fork* (Paris: Black Sun Press, 1931); Spies-Leppien 13.
16. Benjamin Péret, *Je sublime* (Paris: Editions Surréalistes, 1936); Spies-Leppien 16.
17. Paul Eluard, *Chanson complète* (Paris: Gallimard, 1939); Spies-Leppien 19.
18. Georges Limbour, *Soleils bas* (Paris: Editions de la Galerie Simon, 1924); Saphire 1–4; Saphire-Cramer 1.
19. Michel Leiris, *Simulacre* (Paris: Editions de la Galerie Simon, 1925); Saphire 5–11; Saphire-Cramer 2. Saphire states that although there may have been some shared stimulations at play when Leiris and Masson were composing their poems and prints, Leiris maintained that the poems and the prints were for the most part arrived at separately; Lawrence Saphire and Patrick Cramer, *André Masson: The Illustrated Books: Catalogue Raisonné* (Geneva: Patrick Cramer, 1994), 24.
20. Marcel Jouhandeau, *Ximenès Malinjoude* (Paris: Editions de la Galerie Simon, 1927); Saphire 16–21; Saphire-Cramer 4.
21. Saphire 22–26; Saphire-Cramer 5.
22. Michel Leiris, *Glossaire, j'y serre mes gloses* (Paris: Editions de la Galerie Simon, 1939); Saphire 66–81; Saphire-Cramer 13.
23. Margit Rowell, ed., *Joan Miró: Selected Writings and Interviews* (Boston: G. K. Hall, 1986), 208; reprinted from "Joan Miró: Comment and Interview," *Partisan Review* (New York) 15 (February 1948): 206–12.
24. Lise Hirtz, *Il était une petite pie* (Paris: Editions Jeanne Bucher, 1928); Dupin 1–8; Cramer hors catalogue 1.
25. *Lithograph I*, 1930, published by Zervos, Paris; Mourlot 1. Tristan Tzara, *L'Arbre des voyageurs* (Paris: Editions de la Montagne, 1930); Mourlot 2–5; Cramer 1.
26. Rowell, *Joan Miró*, 113.
27. Mourlot 6–55.
28. Tristan Tzara, *Parler seul* (Paris: Maeght éditeur, 1950); Mourlot 102–75; Cramer 17. Paul Eluard, *A toute épreuve* (Geneva: Gérald Cramer, 1958); Dupin 161–234; Cramer 49. Adrien de Montluc, comte de Cramail, *Le Courtisan grotesque* (Paris: Le Degré quarante et un, 1974); Dupin 660–75; Cramer 182.
29. Michael Raeburn, ed., *Salvador Dalí: The Early Years* (London: Thames and Hudson, 1994), 38.
30. Carles Fages de Climent, *Les Bruixes de Llers* (Barcelona: Editorial Políglota, 1924), with cover and illustrations by Dalí.
31. Michler-Löpsinger 1.
32. Salvador Dalí, *Le Mythe tragique de l'Angelus de Millet: Interprétation paranoiaque-critique* (Paris: Société Nouvelle des Editions Pauvert, 1963); translated in Dawn Ades, *Dada and Surrealism Reviewed* (London: Arts Council of Great Britain, 1978), 267.
33. Photomechanical processes involving heliogravure in the creation of the previously discussed frontispieces Dalí contributed to books and the prints for *Les Chants de Maldoror* were the subject of research by Rainer Michael Mason, presented in the exhibition catalogue *Vrai Dali, fausse gravure: L'Oeuvre imprimée, 1930–1934* (Geneva: Cabinet des estampes, Musée d'art et d'histoire, 1992). The techniques are so described in the recently published Michler and Löpsinger catalogue raisonné.
34. Benjamin Péret, *Dormir, dormir dans les pierres* (Paris: Editions Surréalistes, 1927).
35. Spies and Metken, *Oeuvre Katalog*, vol. 4, *Werke, 1929–1938*, no. 1806.

Plates

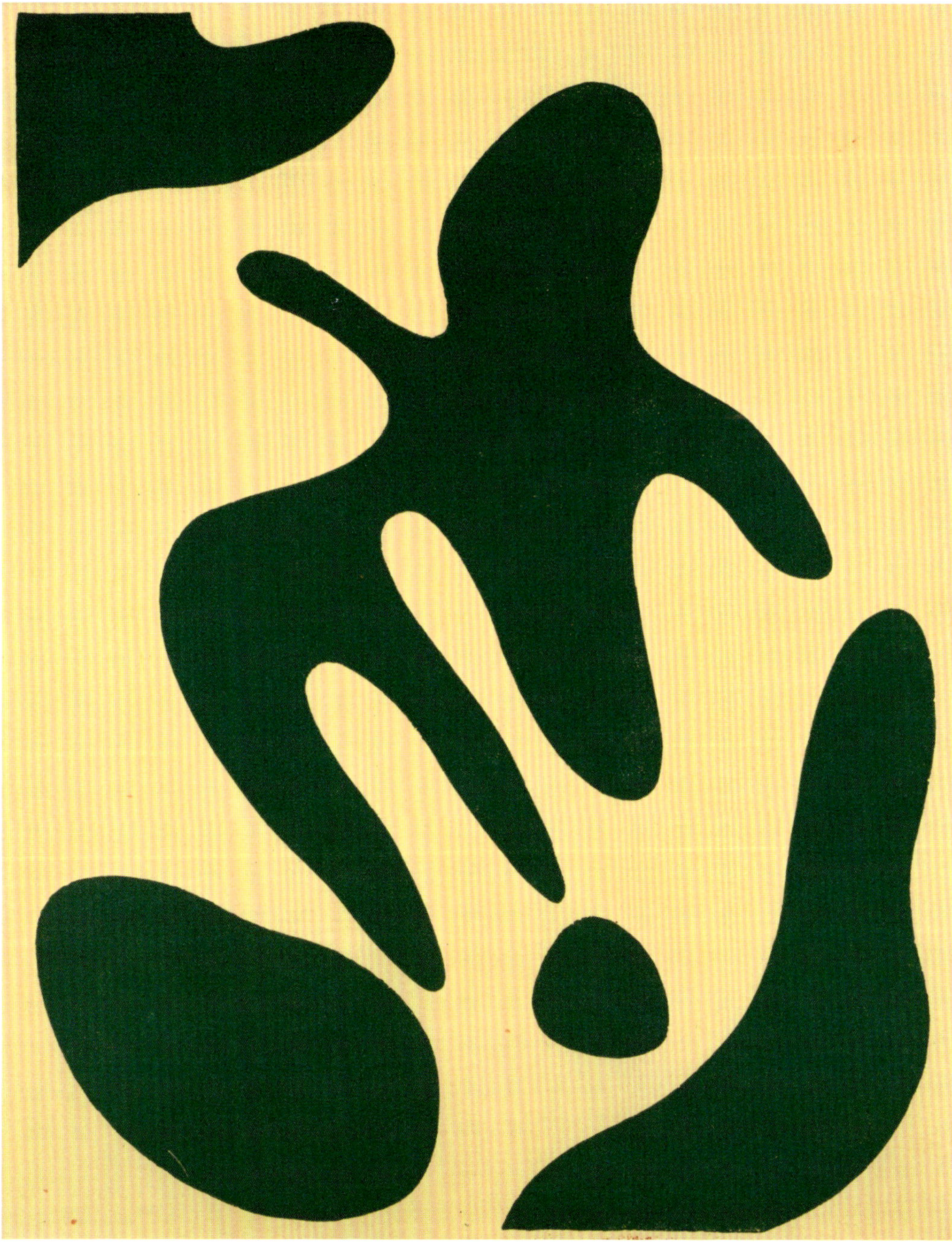

● *Fig. 15*
Jean Arp, *Constellation*, 1938
(cat. no. 1).

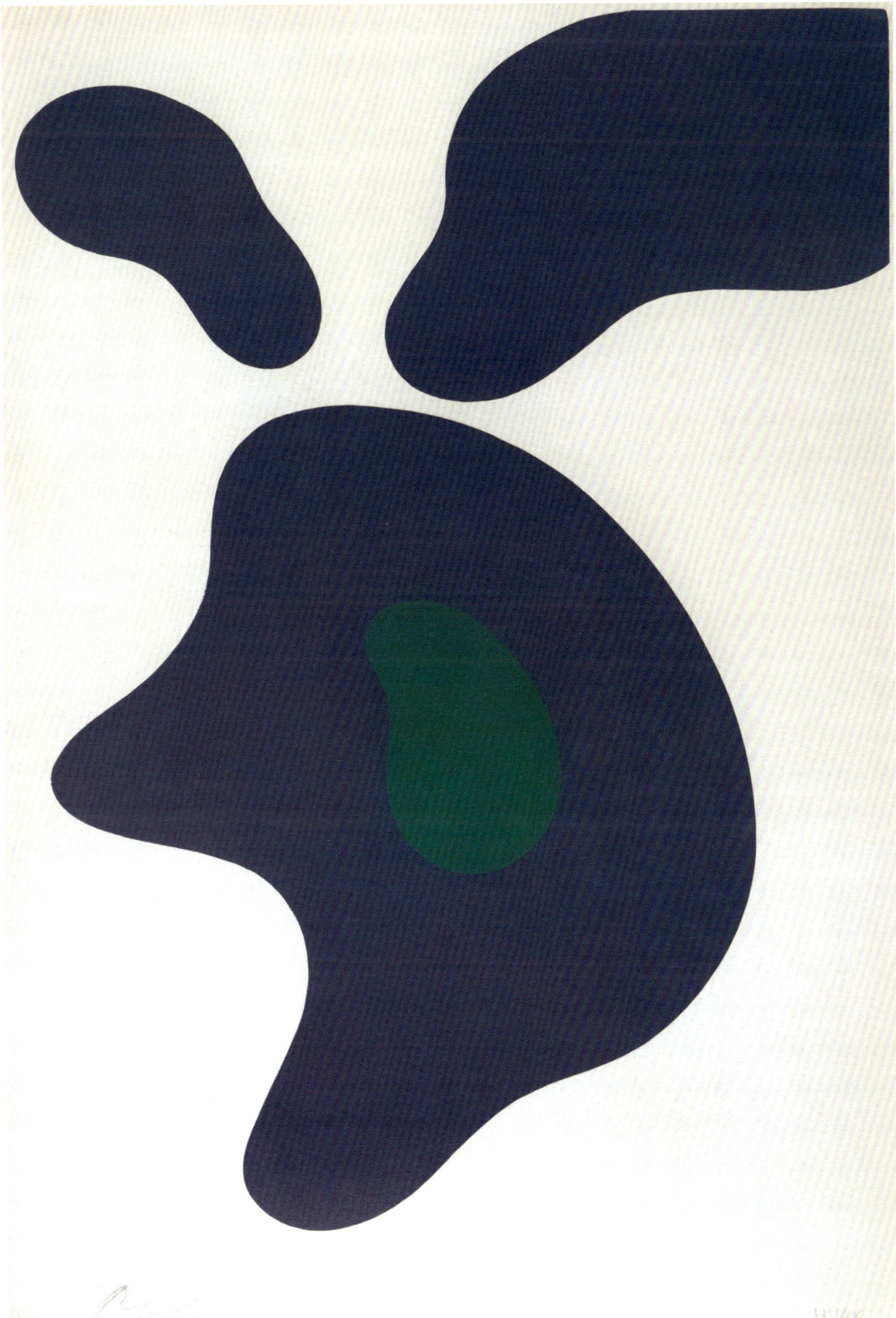

◉ *Fig. 16*
Jean Arp, *Constellation*, 1951
(cat. no. 2).

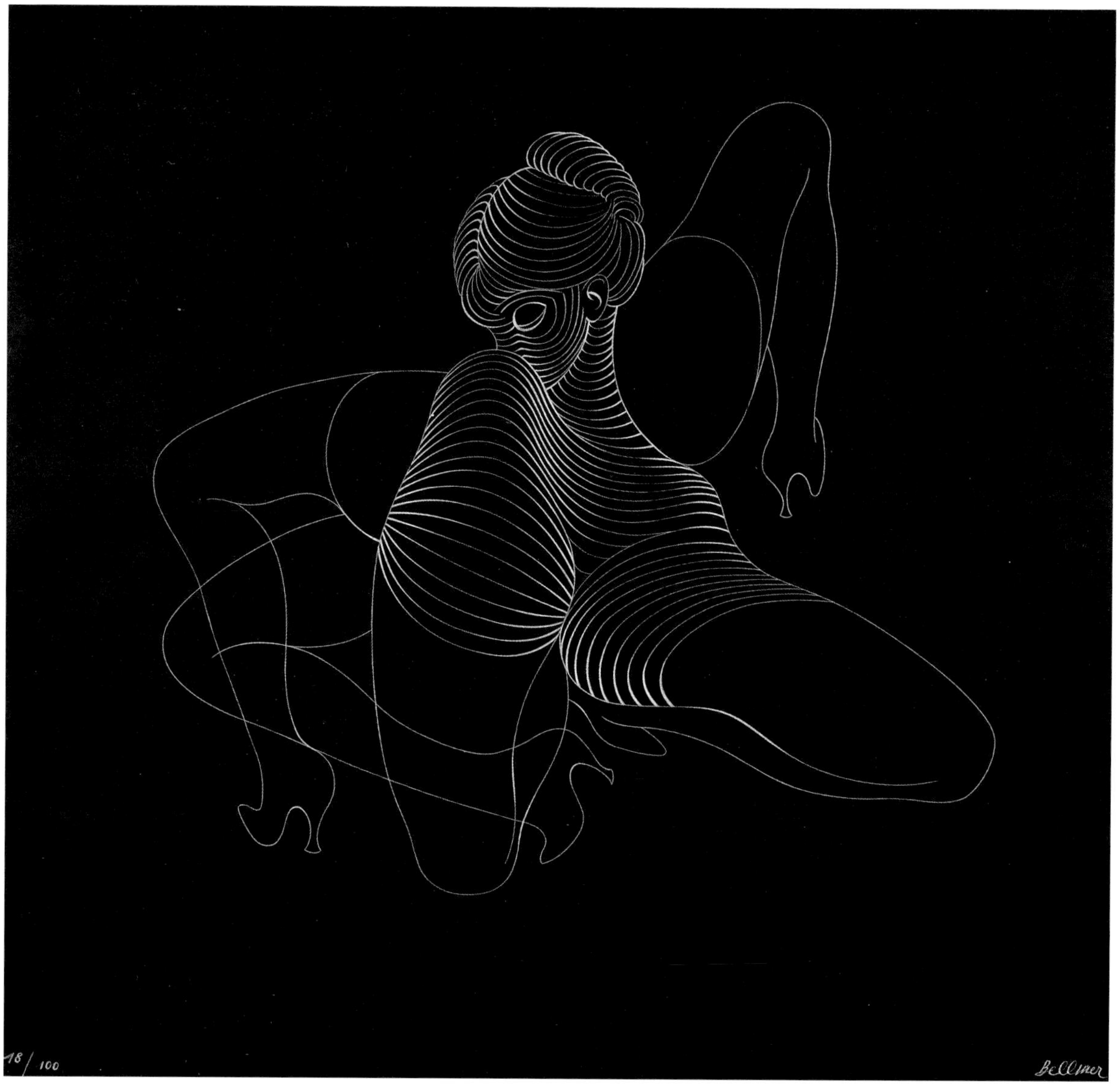

● *Fig. 17*
Hans Bellmer, *Céphalopode double* (Double cephalopod), 1965 (cat. no. 3).

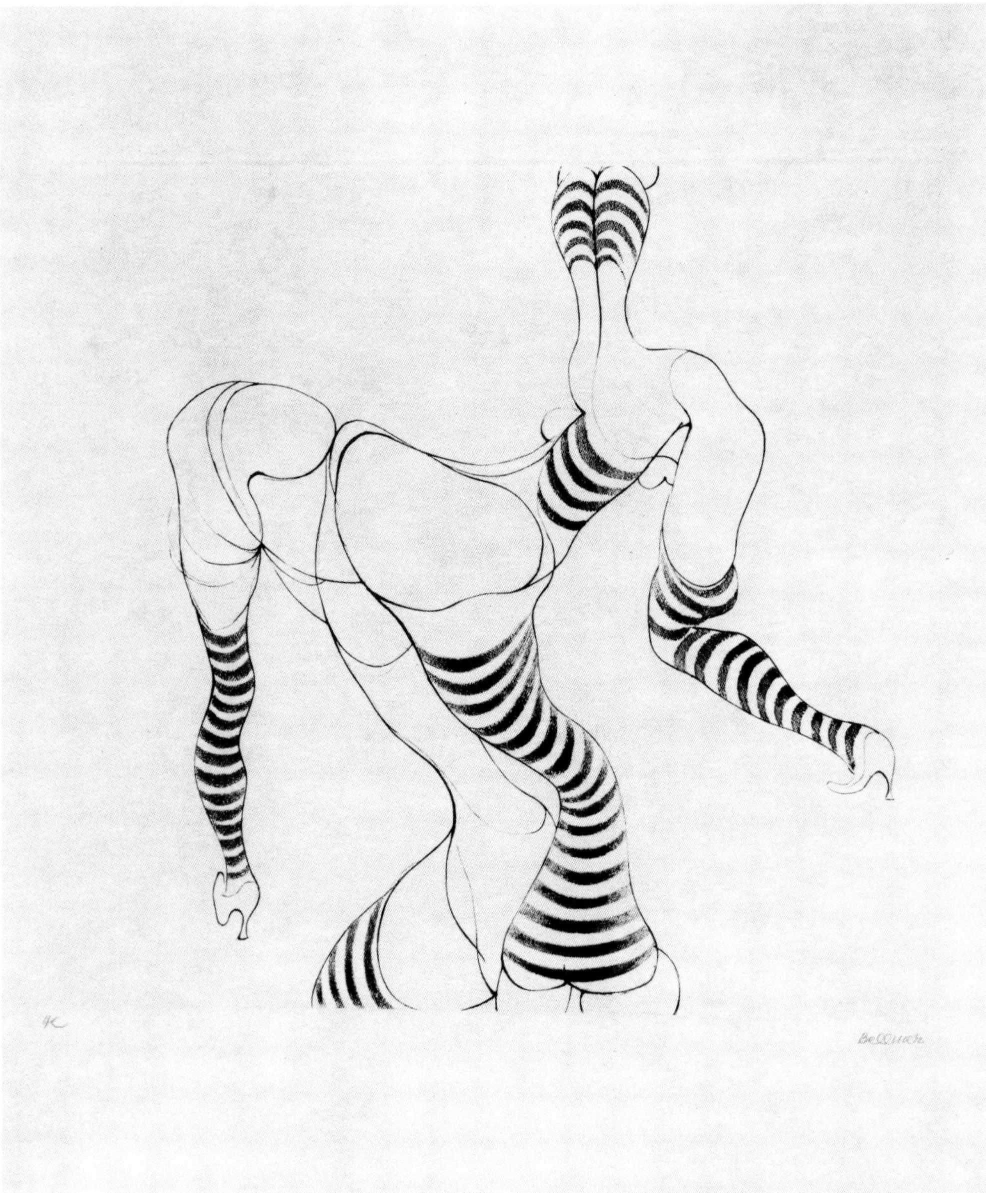

● *Fig. 18*
Hans Bellmer, Untitled, 1967 (cat. no. 4).

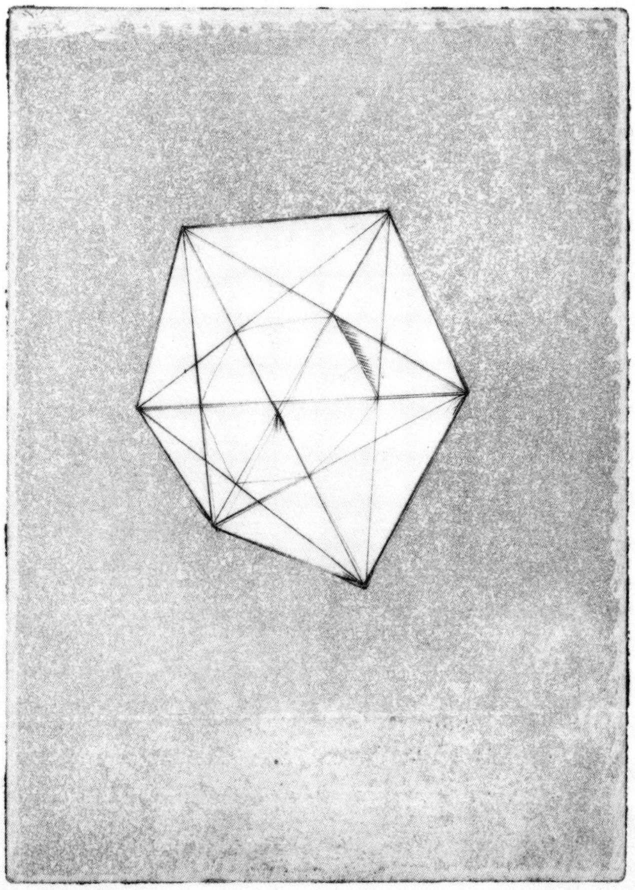

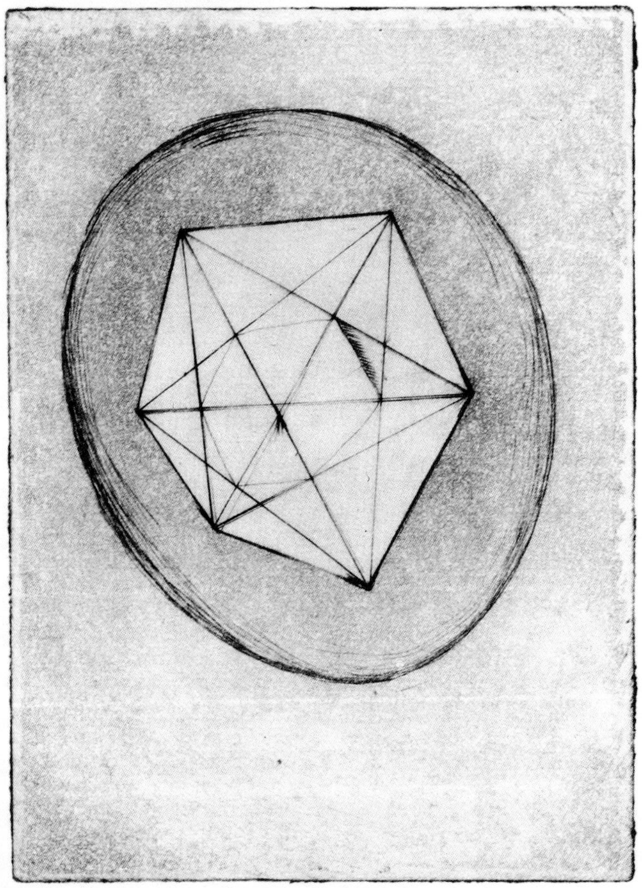

● *Fig. 19*
Victor Brauner, Untitled
(from *Frappe de l'écho*), 1940
(cat. no. 5).

● *Fig. 20*
Victor Brauner, Untitled
(from *Frappe de l'écho*), 1940
(cat. no. 6).

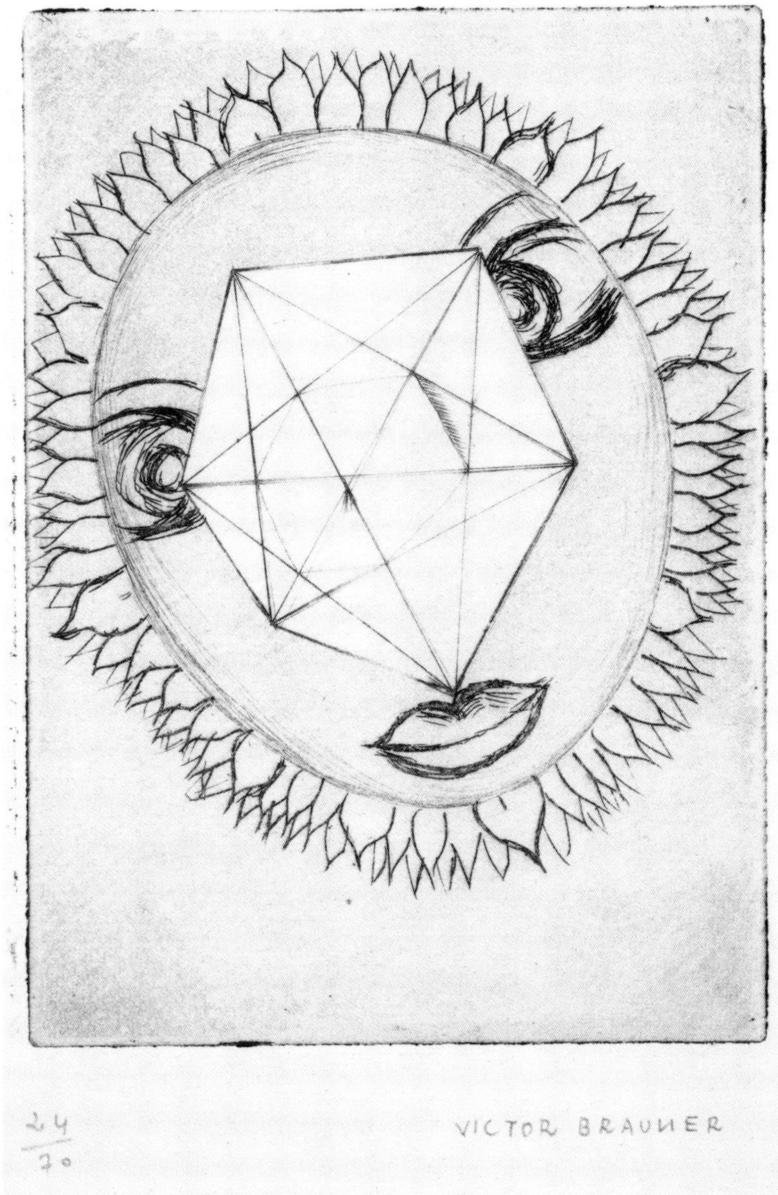

● *Fig. 21*
Victor Brauner, Untitled
(from *Frappe de l'écho*), 1940
(cat. no. 7).

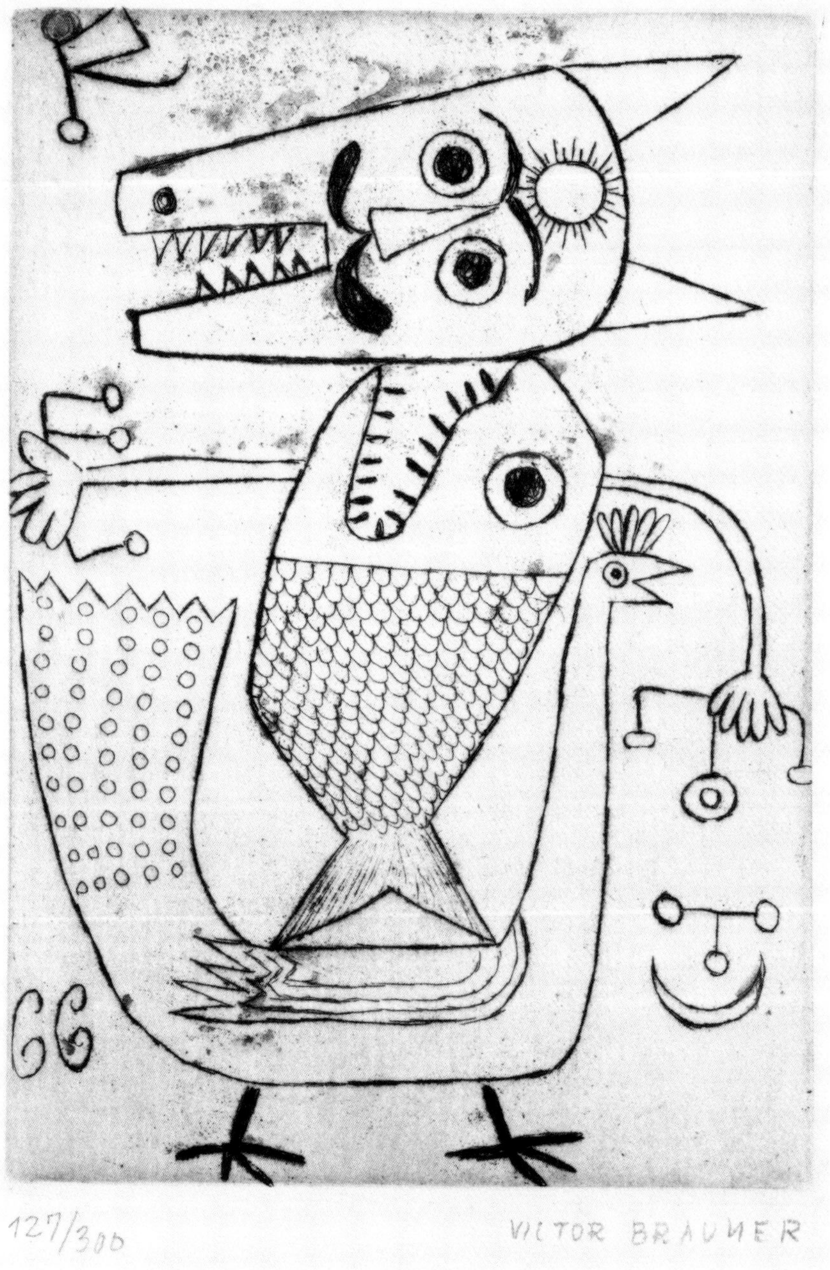

● *Fig. 22*
Victor Brauner, Untitled (from *Le Char triomphal de l'antimoine*), 1949 (cat. no. 9).

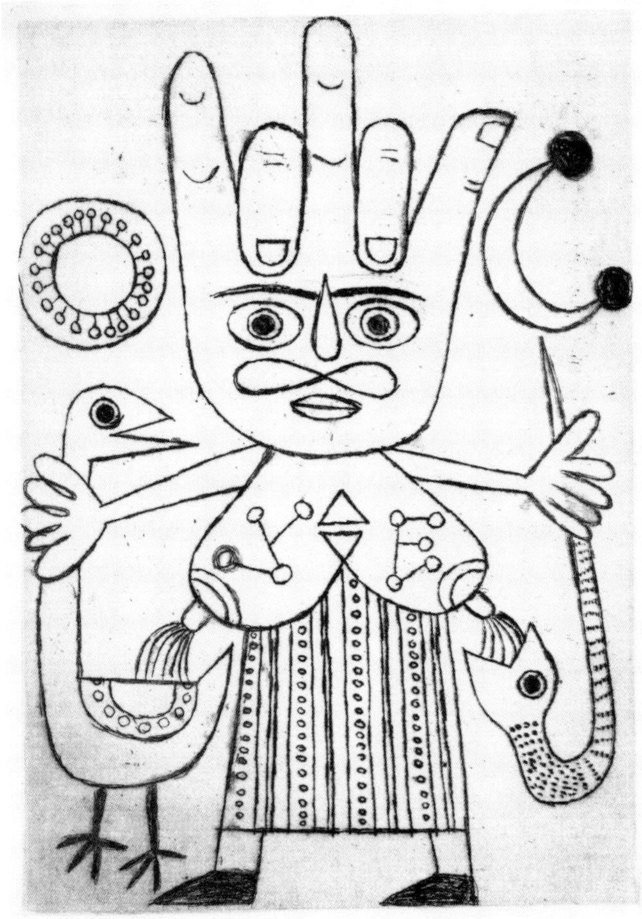

● *Fig. 23*
Victor Brauner, Untitled (from *Le Char triomphal de l'antimoine*), 1949 (cat. no. 10).

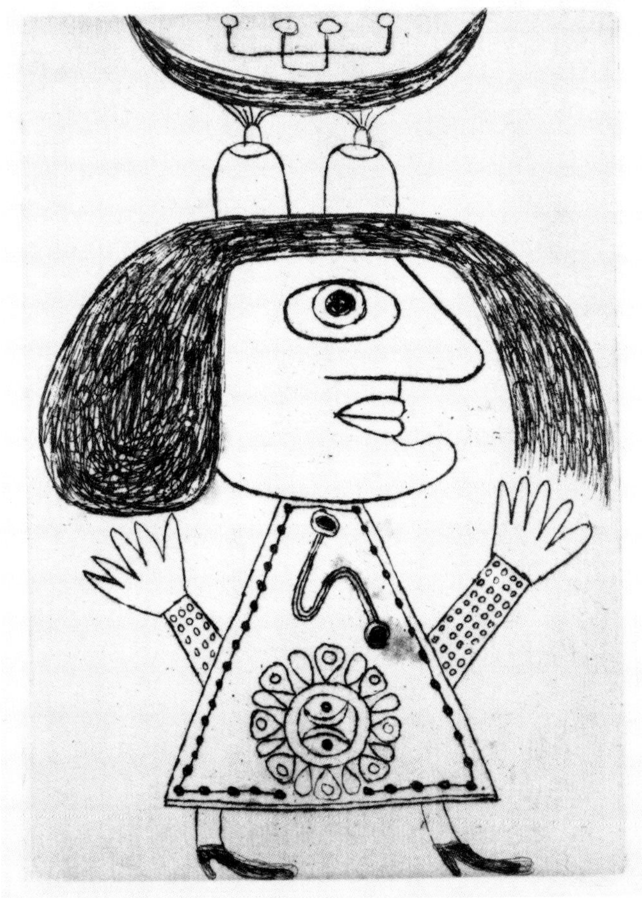

● *Fig. 24*
Victor Brauner, Untitled (from *Le Char triomphal de l'antimoine*), 1949 (cat. no. 11).

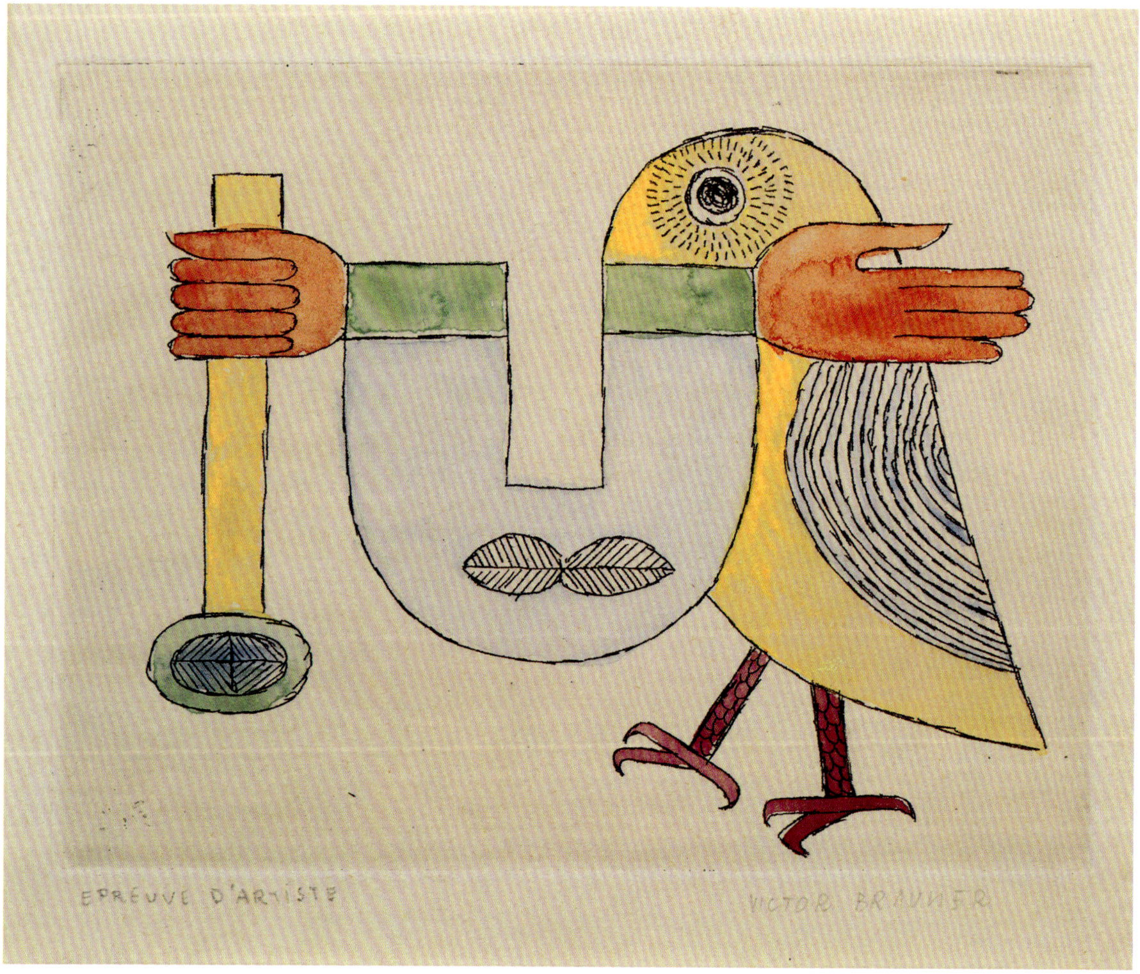

● *Fig. 25*
Victor Brauner, *L'Oiseau innomé* (The unnamed bird), 1958 (cat. no. 12).

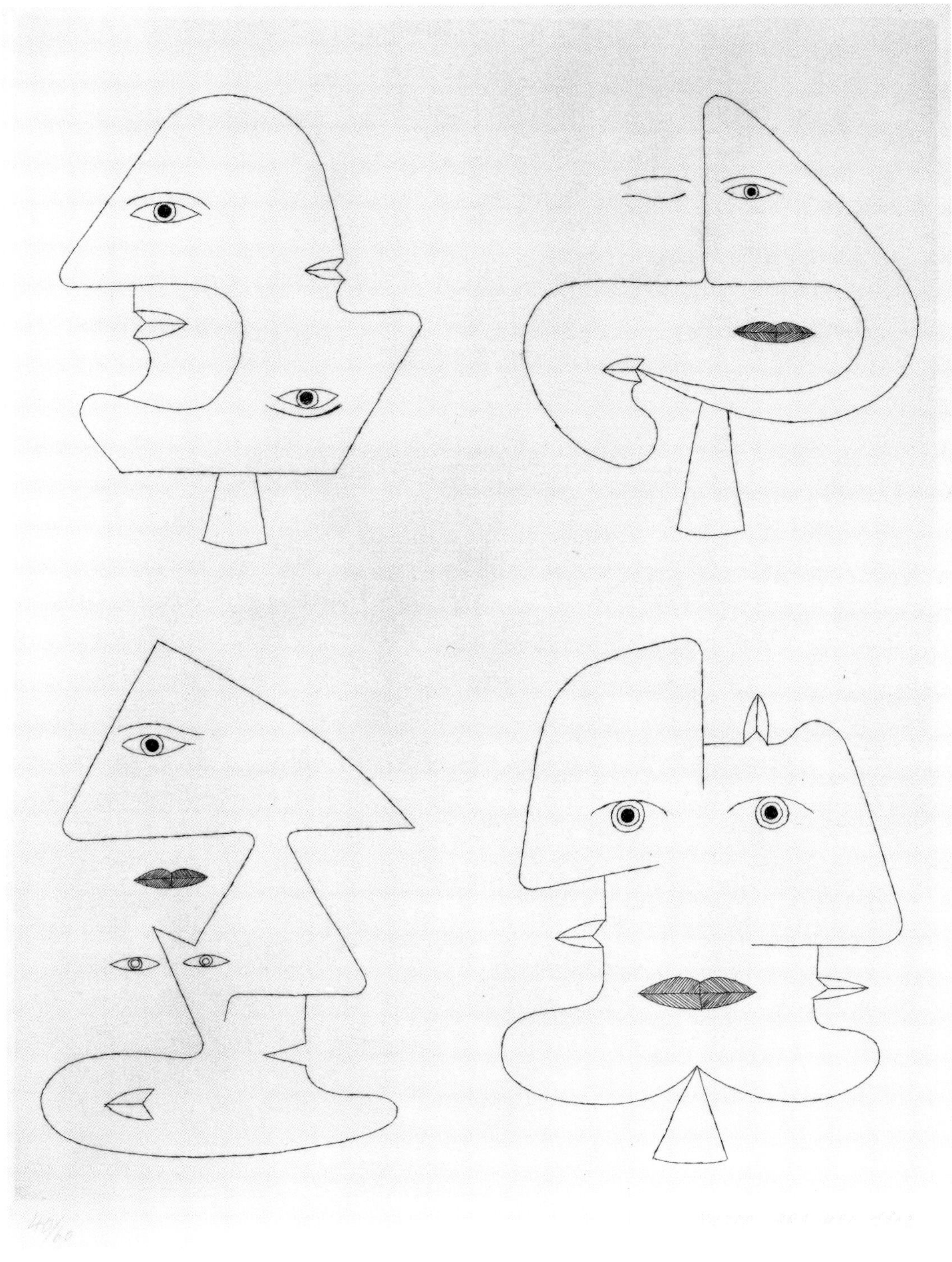

● *Fig. 26*
Victor Brauner, *Révulsion de la fin dans le commencement des mutations inconnues*, 1963 (cat. no. 13).

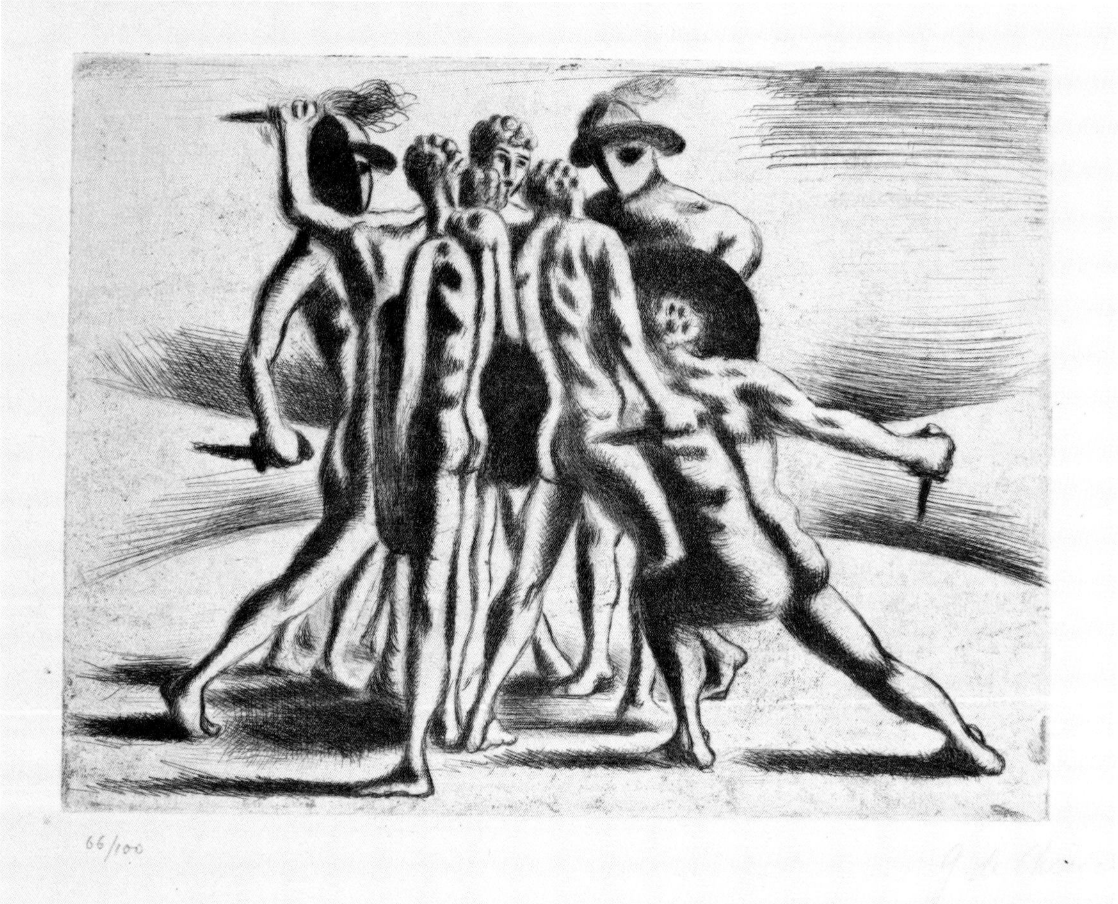

● *Fig. 27*
Giorgio de Chirico,
Combattimento de gladiatori (Battle of the gladiators), 1928 (cat. no. 15). © Foundation Giorgio de Chirico/Licensed by VAGA, New York, NY.

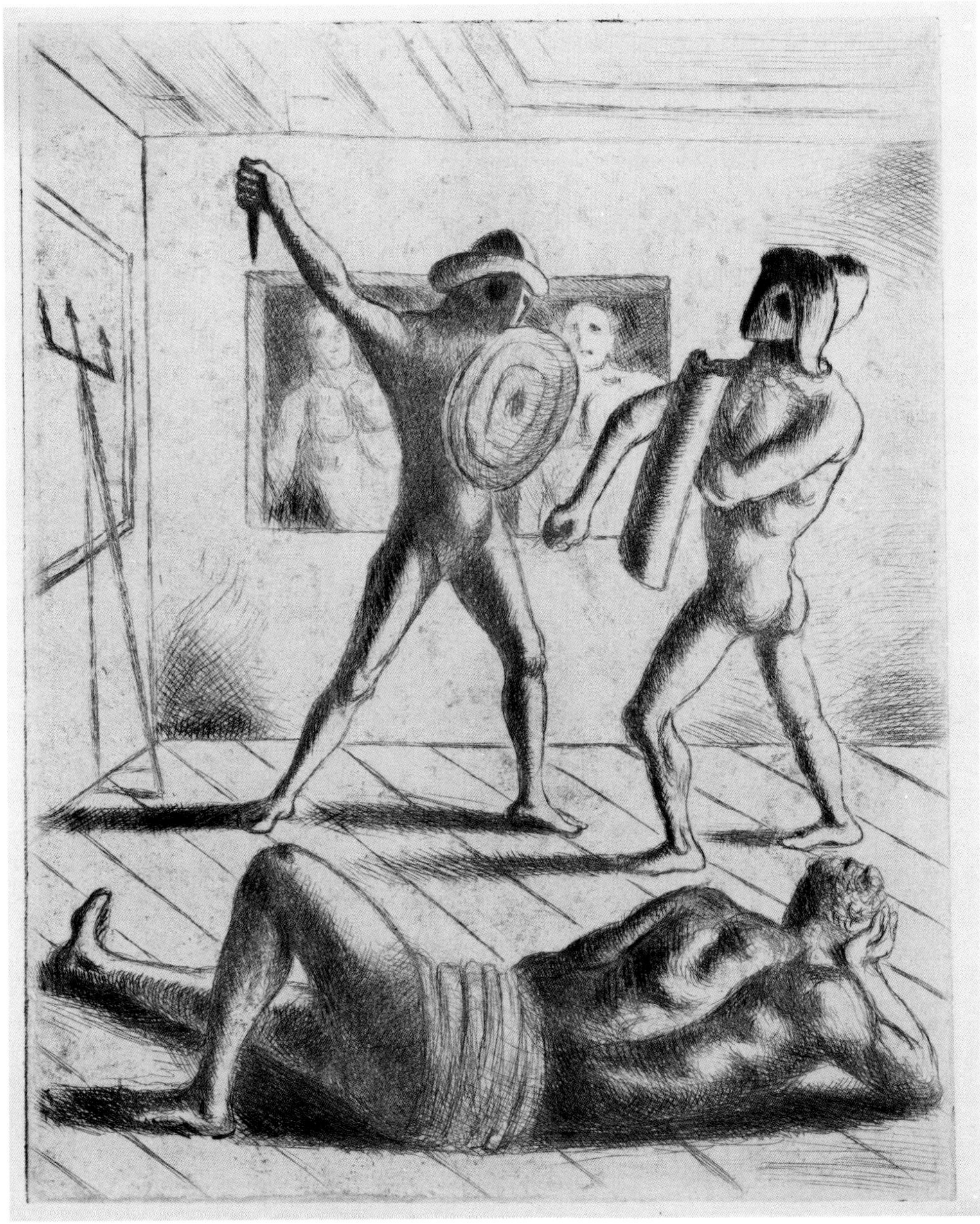

◉ *Fig. 28*
Giorgio de Chirico, *Scuola di gladiatori I* (School of the gladiators I), 1928 (cat. no. 16).

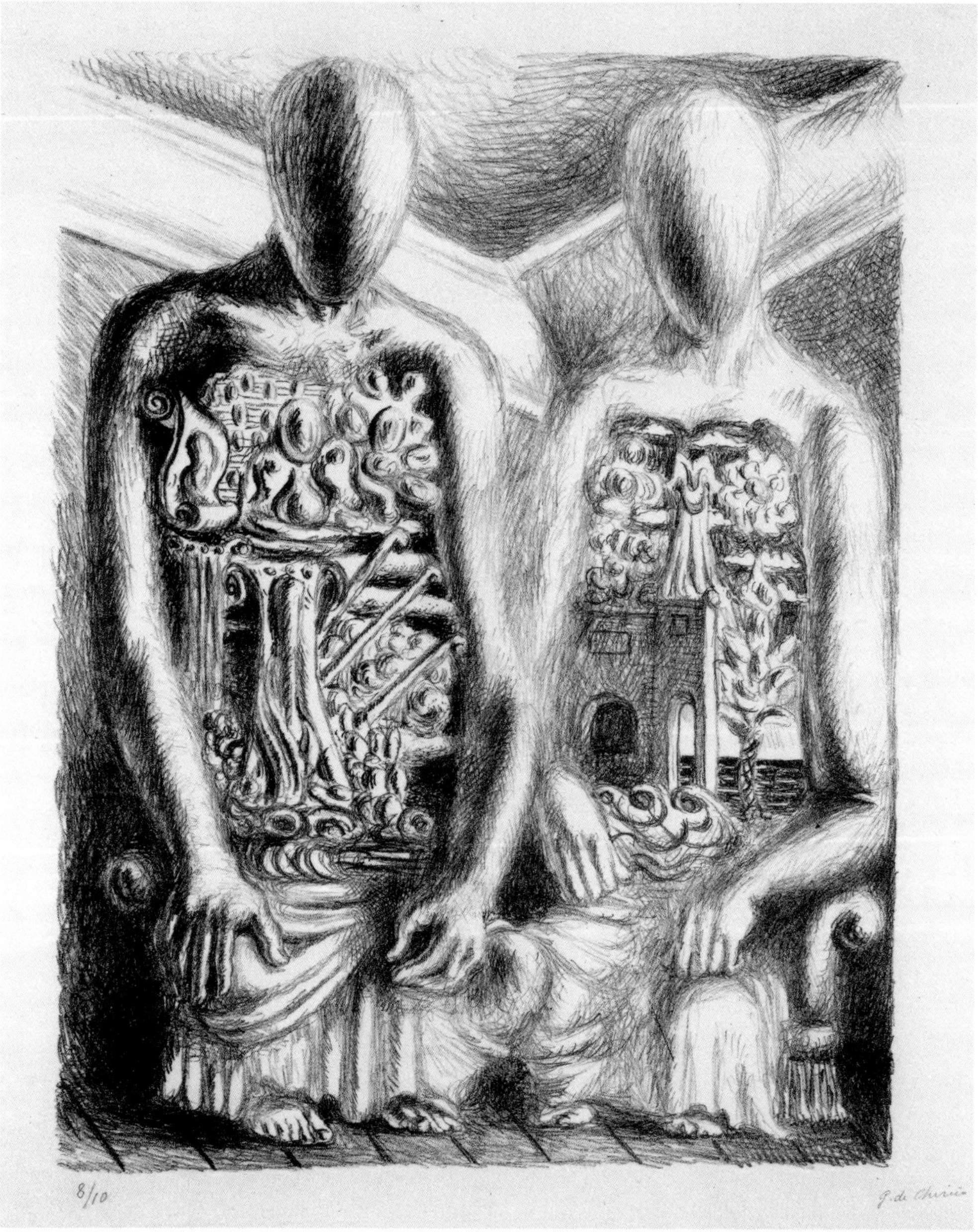

● *Fig. 29*
Giorgio de Chirico, *Gli archeologi IV* (The archaeologists IV), 1929 (cat. no. 17). © Foundation Giorgio de Chirico/ Licensed by VAGA, New York, NY.

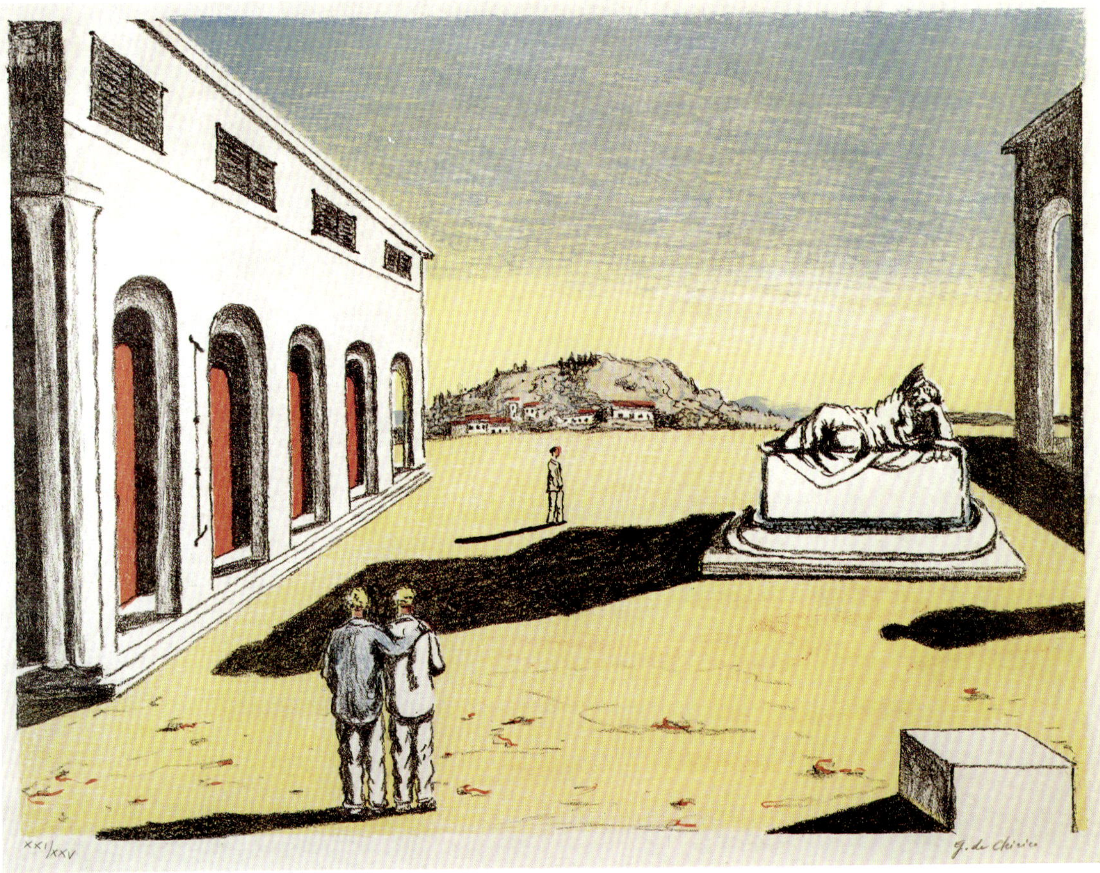

● *Fig. 30*
Giorgio de Chirico, *Ricordo d'autunno* (Memory of autumn), 1969 (cat. no. 18).

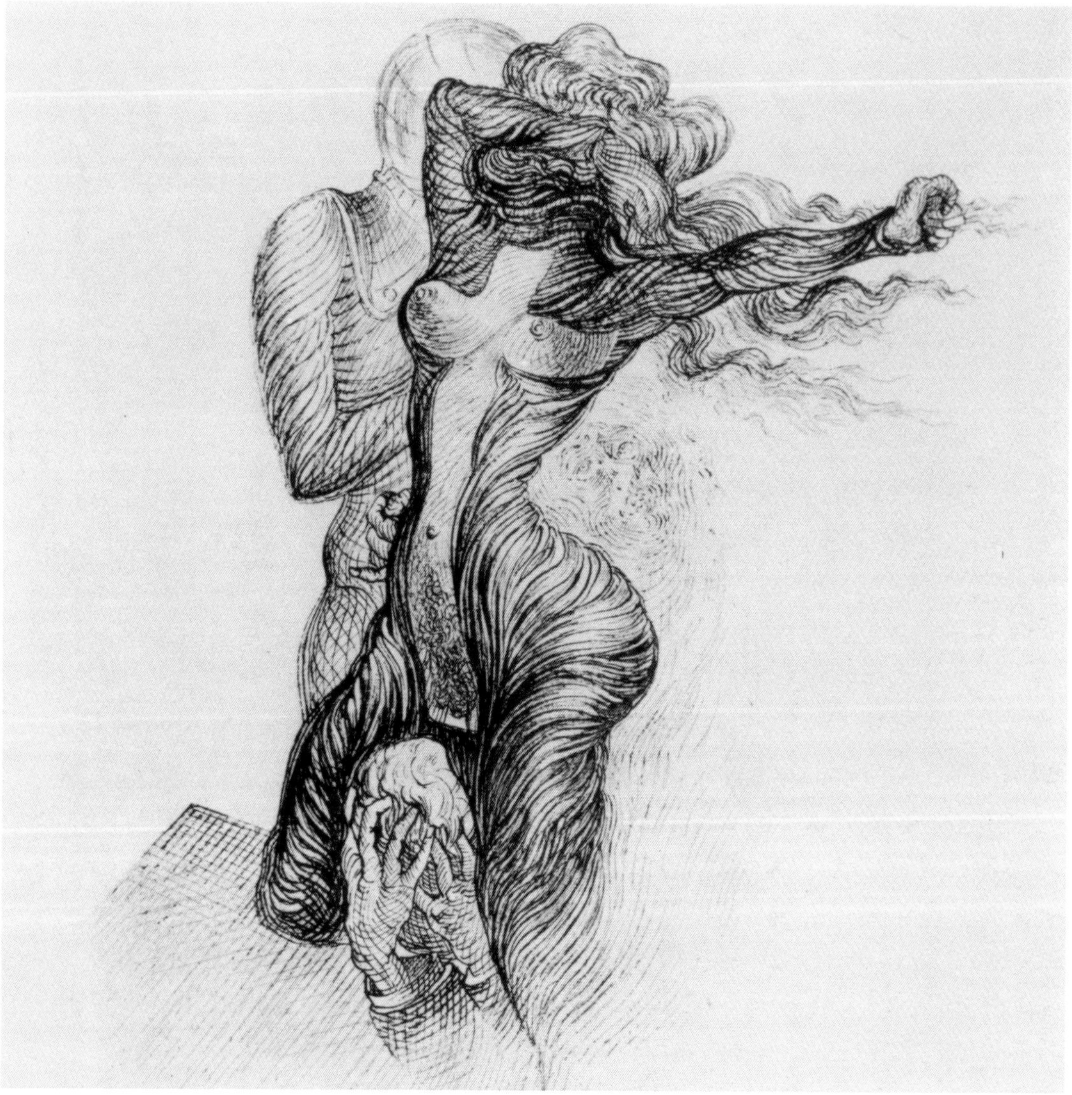

● *Fig. 31*
Salvador Dali, *L'Immaculée Conception* (The Immaculate Conception), 1930 (cat. no. 19).

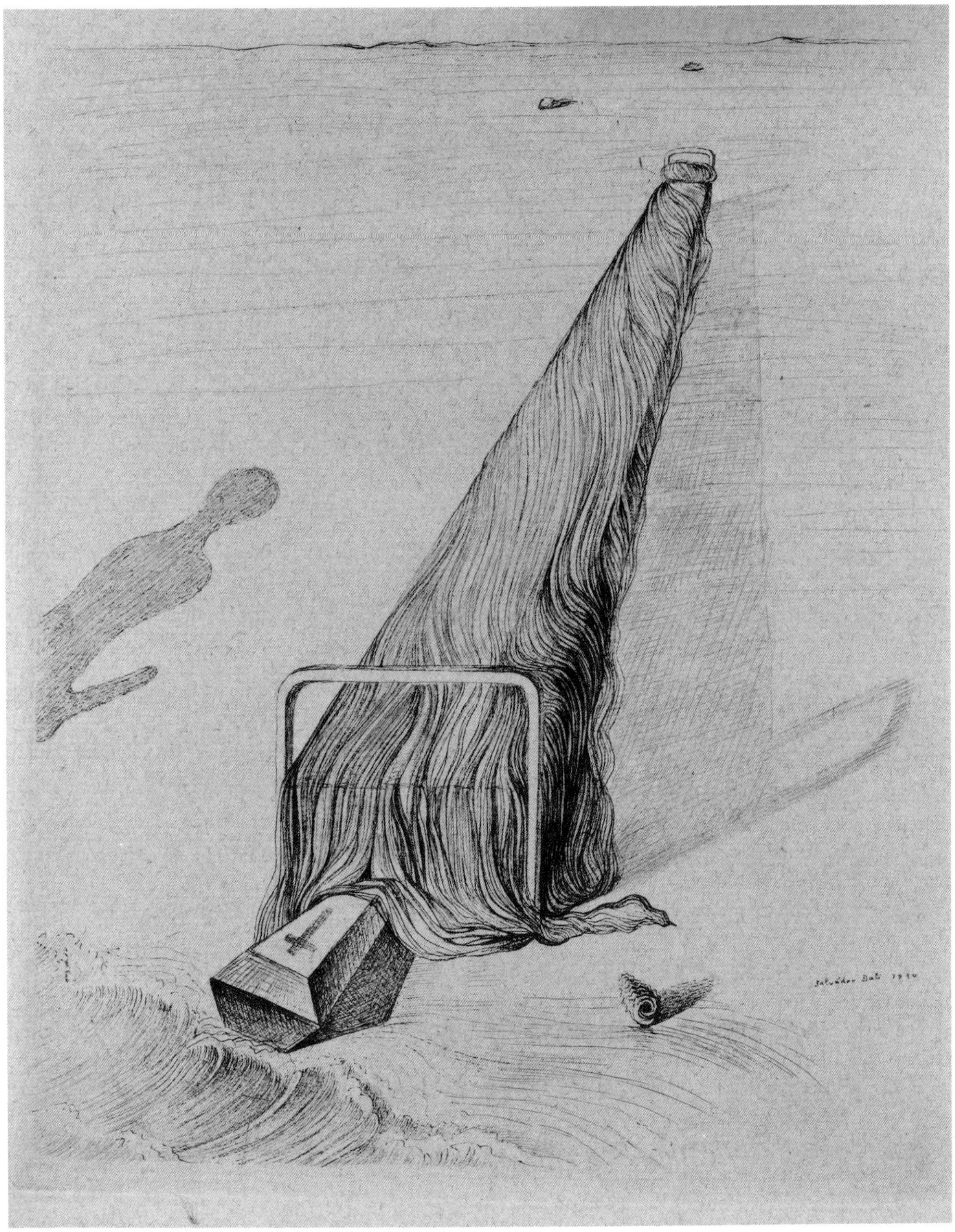

● *Fig. 32*
Salvador Dalí, *Artine*, 1930
(cat. no. 20).

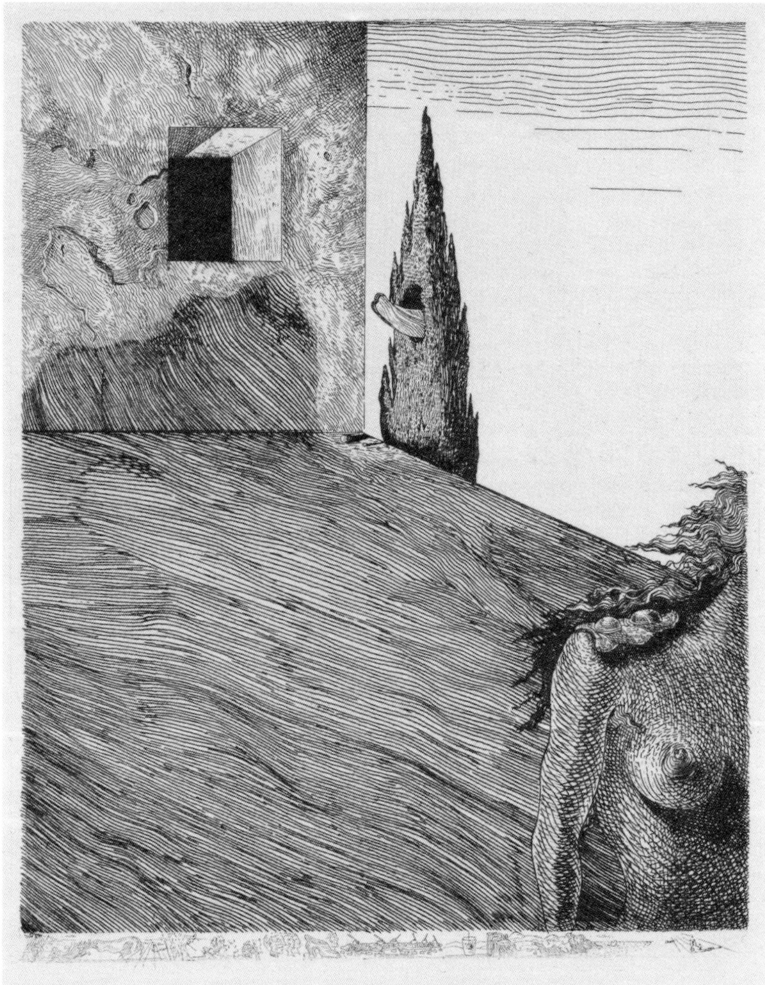

● *Fig. 33*
Salvador Dalí, *Le Revolver à cheveux blancs* (The white-haired revolver), 1932 (cat. no. 22).

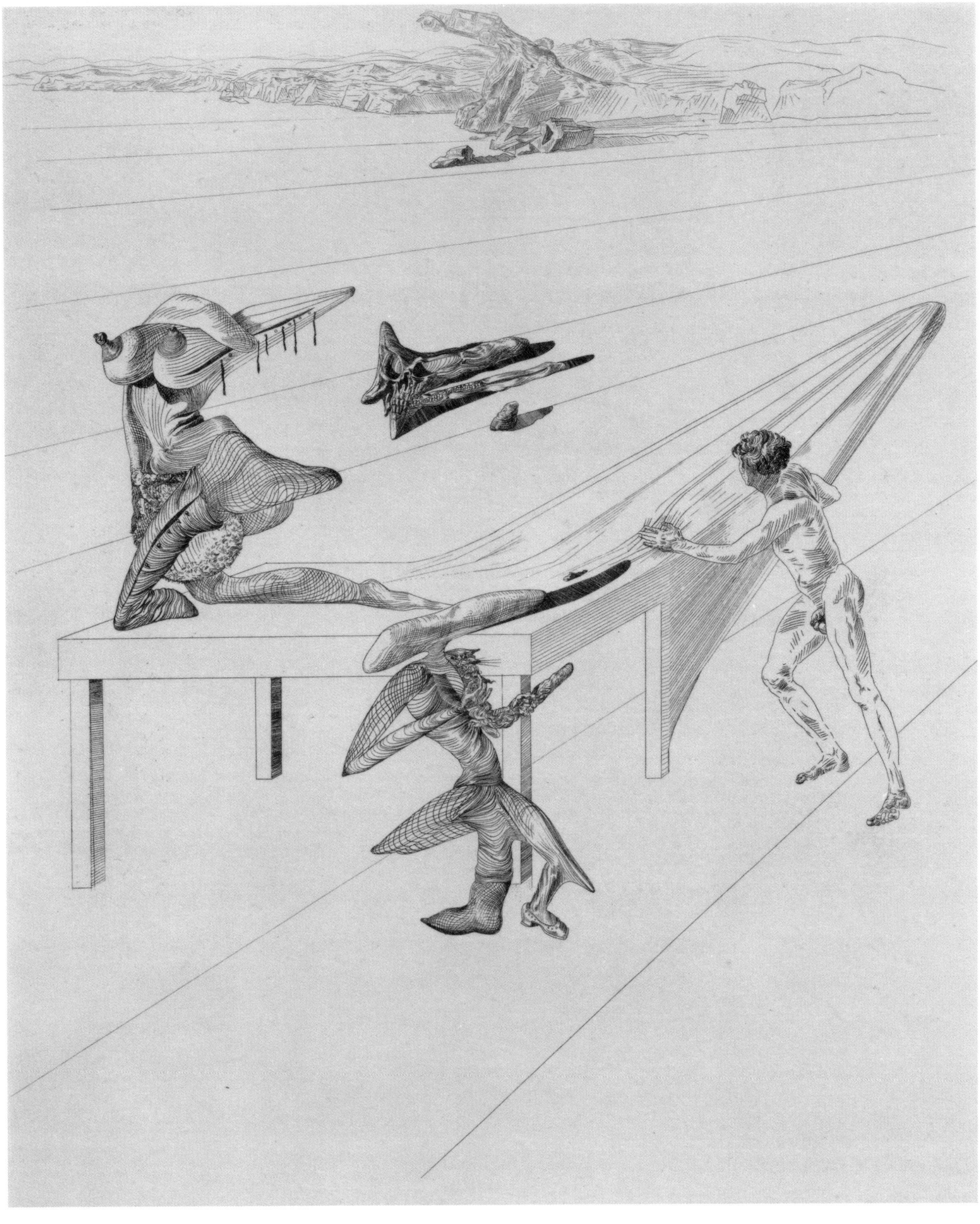

● *Fig. 34*
Salvador Dalí, *L'Enfant-sauterelle* (Grasshopper child), 1934 (cat. no. 23).

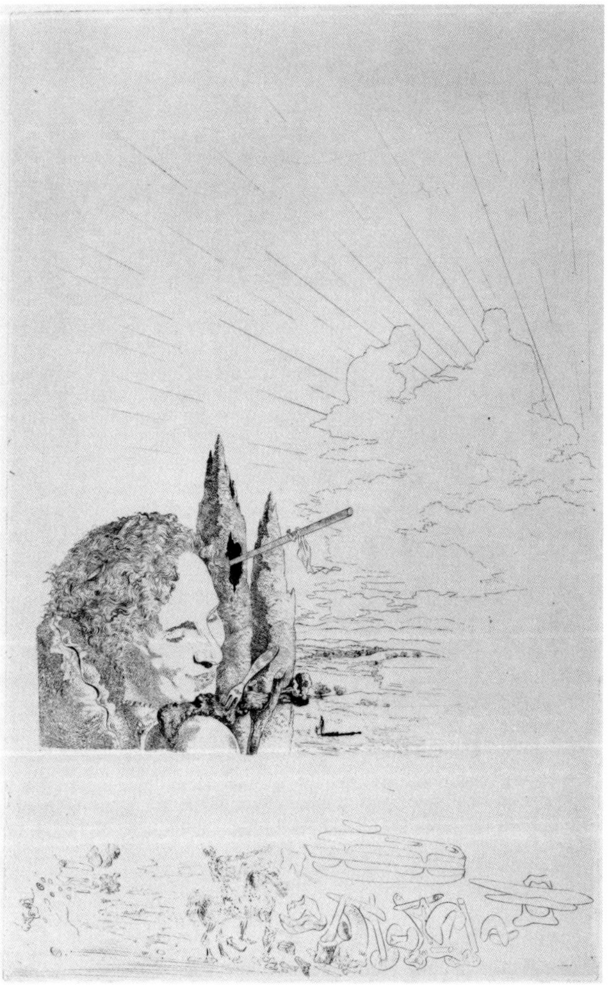

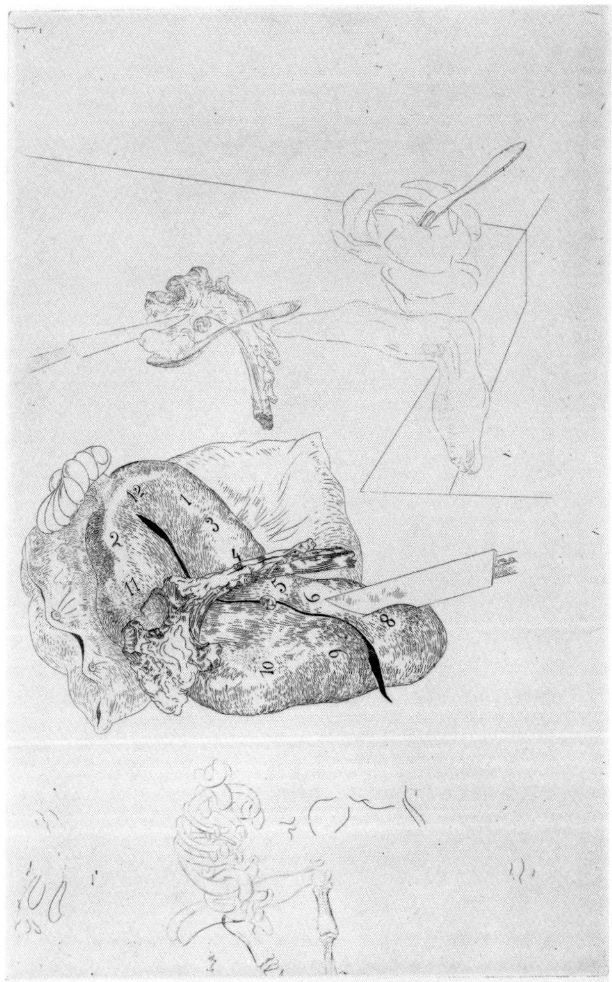

● *Fig. 35*
Salvador Dali, Untitled (from *Les Chants de Maldoror*), 1934 (cat. no. 26).

● *Fig. 36*
Salvador Dali, Untitled (from *Les Chants de Maldoror*), 1934 (cat. no. 27).

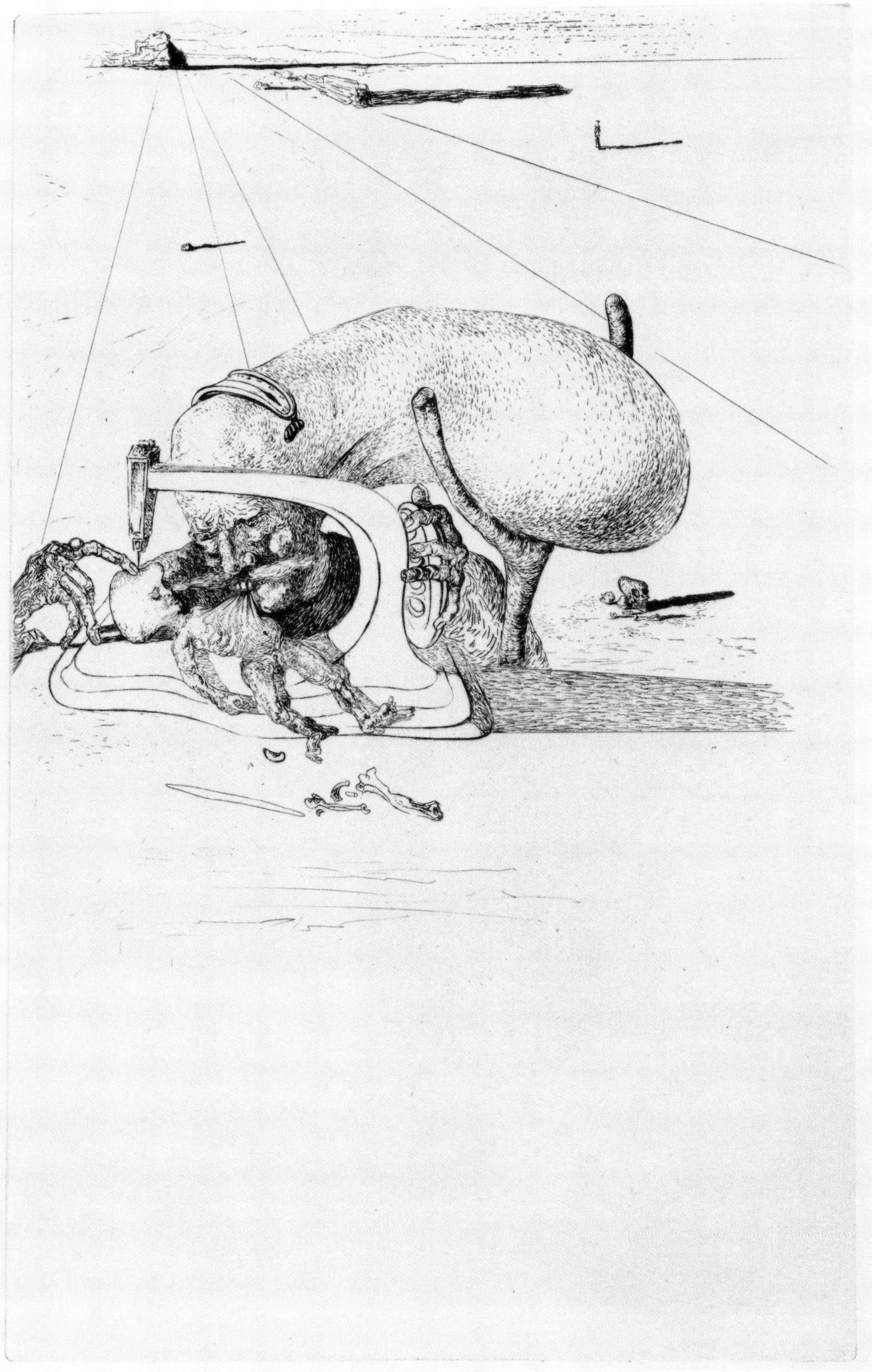

● *Fig. 37*
Salvador Dalí, Untitled (from *Les Chants de Maldoror*), 1934 (cat. no. 28).

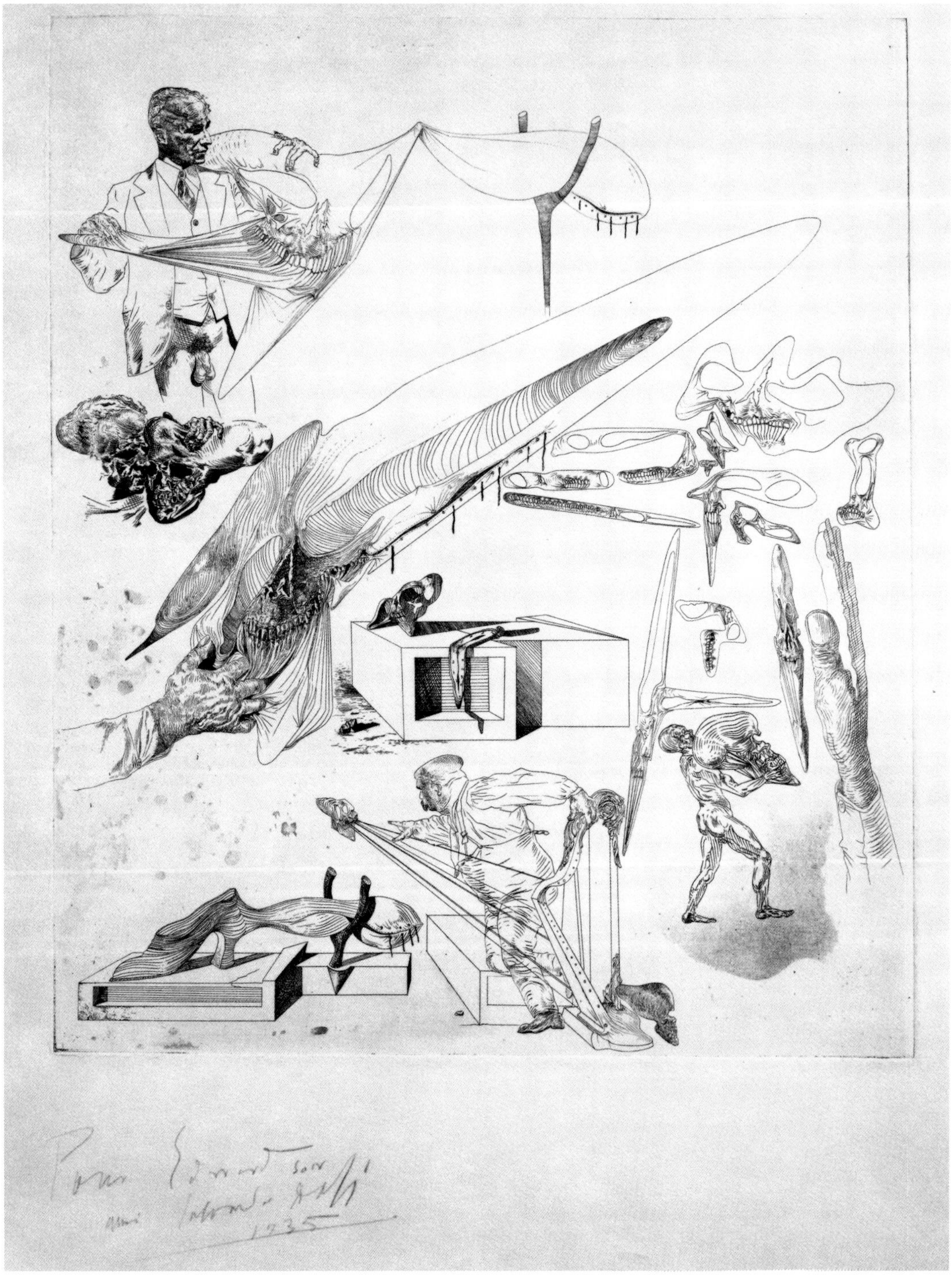

● *Fig. 38*
Salvador Dalí, *Crânes mous et harpe crânienne* (Limp cranes and "cranian" harp), 1935 (cat. no. 30).

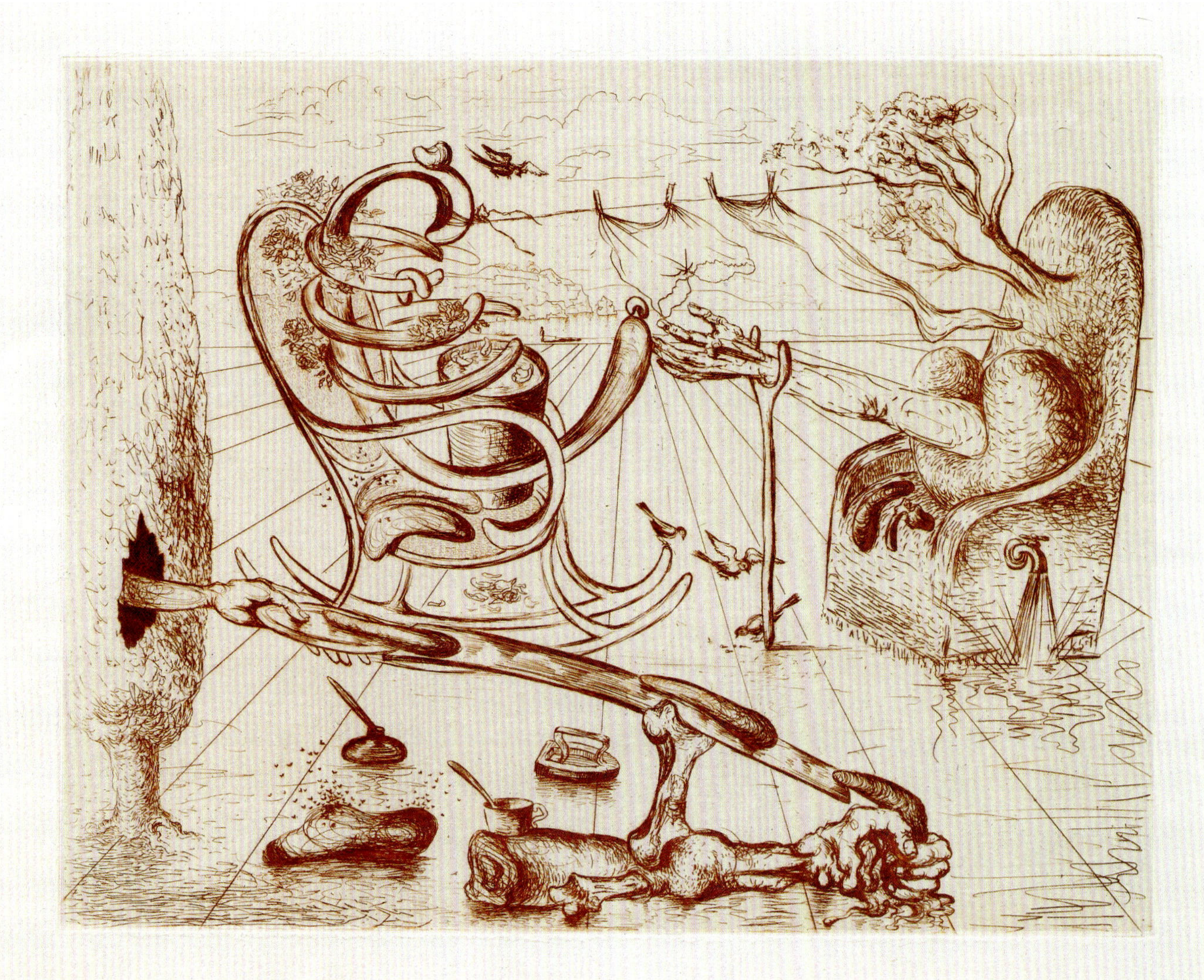

◉ *Fig. 39*
Salvador Dali, *Fantastic Beach Scene*, 1935 (cat. no. 31).

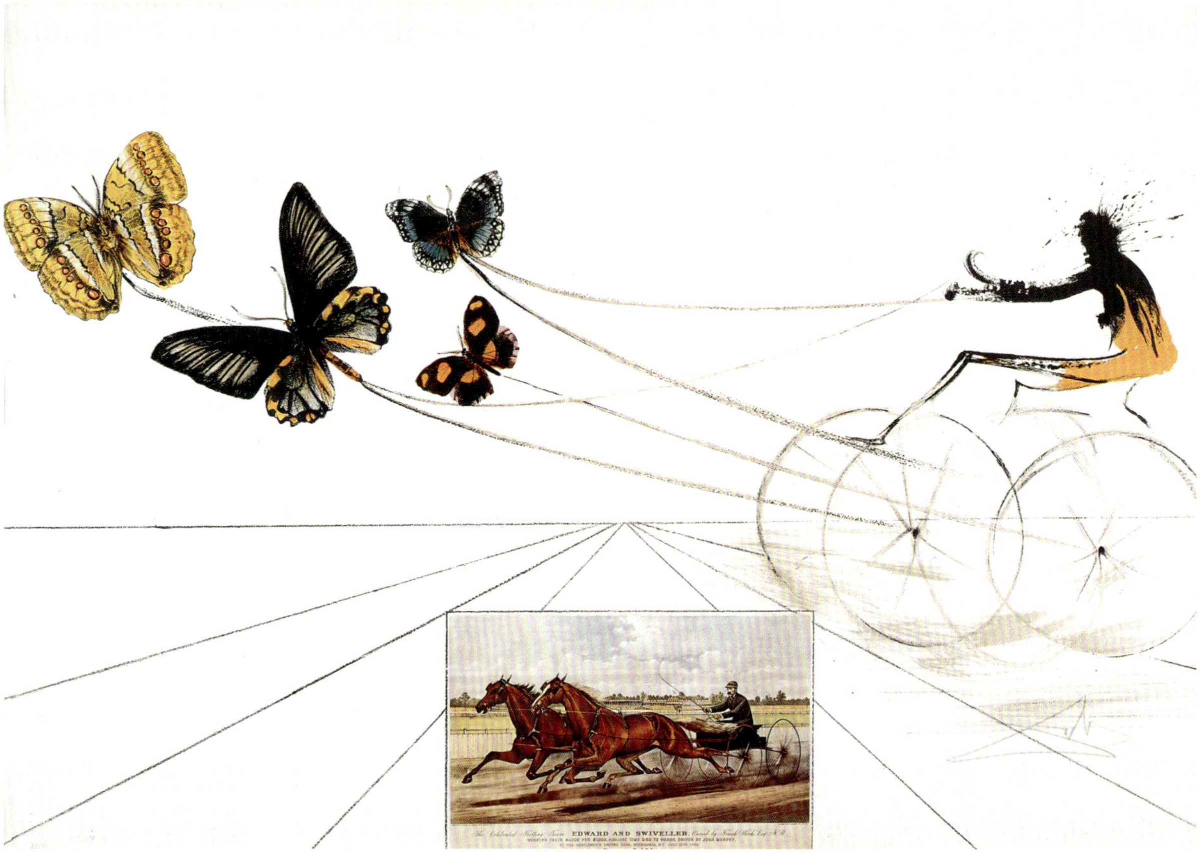

● *Fig. 40*
Salvador Dali, *American Trotting Horses No. 1*, 1971
(cat. no. 32).

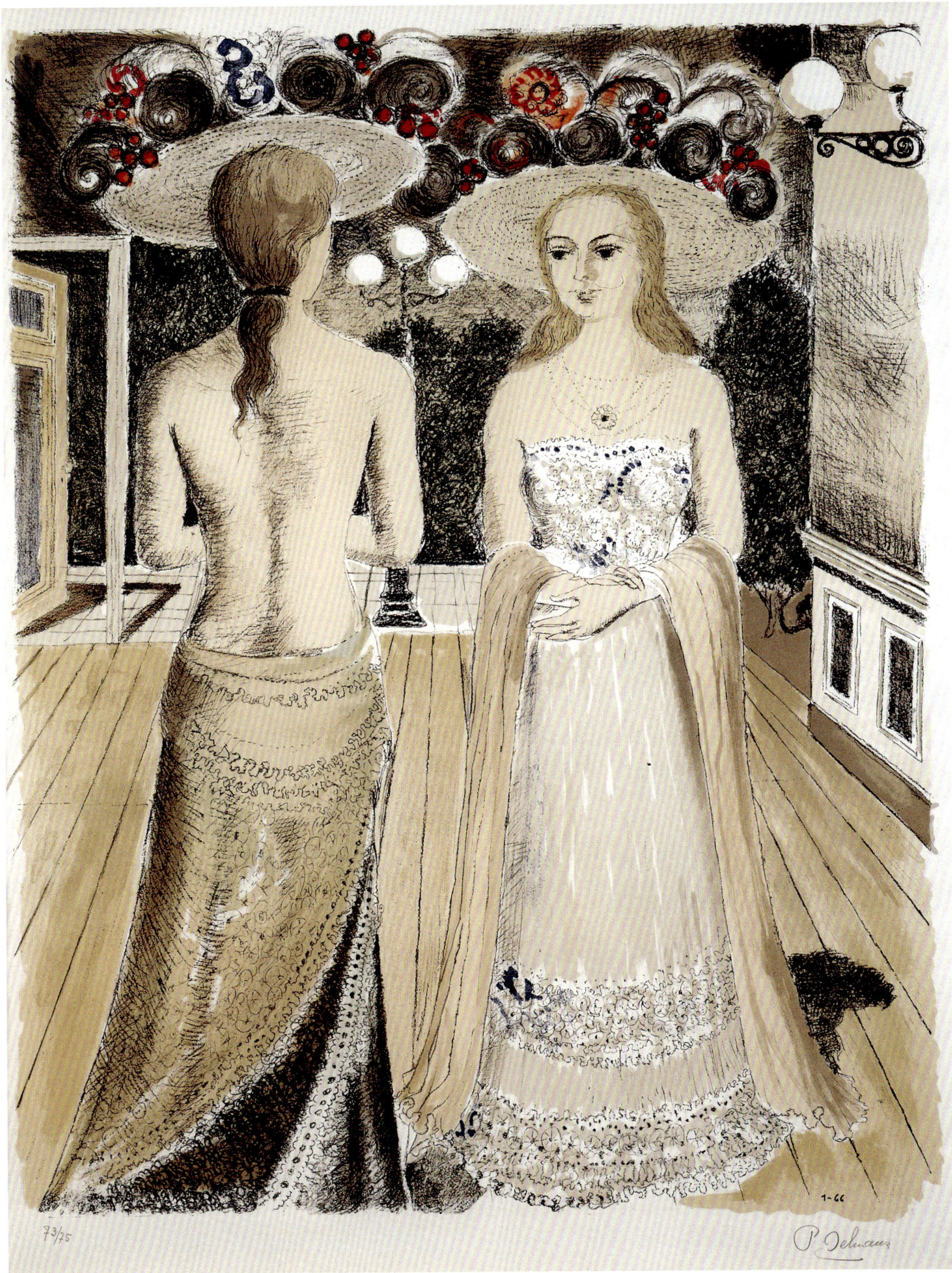

● *Fig. 41*
Paul Delvaux, *Les Deux Rivales* (The rivals), 1966 (cat. no. 34).

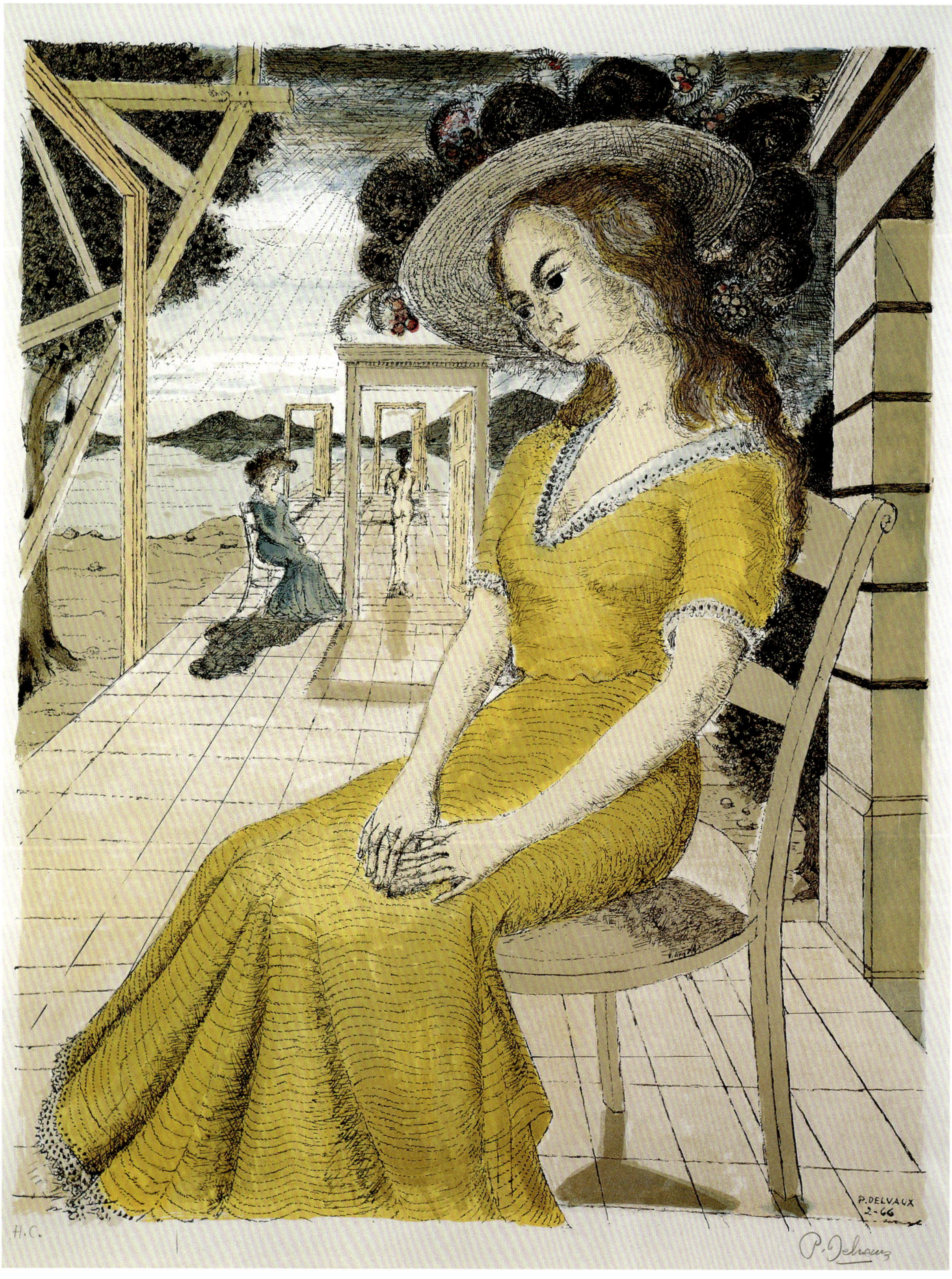

● *Fig. 42*
Paul Delvaux, *Anne songeuse* (Annie lost in thought), 1966 (cat. no. 35). © Estate of Paul Delvaux/ Licensed by VAGA, New York, NY.

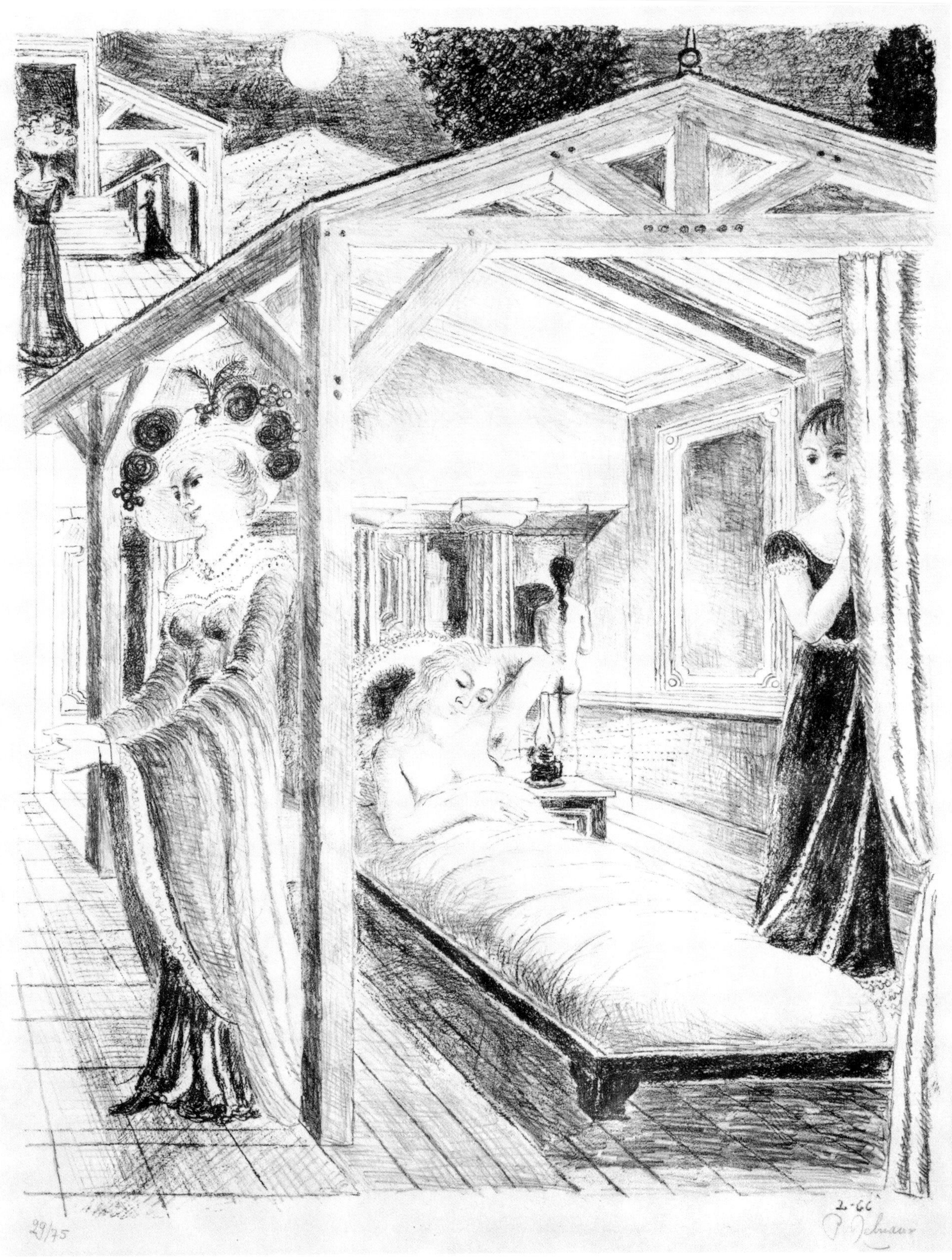

● *Fig. 43*
Paul Delvaux, *La Mer est proche* (The sea is near), 1966 (cat. no. 36).

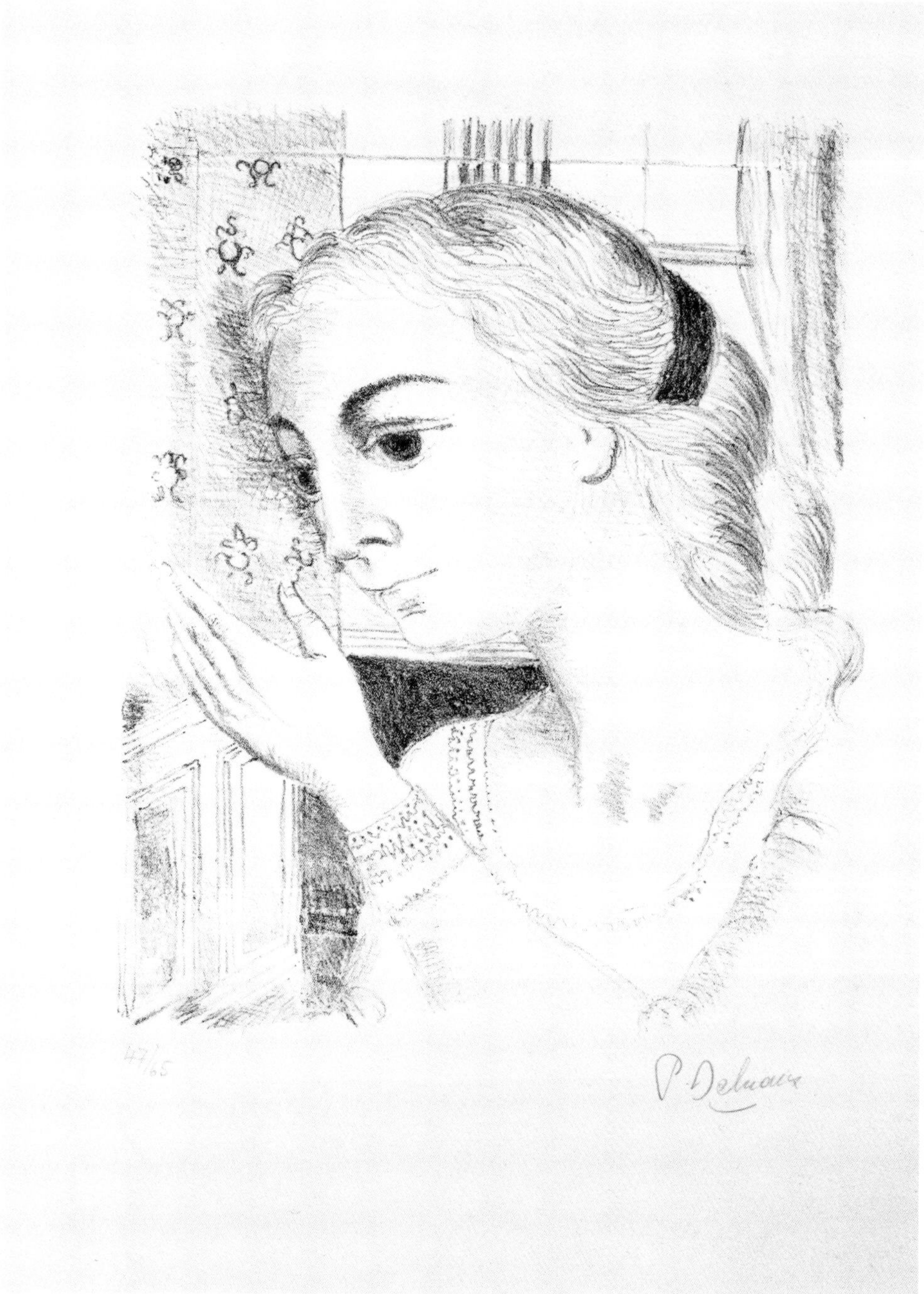

● *Fig. 44*
Paul Delvaux, *La Dame à la bougie* (Lady with the candle), 1966 (cat. no. 37). © Estate of Paul Delvaux/Licensed by VAGA, New York, NY.

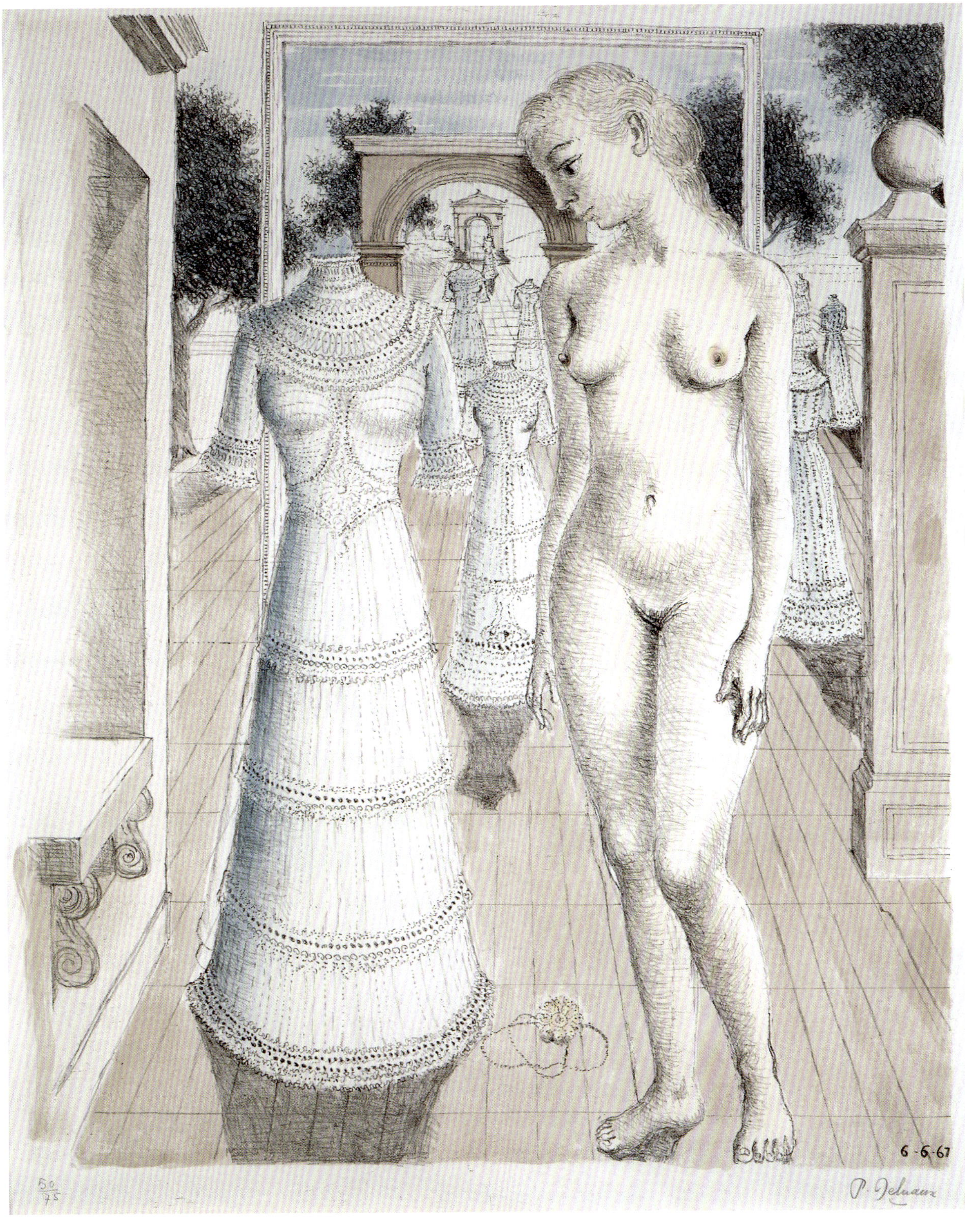

● *Fig. 45*
Paul Delvaux, *La Robe du dimanche* (Sunday dress), 1967 (cat. no. 38).

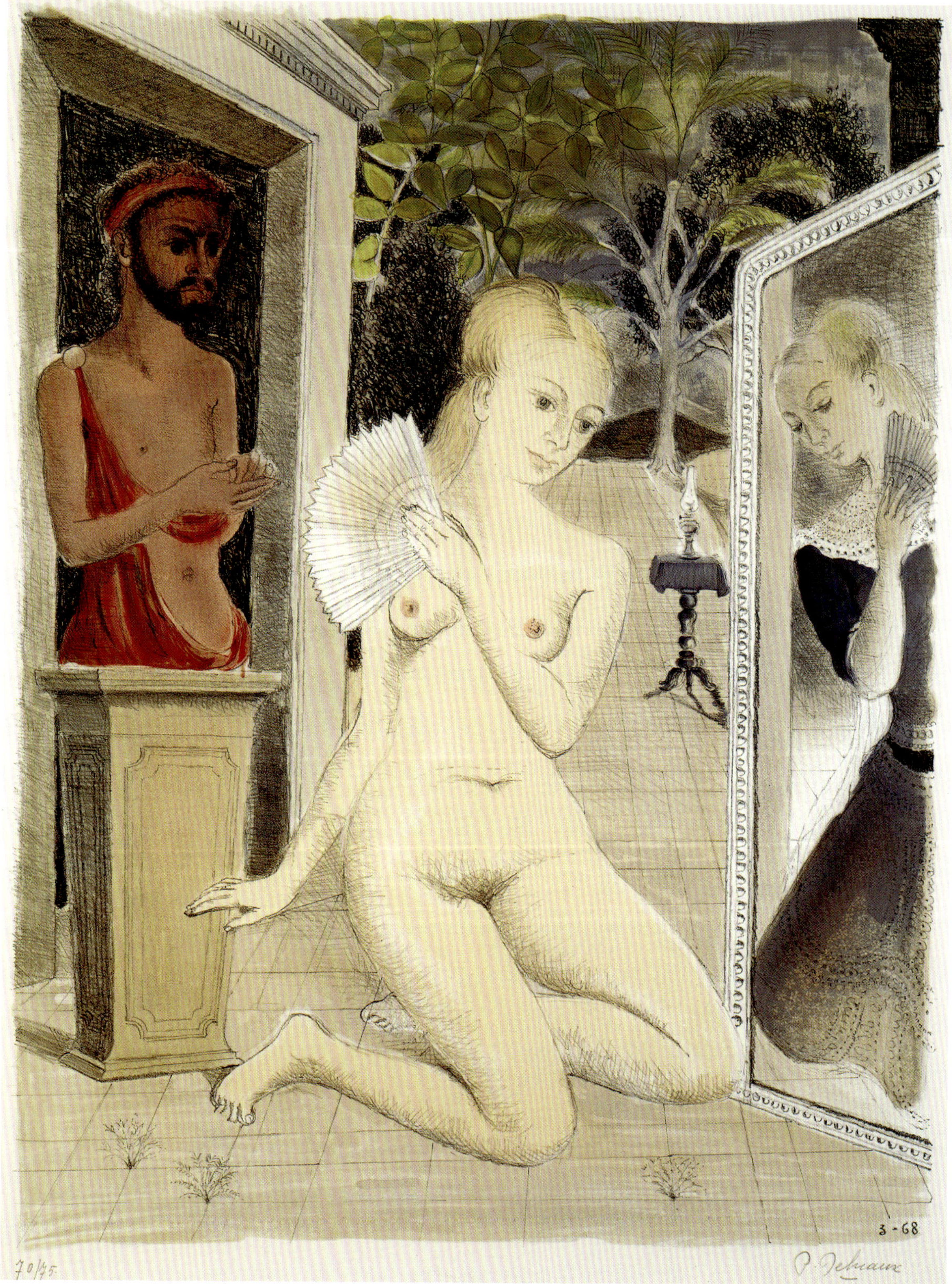

● *Fig. 46*
Paul Delvaux, *L'Eventail* (The fan), 1968 (cat. no. 39). © Estate of Paul Delvaux/Licensed by VAGA, New York, NY.

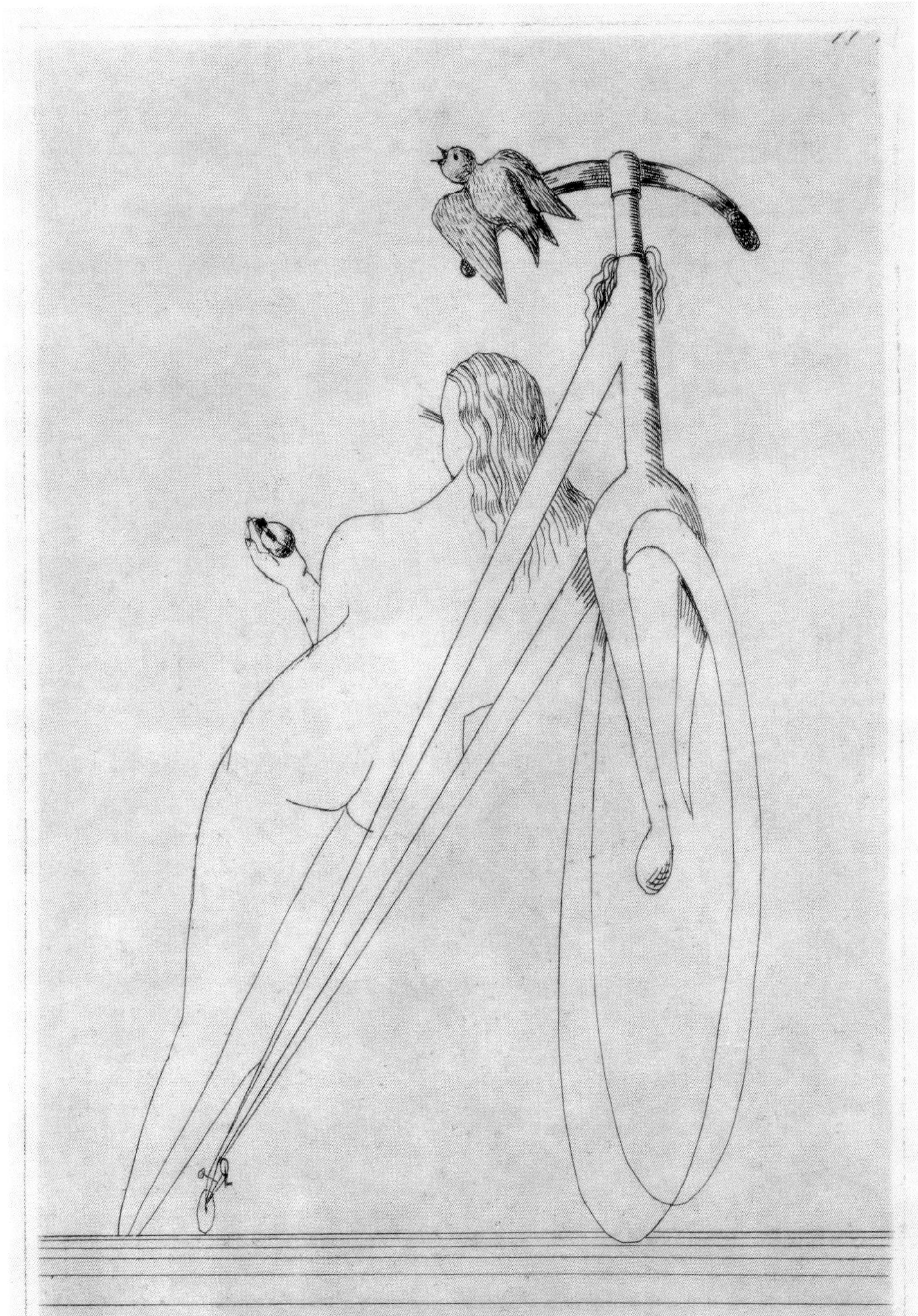

Fig. 47
Oscar Dominguez, *Femme à la bicyclette* (Woman with a bicycle), 1935 (cat. no. 40).

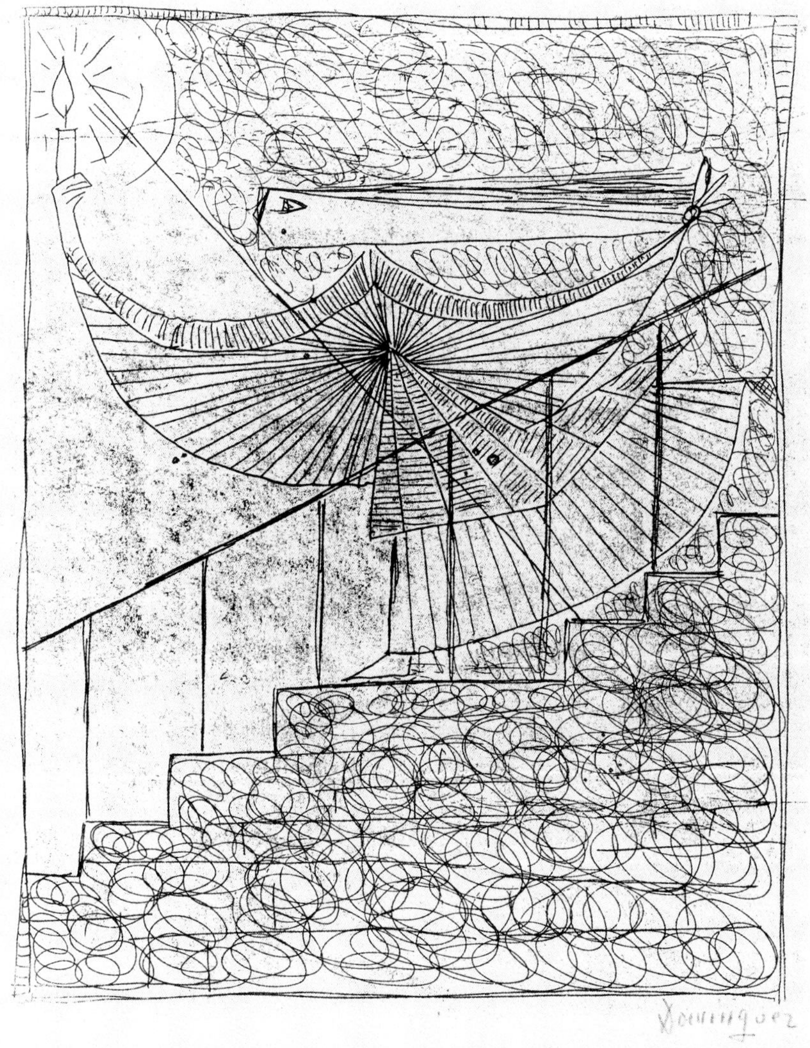

● *Fig. 48*
Oscar Dominguez, Untitled
(from *Sombre est noir*), 1945
(cat. no. 42).

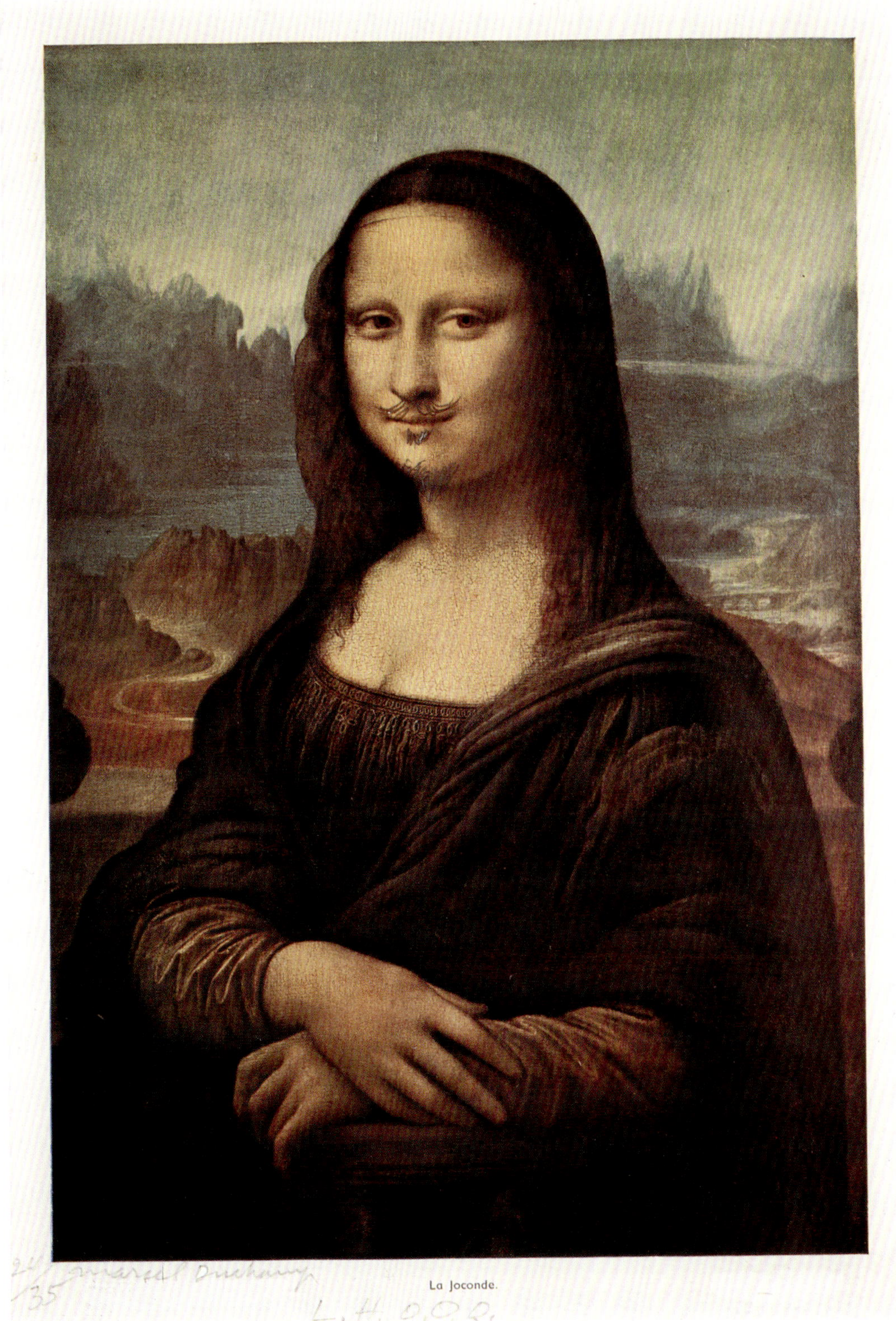

● *Fig. 49*
Marcel Duchamp, *L.H.O.O.Q.*,
1964 (cat. no. 43).

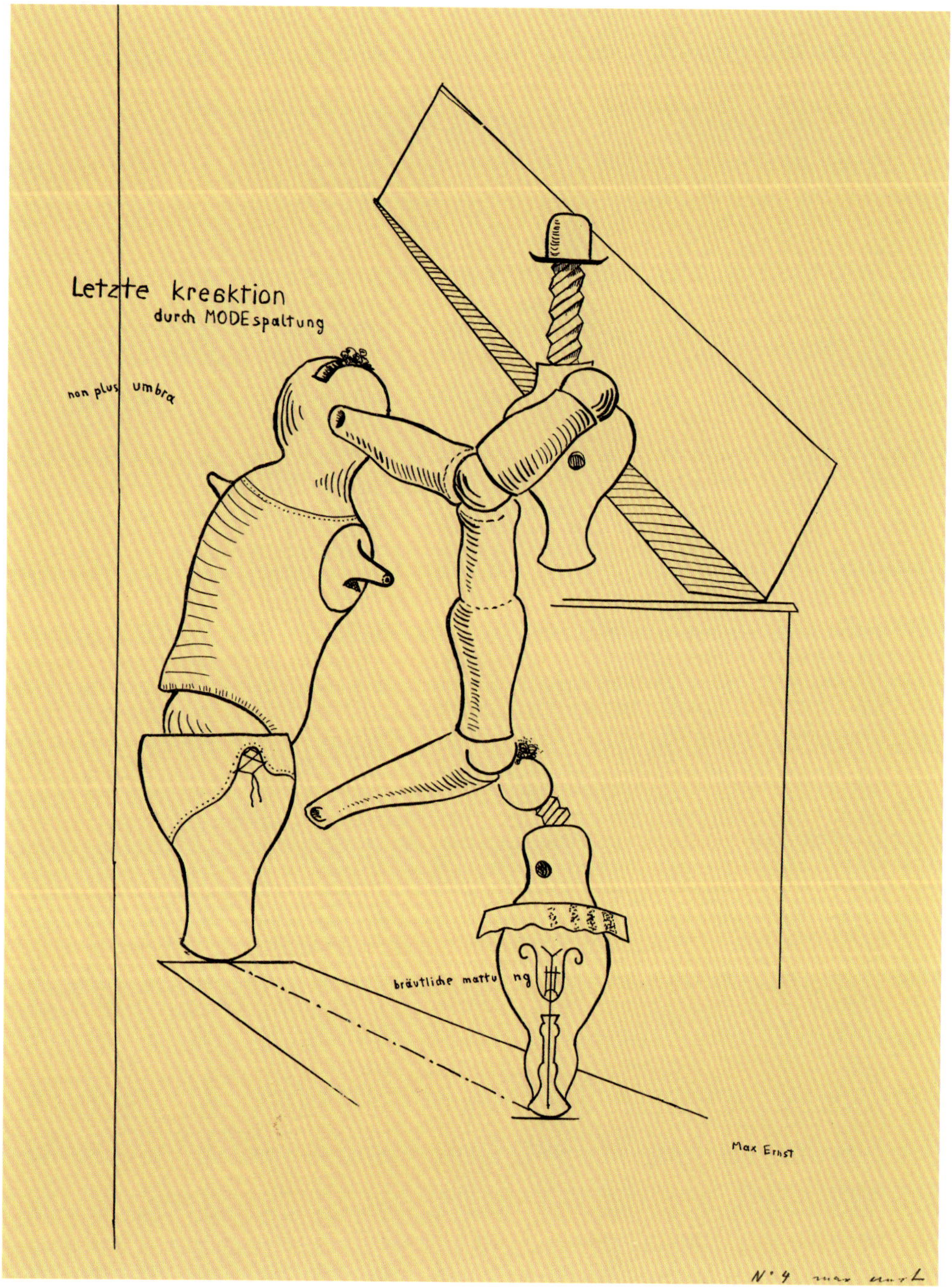

● *Fig. 50*
Max Ernst, Untitled (plate 3 from *Fiat modes pereat ars*), 1919 (cat. no. 46).

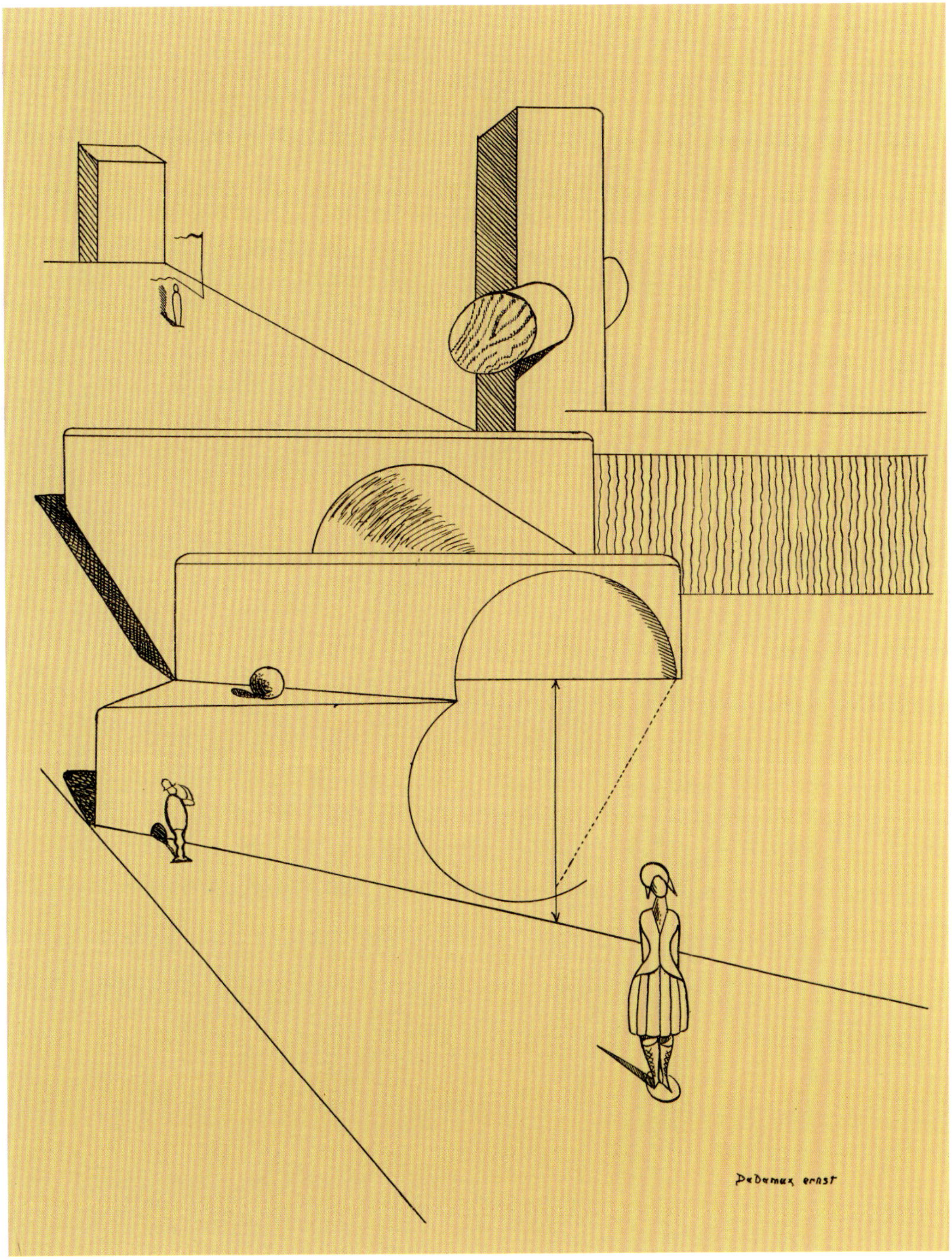

● *Fig. 51*
Max Ernst, Untitled (plate 4 from *Fiat modes pereat ars*), 1919 (cat. no. 47).

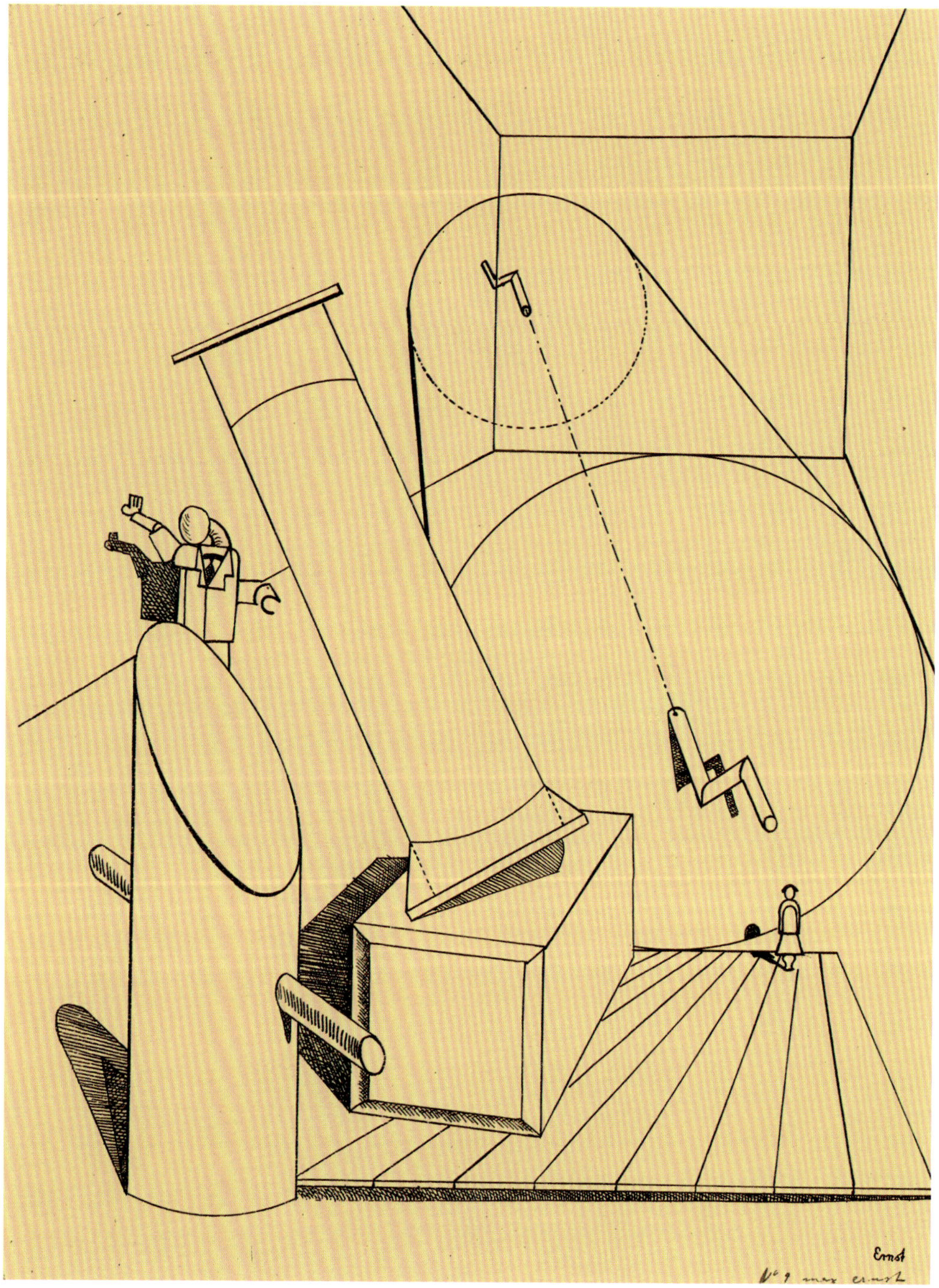

● *Fig. 52*
Max Ernst, Untitled (plate 5 from *Fiat modes pereat ars*), 1919 (cat. no. 48).

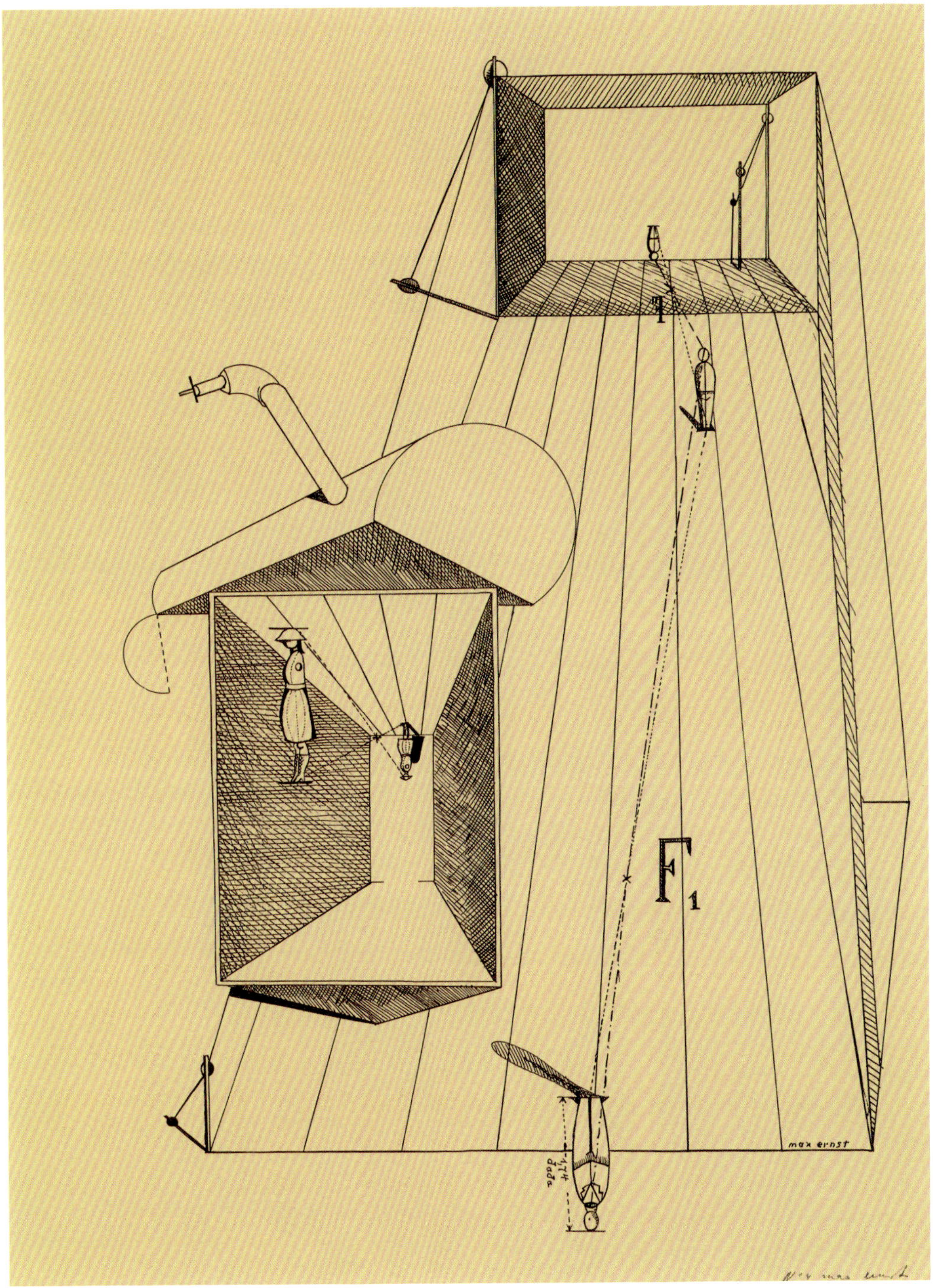

● *Fig. 53*
Max Ernst, Untitled (plate 6 from *Fiat modes pereat ars*), 1919 (cat. no. 49).

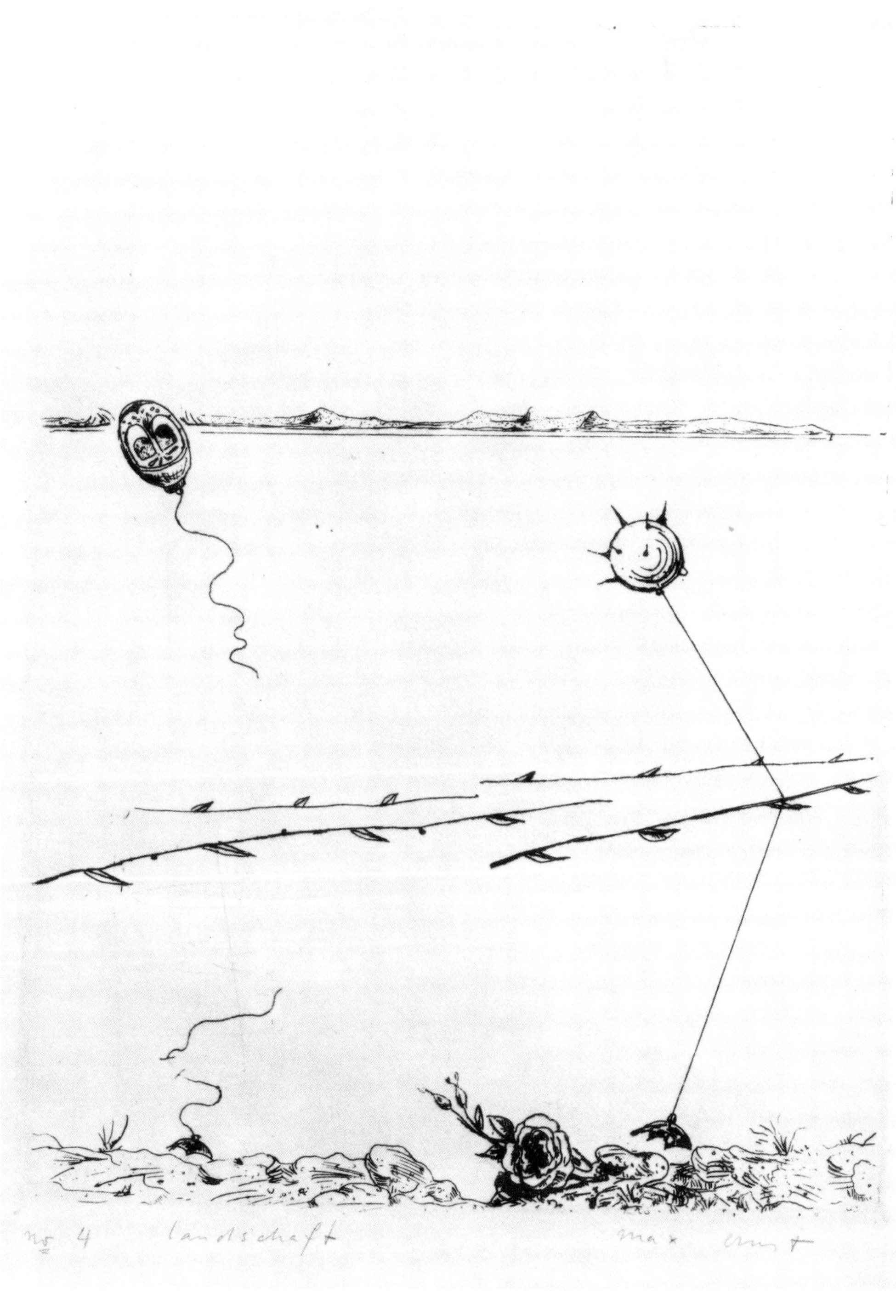

● *Fig. 54*
Max Ernst, *Pays sage II*, 1923
(cat. no. 51).

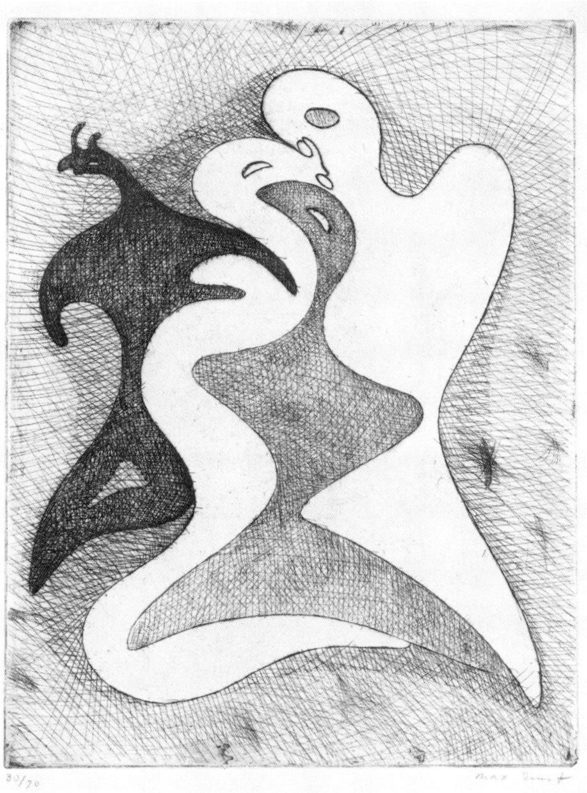

● *Fig. 55*
Max Ernst, *Correspondances dangereuses* (Dangerous harmonies), 1947 (cat. no. 53).

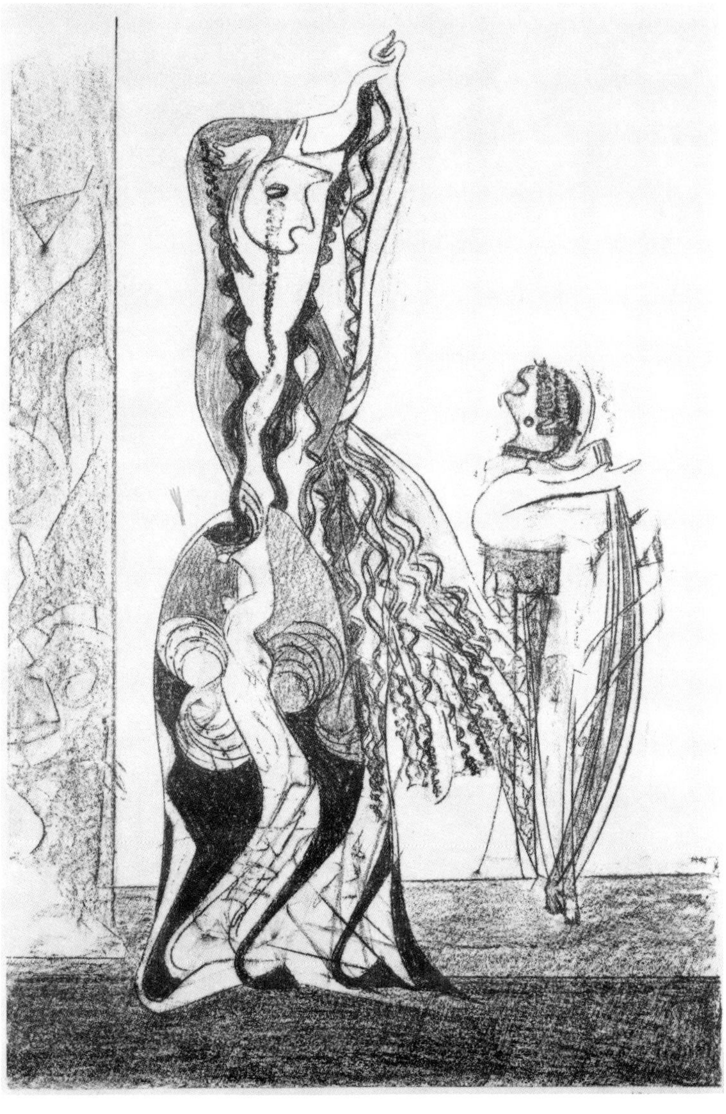

● *Fig. 56*
Max Ernst, *Danseuses* (Dancers), 1950 (cat. no. 54).

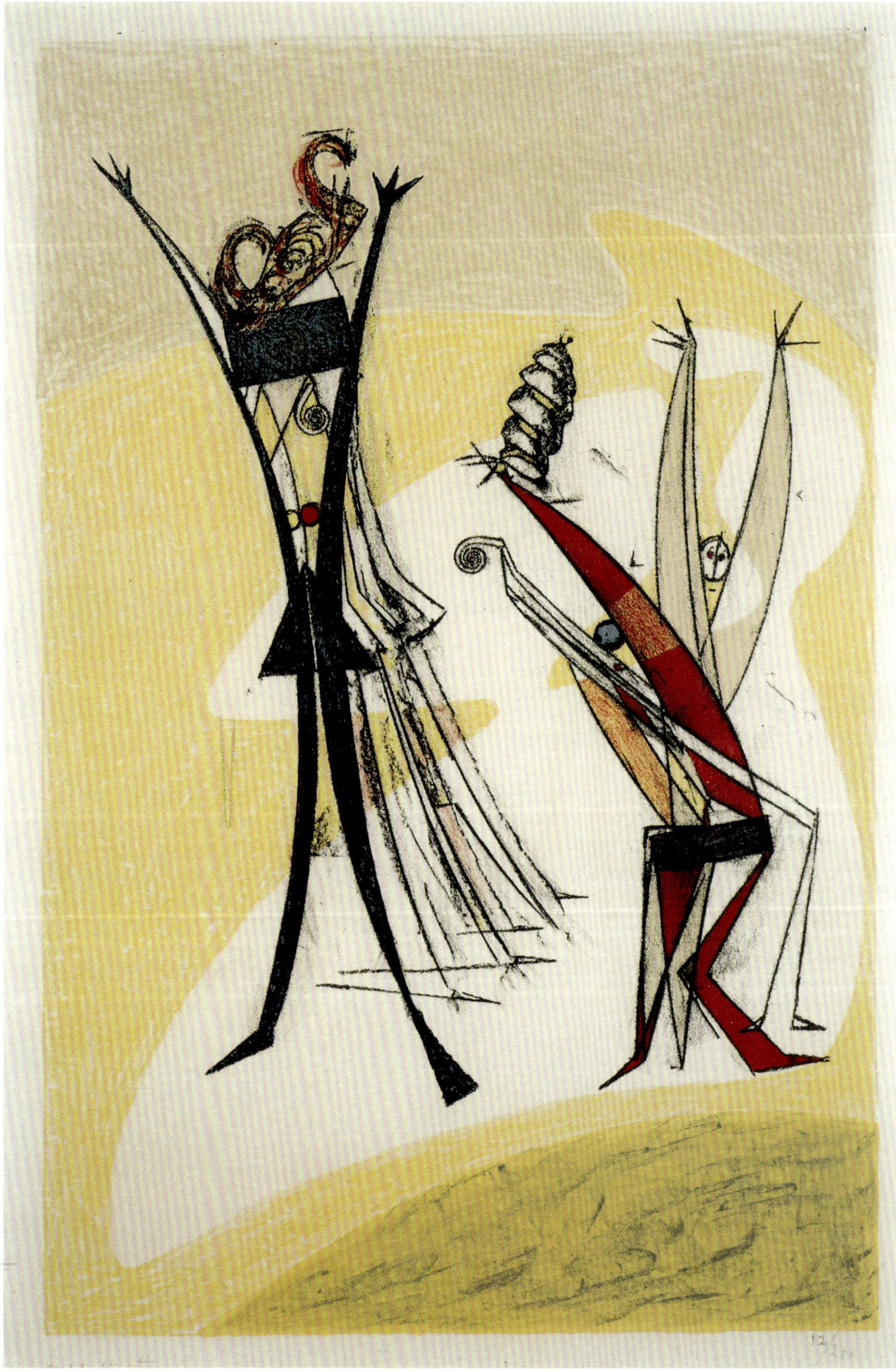

◉ *Fig. 57*
Max Ernst, *Rhythmes*
(Rhythms), 1950 (cat. no. 55).

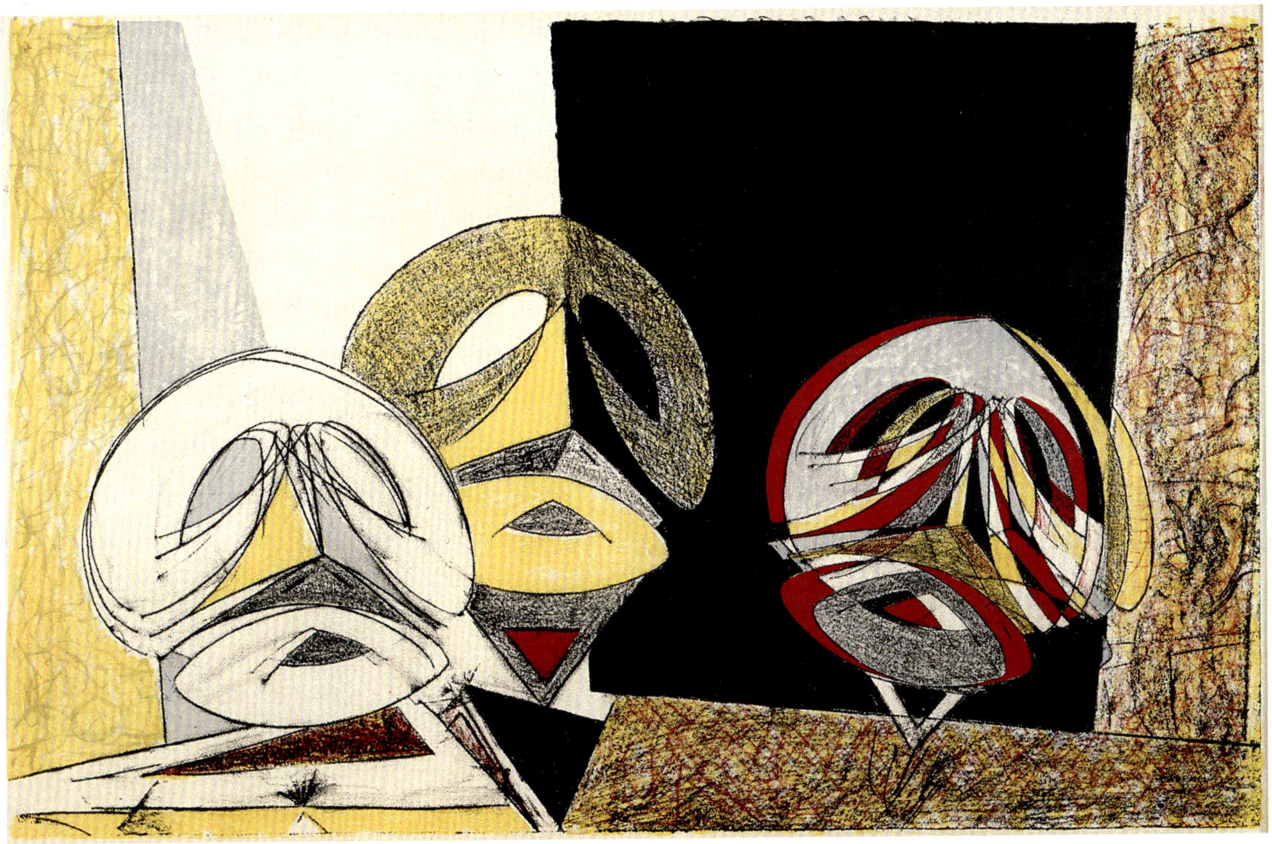

● *Fig. 58*
Max Ernst, *Masques* (Masks), 1950 (cat. no. 56).

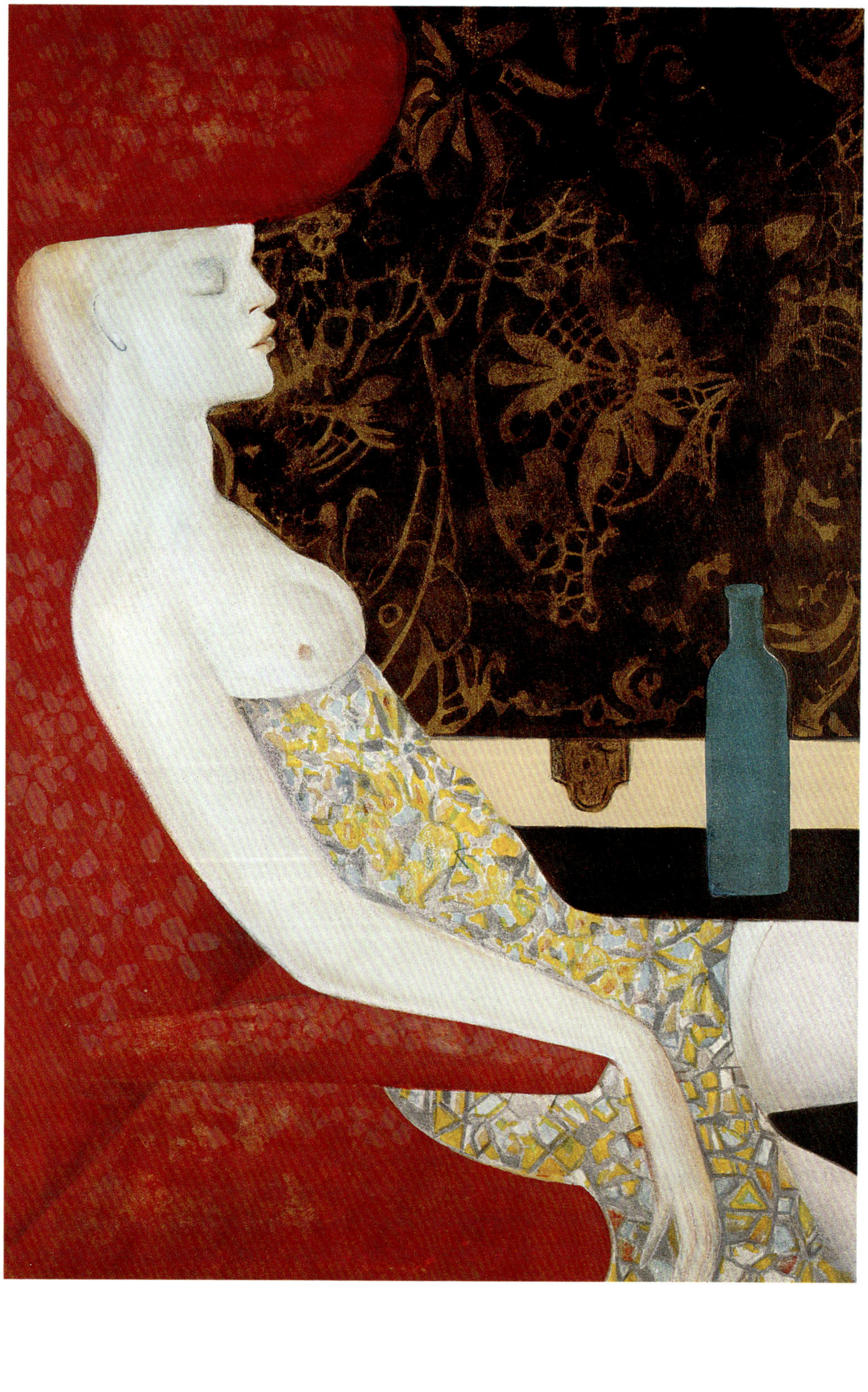

◉ *Fig. 59*
Leonor Fini, *La Nuit vaincue*
(Night conquered), 1967
(cat. no. 57).

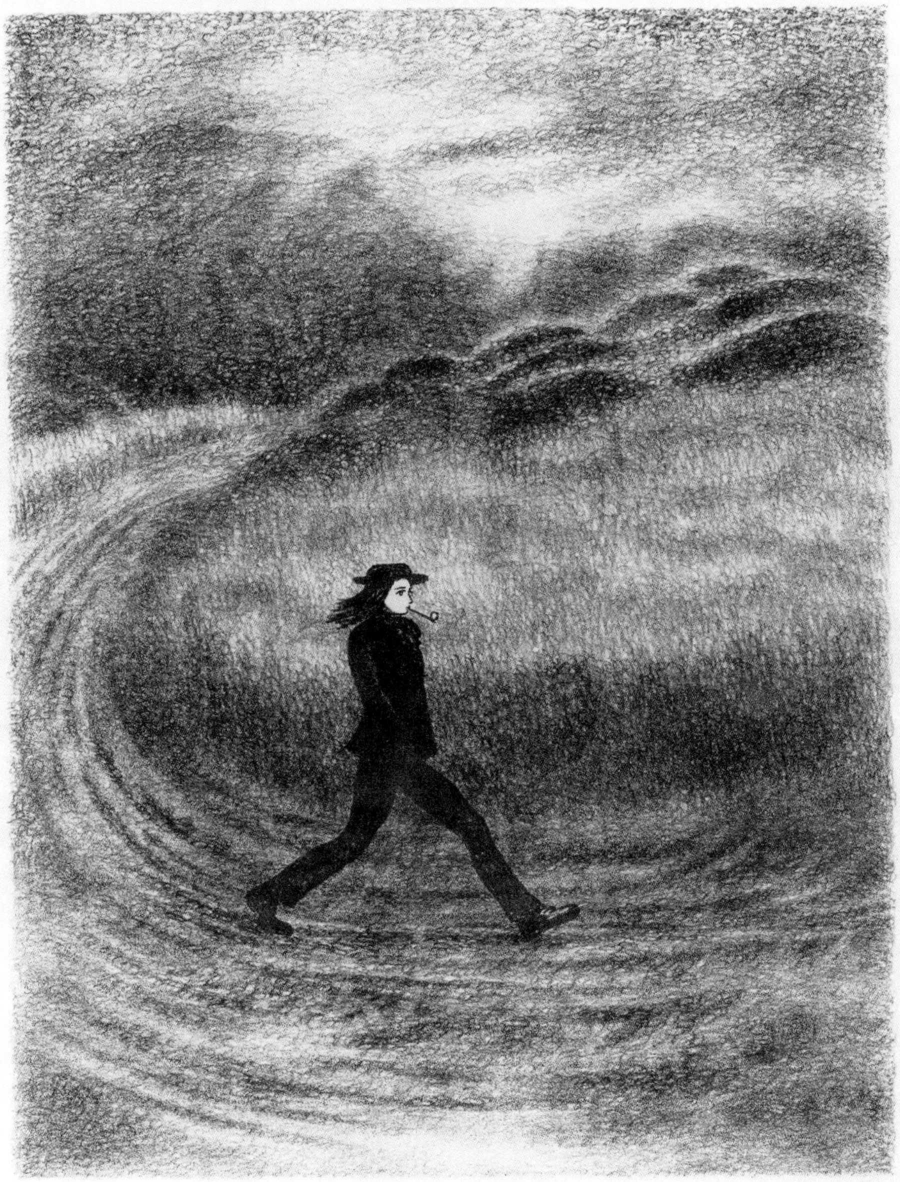

● *Fig. 60*
Valentine Hugo, *Portrait of Rimbaud*, 1961 (cat. no. 58).

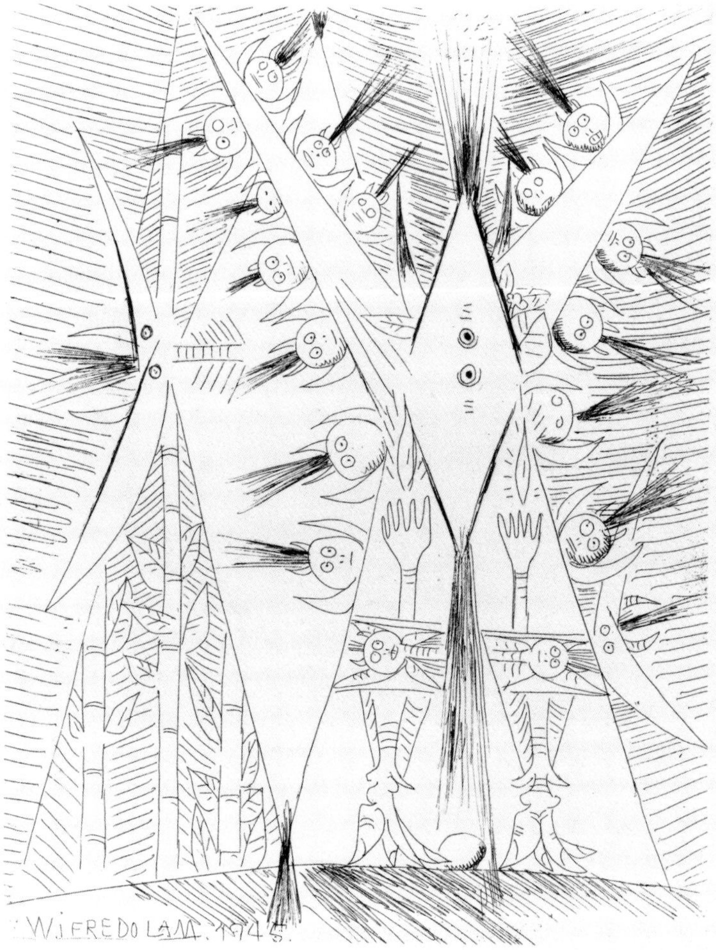

◉ *Fig. 61*
Wifredo Lam, Untitled, 1945
(cat. no. 59).

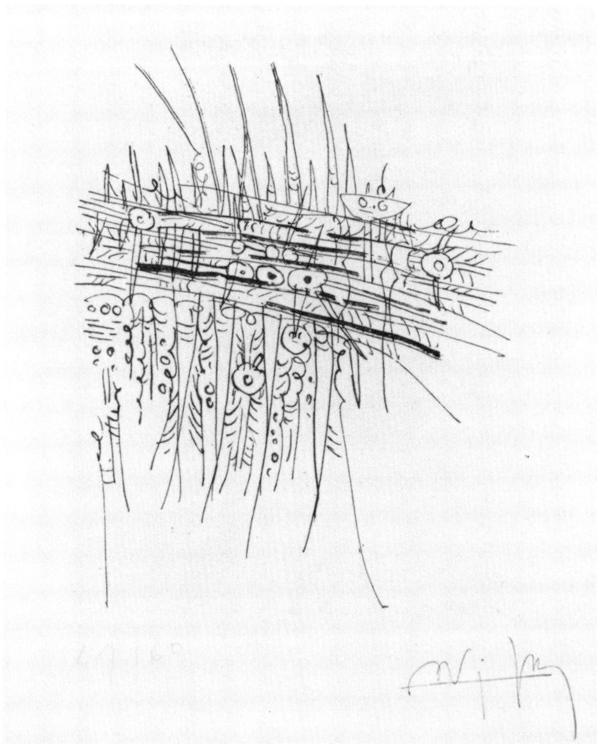

◉ *Fig. 62*
Wifredo Lam, Untitled, 1966
(cat. no. 61).

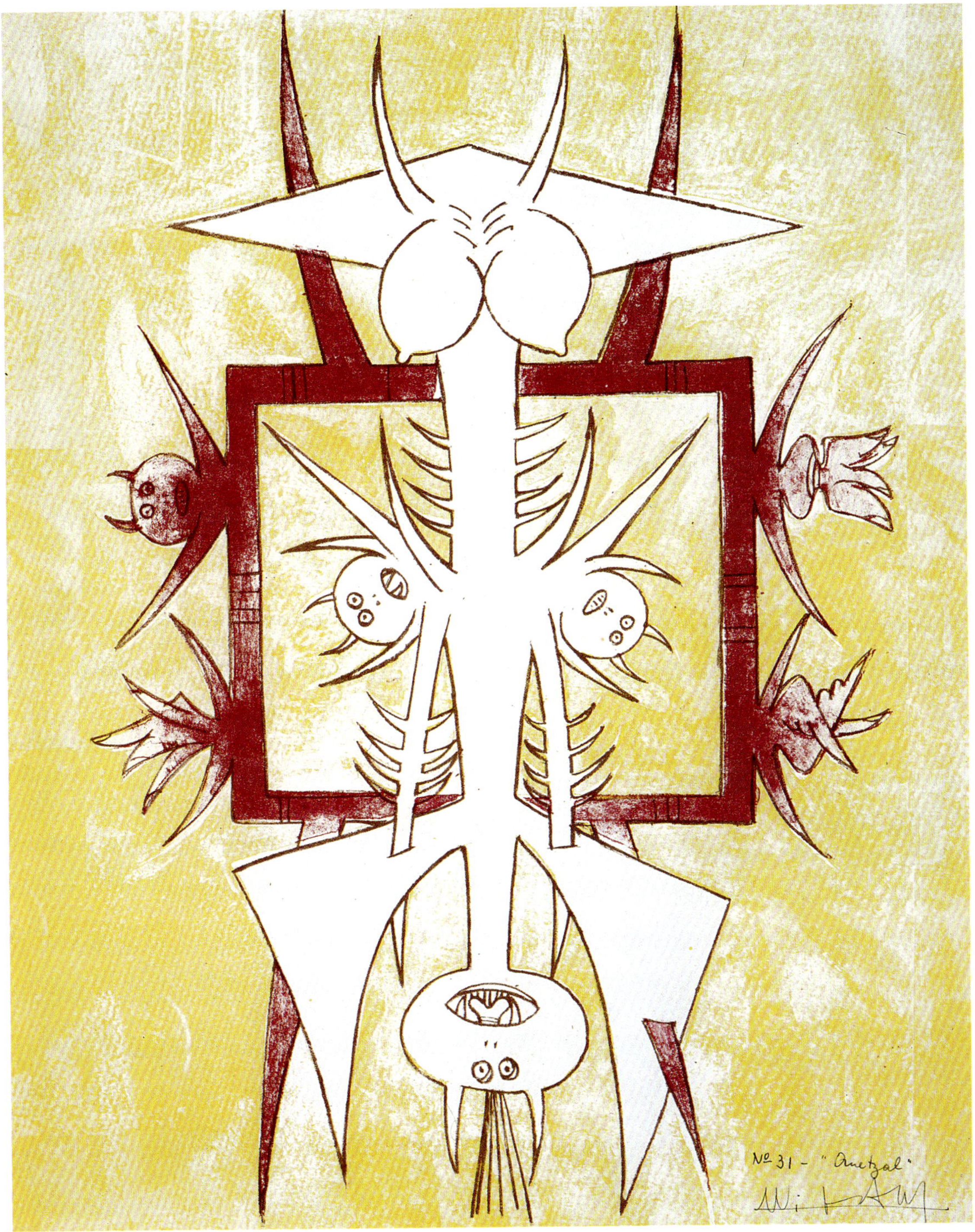

Fig. 63
Wifredo Lam, *Quetzal*, 1947
(cat. no. 60).

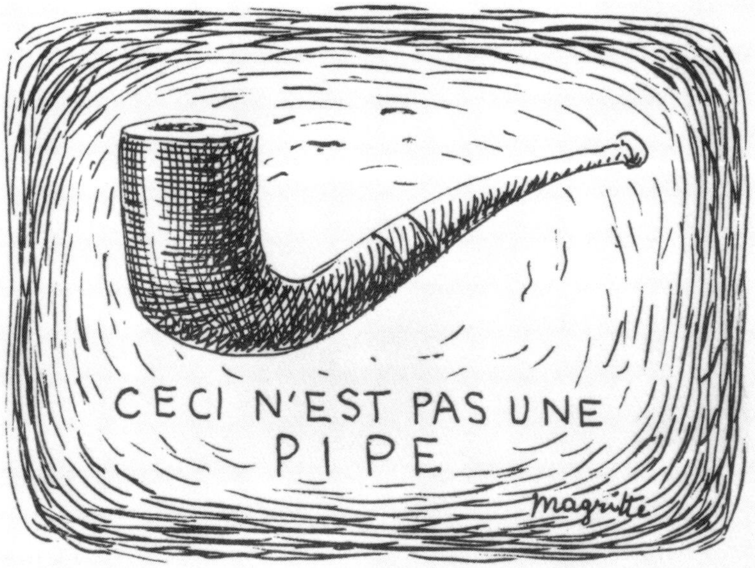

● *Fig. 64*
René Magritte, *Ceci n'est pas une pipe* (This is not a pipe), 1962 (cat. no. 62).

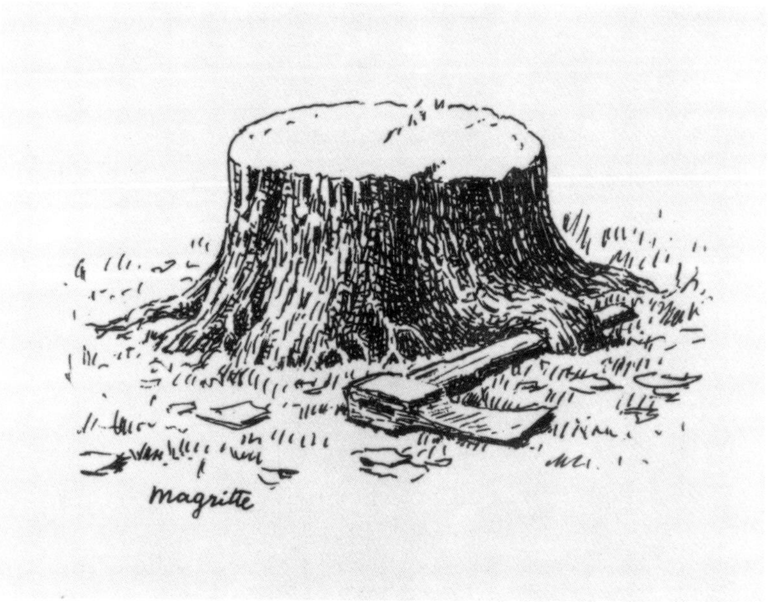

● *Fig. 65*
René Magritte, *Les Travaux d'Alexandre* (The Labors of Alexander), 1962 (cat. no. 63).

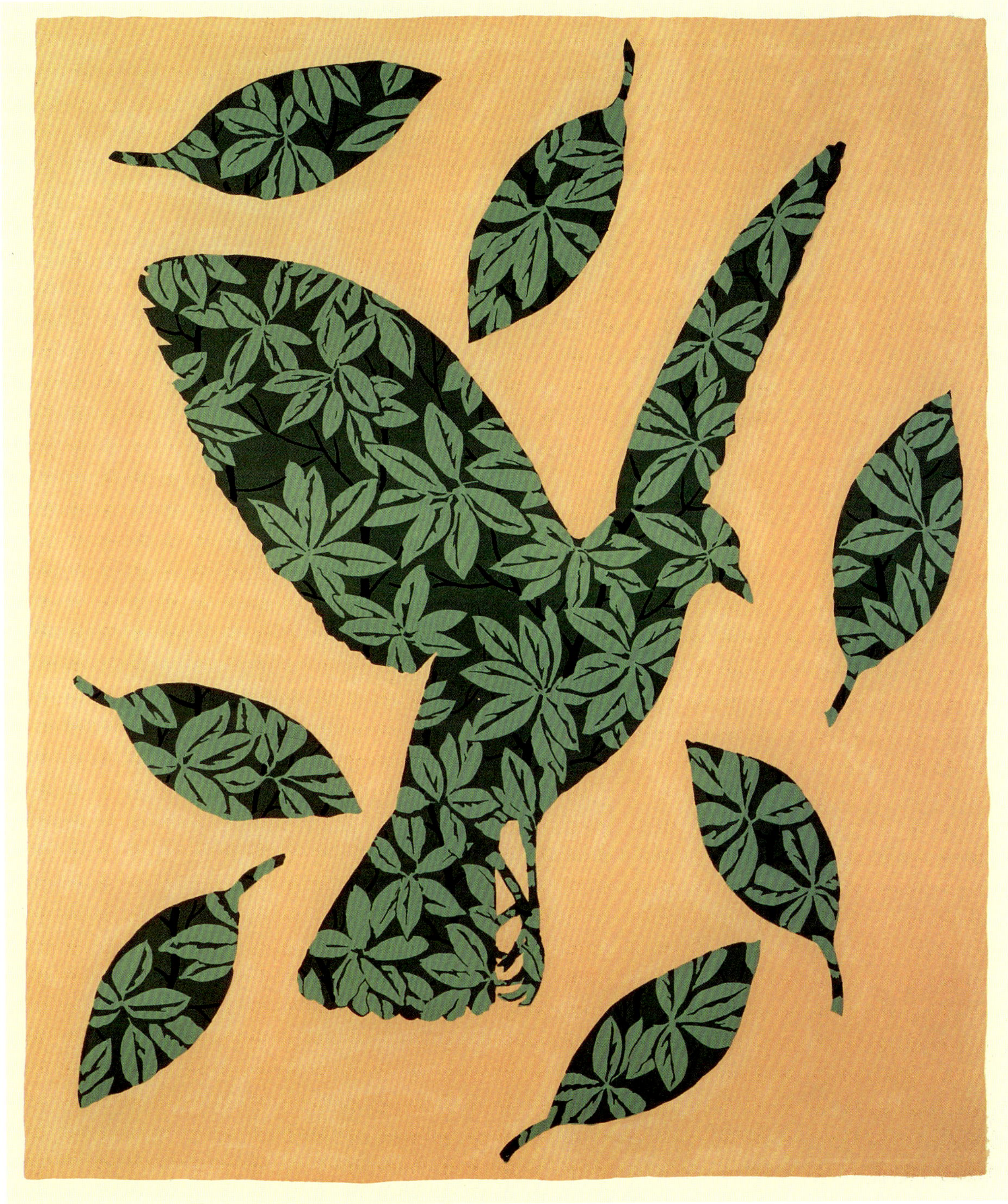

◉ *Fig. 66*
René Magritte, *Salon de mai* (The May salon), 1965 (cat. no. 65).

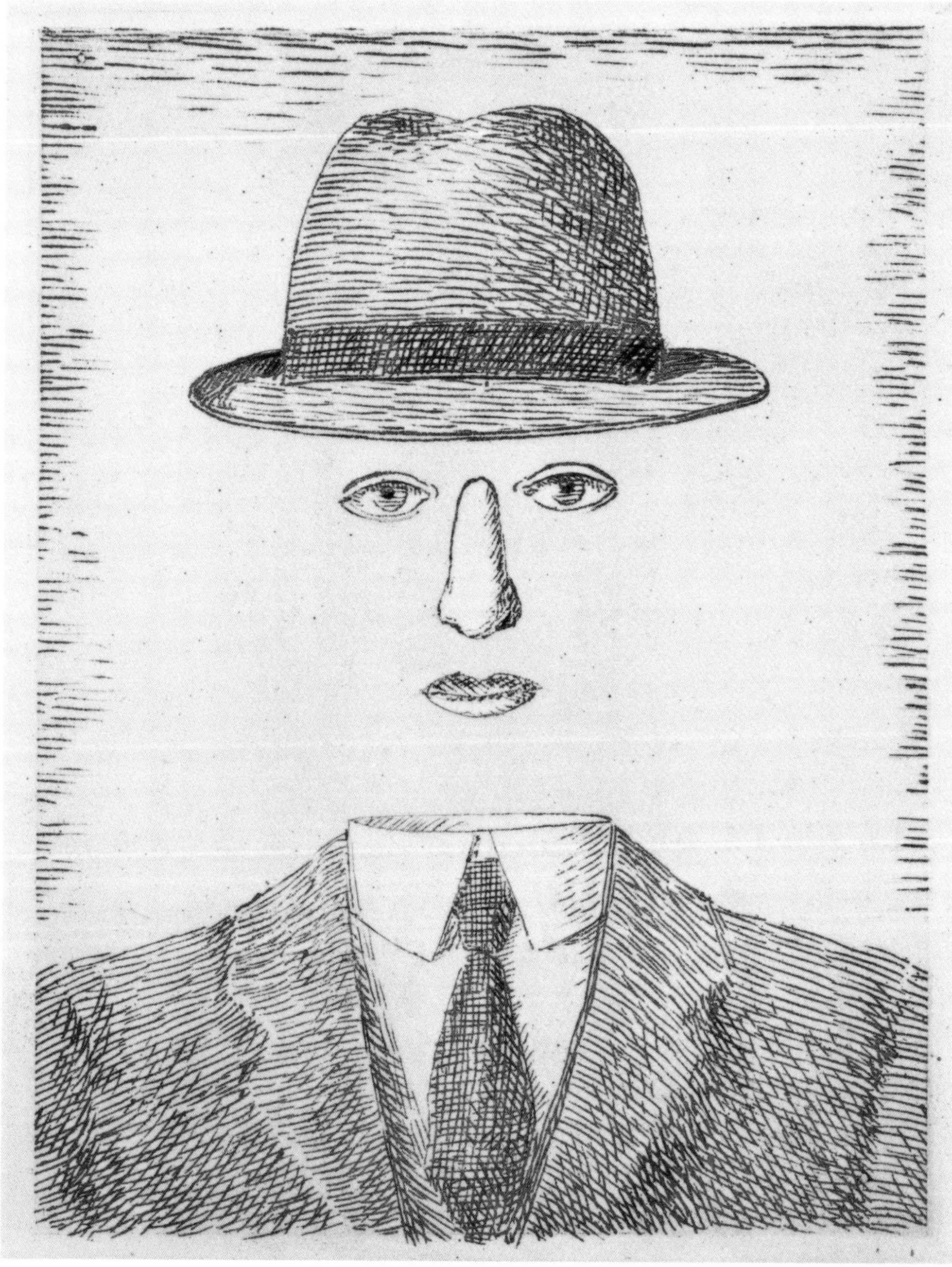

● *Fig. 67*
René Magritte, *Paysage de Baucis* (Baucis's landscape), 1966 (cat. no. 66).

The Surrealist as Printmaker

TIMOTHY BAUM

THE OFFICIAL HISTORY OF SURREALISM began in 1924, as proclaimed by its founder, André Breton, with the publication of his first *Manifesto of Surrealism* and related manifestations. The history of surrealist printmaking, however, began in the decade prior to the birth of the movement itself, for before surrealism was Dada, and among the brigade of dadaists were two in particular, Hans (later known as Jean) Arp and Max Ernst, who began their careers as printmakers during the Dada era—careers that would burgeon and continue to flourish in the surrealist decades that followed.

I will begin my discussion with Arp, appropriate not only to his place at the top of the list by alphabetization but also to his role as one of the members of the original Dada group, founded in Zurich in 1916, and thus one of the eventual elder statesmen of the surrealist circle. Arp, as a sculptor of playful and sensual offerings in metal or stone and as a creator of collages formed from randomly torn paper fragments, adapted with ease to the craft of woodcut and was soon providing fanciful and eye-catching designs for the early Dada publications: poetry reviews (such as the magazine *DADA* itself) and illustrated volumes of poetry by his friends from the early Dada fraternity, in particular, Richard Huelsenbeck and Tristan Tzara, cofounders of the movement. Of especial merit are the suites of black-on-white woodcuts created for Huelsenbeck's

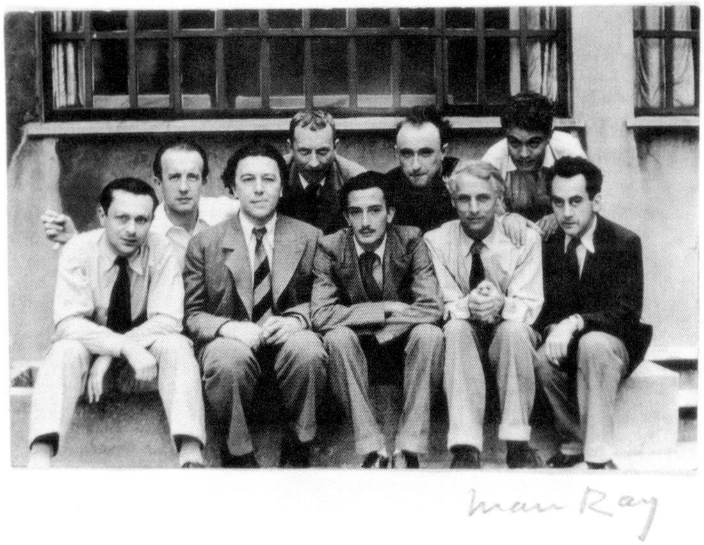

● *Fig. 68*
Man Ray, members of the surrealist group at Tristan Tzara's house, Paris, 1930 (left to right, front row: Tristan Tzara, André Breton, Salvador Dalí, Max Ernst, Man Ray; back row: Paul Eluard, Jean Arp, Yves Tanguy, René Crevel); photograph, 2⅜ x 3½ in. Private collection, New York.

Phantastische Gebete (1916) and Tzara's *Vingt-cinq Poèmes* (1918) and the series of nineteen dispersed through Tzara's *Cinéma calendrier du coeur abstrait* (1920).[1]

Contemporary with Arp but a few years behind in advancing his career because of the years sacrificed to his military obligation during World War I, Ernst, already skilled at the art of linoleum engraving, produced his first major print offering in 1919: *Fiat modes pereat ars* (see figs. 3, 50–53, cat. nos. 45–49), a splendid portfolio of eight line-drawing lithographs. *Fiat modes*, or so the story goes, was Ernst's contribution to a competition sponsored by the local council of Cologne, open to certain young artists of the town. Most of the invited participants produced portfolios of traditional offerings: landscapes, still lifes, and the like. The ever-twinkling, Dada-inspired Ernst created eight images that paid respect to the extended avant-garde of the time: pistonlike pulley systems, geometrical architectural sites and interiors, mannequin creatures (à la Carlo Carrà or Giorgio de Chirico), a sprinkling of words (in the Apollinairean manner), and so forth. When the presentation, supposedly at the town hall itself, came to pass, Ernst's offering was ceremoniously rejected as insulting and useless and, with its creator, turned away in no uncertain disgrace. Ernst, undaunted (as legend would have it), shrugged off the effrontery and burned in a spectacular bonfire the greater part of the print edition (the colophon called for an intended printing of three hundred copies). Luckily for those fortunate enough to possess one of the surviving sets and for those able to view this *chef d'oeuvre* of Dada creativity in various museums and exhibitions, a small number survived.

In the early 1920s Ernst produced another handful of Dada or early surrealist etchings and drypoints, notably an untitled plate of a man and his uncaught fish, one of a nude man in a fish-populated storeroom,[2] and two bizarre landscapes (of sorts!), *Pays sage I* and *Pays sage II*, both of 1923 (figs. 5, 54, cat. nos. 50–51). From that date on, all became officially surrealism.

Printmaking has been an important aspect of artistic activity during every period of art history from the fifteenth century on. The earliest prints were rendered as illustrations for books, and this tradition continues to the present day. Surrealism was as much a literary movement as an artistic one, and because of the proximity of the surrealist artists to the movement's poets, the creation of prints as book illustrations was especially prevalent during the surrealist decades. Many of the prints discussed below originated in this fashion.

At the time of the emergence of surrealism, only one of its new members was a printmaker as well as a painter. (De Chirico, a surrealist whose most famous works preceded the birth of the movement by a decade or more, had made a single print, a lithograph, in 1921 but engaged in no further printmaking activity until the conclusion of the decade.) The artist to whom I refer is André

Masson. From 1924 on, Masson designed beautiful etchings and lithographs for limited-edition books presenting the work of many of his close friends. He had the great fortune to be represented by the prominent, far-seeing dealer-publisher Daniel-Henry Kahnweiler of the Galerie Simon, Paris. Kahnweiler published a series of books under the imprint of his gallery and generously allowed Masson to illustrate many of them.

In 1924 Masson executed a series of four dreamlike etchings for the first book of his friend Georges Limbour, a volume of poems entitled *Soleils bas.*[3] This was followed a year later by a series of seven lithographs—basically spontaneous, automatic images of whimsical subjects—accompanying a volume of poems by Michel Leiris, *Simulacre.*[4] Nineteen twenty-six produced four etchings (printed attractively in bistre) for a volume of poems by Robert Desnos, *C'est les bottes de 7 lieues cette phrase "Je me vois"* (figs. 6, 69, 85, cat. nos. 67–69), and again the images were infused with whimsy and spontaneity. Masson's final project of the decade published under the Galerie Simon imprint was a group of etchings for a novel by Marcel Jouhandeau, *Ximenès Malinjoude* (1927), and here for the first time the images related specifically to the text (though still in the free spirit of automatism).

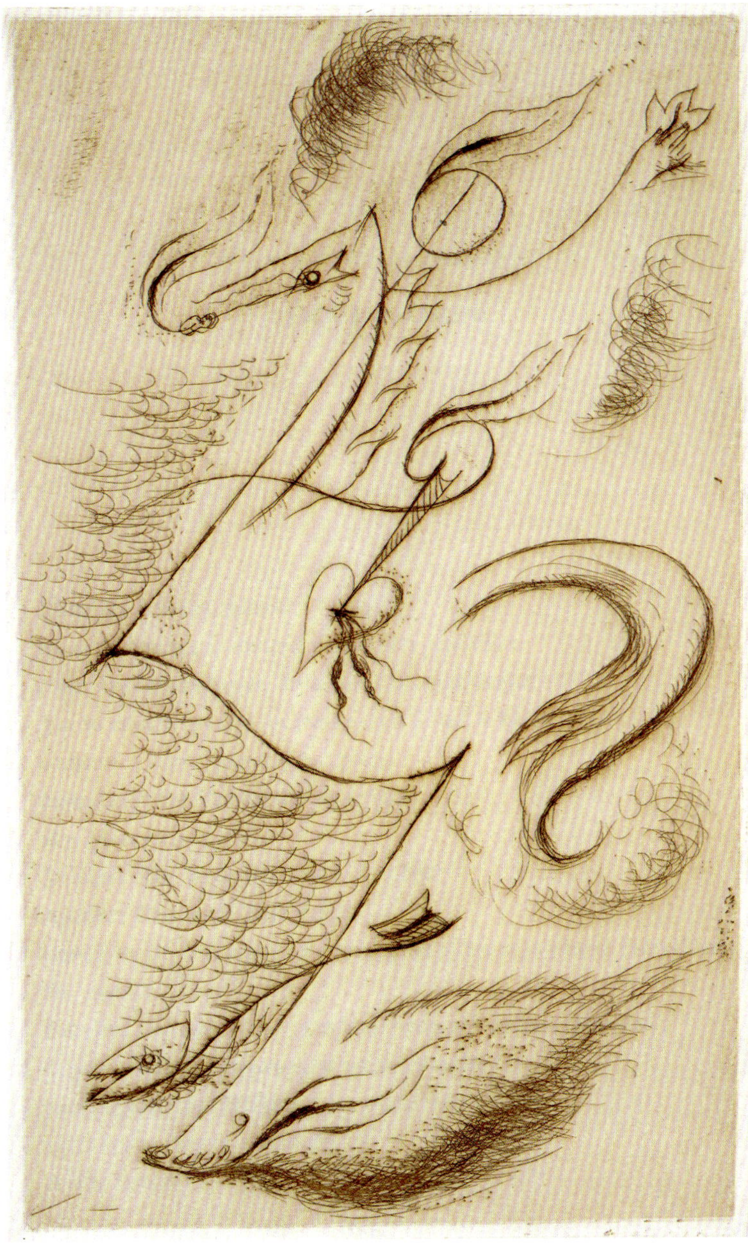

Nineteen twenty-eight saw the publication of two extremely risqué prose books, one by Louis Aragon (though published anonymously) and the other written under the pseudonym Lord Auch by the young master of erotic storytelling of the period, Georges Bataille. Masson's etchings for the Aragon book, provocatively titled *Le Con d'Irène*,[5] are as explicit as any illustrations for any such clandestine work of any earlier or future time. The lithographs (eight in all) drawn to accompany Bataille's *Histoire de l'oeil* are equally shocking.[6] The following decade began with an interesting compromise, as Masson illustrated yet another

● *Fig. 69*
André Masson, Untitled (from *C'est les bottes de 7 lieues . . .)*, 1926 (cat. no. 68).

Bataille volume, *L'Anus solaire*,[7] but this time the imagery of the etchings, though still erotic, was much more subdued. The publisher was once again Editions de la Galerie Simon.

The decade of the 1930s, in relation to the subject of printmaking by surrealists, began as a quiescent landscape suddenly jolted by the metamorphosis of soft, gentle hills into erupting volcanoes. I speak here metaphorically of the entrance of Joan Miró and Salvador Dalí.

Miró, the first of these Spanish artists to arrive and join the surrealist ranks, approached printmaking with a certain caution. His first project—befitting the fashion of the time—was a series of pochoir (silkscreen) illustrations, rendered in true, electric colors, for a happy little book by the poet Lise Deharme (writing under the surname Hirtz), *Il était une petite pie* (1928).[8] One year later he began an investigation of the art of lithography, and the first successful result was the series of four simple but diverting images contained with the poems of Tzara in *L'Arbre des voyageurs* (1930).[9] The next step of the program was to study and master the techniques of etching and drypoint. The splendid results of this bit of schooling will be discussed a little farther along.

And then there was Dalí, the 1930s and the surrealists awaiting, then adoring him: Dalí the dashing one, Dalí the ultimate in surrealist personality and artistic virtuosity. Strangely Dalí's adventures in printmaking were dignified and classical, not wild or overly daring. The imagery of his early prints (etchings and/or heliogravures rendered from his preparatory drawings) was magnificent but rarely intricate from a technical standpoint. Shock value was ever-present (scatological references; the print serving as frontispiece for Georges Hugnet's *Onan* [fig. 10, cat. no. 24], with a tiny text engraved in the lower corner explaining that the artist had drawn the image with one hand while masturbating with the other; nudity; cannibalism), but the general tone of the work was steady and academic, not frantic or overly experimental.

One can only admire Dalí for the exquisiteness of his line and his immaculate brushwork. In the etchings and heliogravures of the 1930s the wonder of his line remained. One plate after another appeared, testifying to the skill of this extraordinary draftsman: illustrations for André Breton and Paul Eluard's *L'Immaculée Conception* (fig. 31, cat. no. 19), René Char's *Artine* (fig. 32, cat. no. 20), and Dalí's own *La Femme visible* (fig. 11, cat. no. 21), all from 1930; Breton's *Le Revolver à cheveux blancs* of 1932 (fig. 33, cat. no. 22); the splendid, single copperplate engraving of 1933, *L'Enfant-sauterelle* (fig. 34, cat. no. 23);[10] the remarkable scatological image serving as the frontispiece for the fifteen deluxe copies of Tzara's *Grains et issues* of 1935 (fig. 70, cat. no. 29); an anthological plate with a dozen or so vignettes juxtaposed, *Crânes mous et harpe crânienne* (fig. 38, cat. no.

30), of which only a handful of proofs were ever printed; and the *Fantastic Beach Scene* (fig. 39, cat. no. 31; titled thus in English in the recent Michler and Löpsinger catalogue raisonné), both from 1935 as well. This group of prints, alongside the famous series of forty-two etchings and engravings illustrating Lautréamont's *Les Chants de Maldoror* (1934; see figs. 9, 35–37, cat. nos. 25–28), constitute the classic period of Dalí's graphic oeuvre. It is necessary to note, and truly in the form of a postscript, that during the forty-five years subsequent to this period, Dalí (at the constant demand of his agents and publishers) hosted the creation of an additional nine hundred editions, encompassing every imaginable subject and printmaking technique, all honored by his untiring pen or pencil signature.

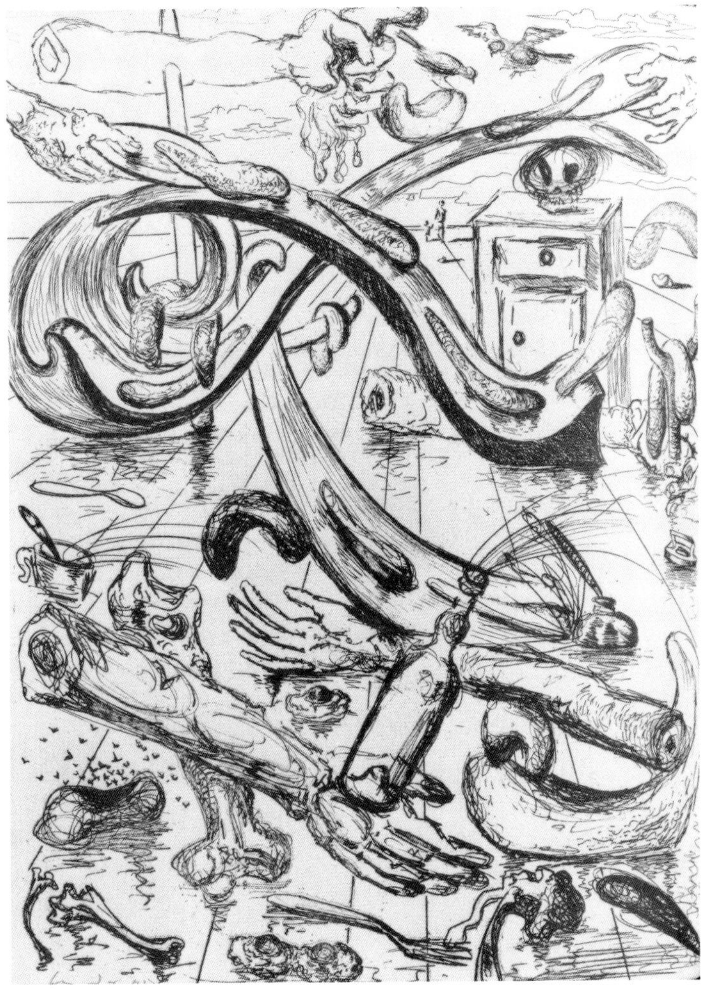

The 1930s were the decade of greatest activity for the surrealists. New members entered the group in profusion (while occasionally, by Breton's decree, others were requested to depart), including talented poets and painters from all over the European continent, Great Britain, and the Americas. Breton remained the leader of most surrealist activities: publications, collective statements (usually issued in the form of manifestoes or related printed circulars), group exhibitions. As the fame of surrealism, and especially of its more eminent members (Breton himself, Dalí, Ernst, Eluard, Miró, Man Ray, etc.), swelled before the public's wary eye, more galleries proffered their hospitality to the artists, and more publishers became interested in surrealist writings. The profusion of publishers sympathetic to the growing number of talented surrealist writers afforded that much more opportunity for the artists of the group to collaborate as illustrators. Many of these artists had never received training in printmaking, but few passed up the challenge of learning these skills.

In the early 1920s, when the surrealist movement began, the principal ateliers in Paris where prints—in particular, etchings, engravings, and drypoints—were made according to the highest professional standards numbered a mere handful. Prominent among them were Lacourière, Haasen, Charlot Frères,

● *Fig. 70*
Salvador Dalí, *Grains et issues* (Grain and chaff), 1935 (cat. no. 29).

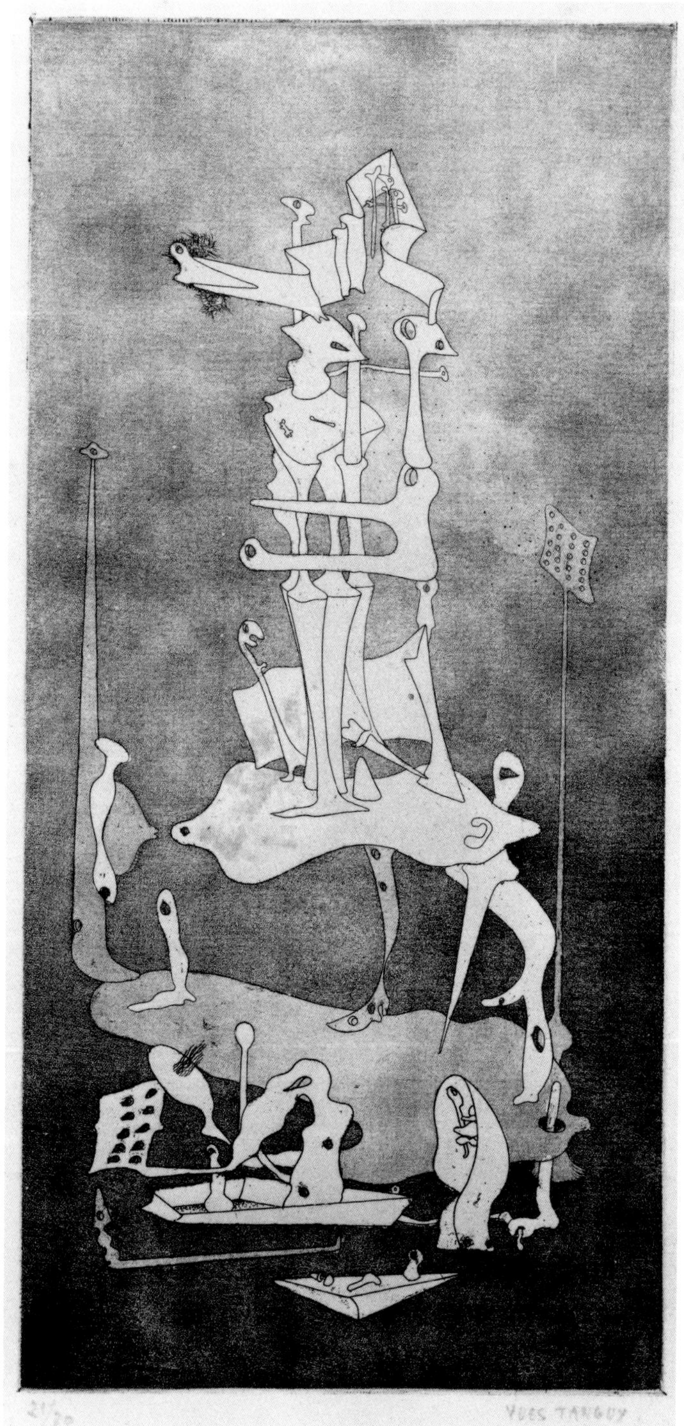

Tanneur, and Leblanc. Here master printers were available to provide instruction to young artists interested in pursuing printmaking in earnest. The seriousness of the surroundings discouraged dabblers from wasting the time of these veteran craftsmen, and many of the younger or less academic artists shied away from such demanding challenges.

In 1927 a young Englishman named Stanley William Hayter, who had recently moved to Paris, opened a small printmaking atelier in association with a master printer named Joseph Hecht. Little by little their quality standards came to the attention of artists and publishers. It was not until the early years of the following decade, however, that many of the surrealist artists turned to Hayter and his Atelier 17, as it came to be called, for instruction in the arts of engraving, but those who came to learn from him learned well.

In 1933 Hayter moved his atelier from the out-of-the-way fifteenth arrondissement to a small street, Campagne-Première, which was already home to many artists, including Man Ray, and which opened onto the popular Boulevard Montparnasse. Alberto Giacometti, an early, successful follower of Hayter's guidance, began a group of surrealist etchings on these new premises that year, and by 1934 Yves Tanguy had joined Hayter's coterie as well. By the end of the decade—at which time Hayter decided to move his operation to the United States—most of the surrealists who were dedicated printmakers had created at least some of their most successful engravings and etchings there, among them, Oscar Dominguez, Ernst, Masson, and, in particular, Miró.

Tanguy's graphic oeuvre, although totaling only about thirty-odd prints (all some form of etching or aquatint), constitutes one of the most elegant of any of the surrealist artists. His first print (fig. 12, cat. no. 115), an etching drawn in 1932 to accompany the deluxe examples of Eluard's *La Vie immédiate*, was print-

● *Fig. 71*
Yves Tanguy, Untitled (from *L'Ile d'un jour*), 1938 (cat. no. 119).

ed at Lacourière's atelier. From his second print (fig. 129, cat. no. 116)—an exquisite and intricate image with shaded background tone from 1934—onward, all of his graphic works (with one, unimportant exception) were printed at Hayter's Atelier 17 (first in Paris, then in New York, with a final handful executed during visits to Paris toward the end of his life, though he never lived in France again). One marvels at the dexterity and technical superiority of certain of Tanguy's etchings. The 1934 etching, which illustrates a book by Tzara and was printed in an edition of fewer than fifteen examples, is a treasure indeed. Likewise, we can only shake our heads and wonder at the perfection (such balance!) of the etching of 1938 that serves as the frontispiece for Marcelle Ferry's *L'Ile d'un jour* (fig. 71, cat. no. 119). This sort of imaginative and extremely skilled printmaking can be achieved only under the tutelage of a true master (in this case, Hayter). Tanguy merely dabbled in color in his graphic activity, and only in some of his prints, but the delicate registration of the blue and the yellow tones in *Rhabdomancie*, the Brunidor etching from 1947 (fig. 13, cat. no. 120), is wonderfully soothing to the eye, and the quality of the merging of the color and the raised intaglio printing in the 1954 etching with monoprinting for Jean Laude's *Grand Passage* (fig. 125, cat. no. 122) is as fine as the medium can offer.

Earlier I made brief mention of Miró: that he began his printmaking career with the illustrations for two books at the end of the 1920s. He also made a sprinkling of other lithographs (all in black-and-white) at that time, but none is of any great interest. His first major print was a large-format drypoint of a neoclassical-looking surrealist landscape, *Daphnis et Chloé* (fig. 7, cat. no. 79). This print was commissioned by the successful publisher Tériade, and for the occasion Miró studied the technique of drypoint with the master himself, Roger Lacourière, at whose atelier the work was produced. This was in 1933. That same year Hugnet requested that his friend furnish the illustrations for his forthcoming book of poems, *Enfances*, and Miró returned to Lacourière's, creating three more etchings (see fig. 95, cat. no. 80).

The next few years were quiescent in the chronology of Miró's printmaking activities, with only one etching produced (fig. 72, cat. no. 83), for *24 Essais* (also known as the *Album de 23 gravures*), an album of prints by twenty-three different artists, with text by Anatole Jakovski, published by G. Orobitz et Cie in 1935. The official printer for this project was

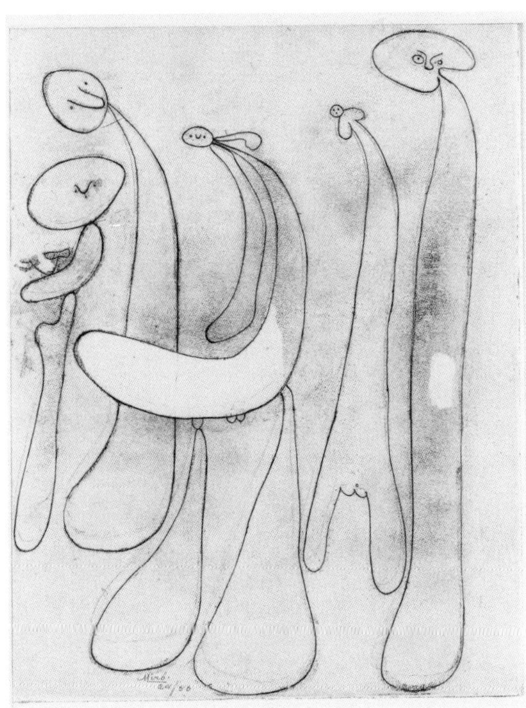

● *Fig. 72*
Joan Miró, Untitled (from *24 Essais*), 1935 (cat. no. 83).

Tanneur, an atelier never before or again frequented by Miró, but one of the most prestigious of that era. Under such auspices Miró was again able to augment his knowledge of printmaking technique.

Miró's only other printmaking activity during the mid-1930s was the production of a small group of brightly colored pochoir prints: two extremely beautiful images published in 1934 in the popular deluxe art journal *Cahiers d'art* (figs. 97–98, cat. nos. 81–82); one large-format, grandly dramatic image entitled *Femme et chien devant la lune*, published in Barcelona in 1935; and a small but vivid work expressing his agitation about the situation in his beloved Spain during the Civil War, entitled *Aidez l'Espagne* (1937).[11]

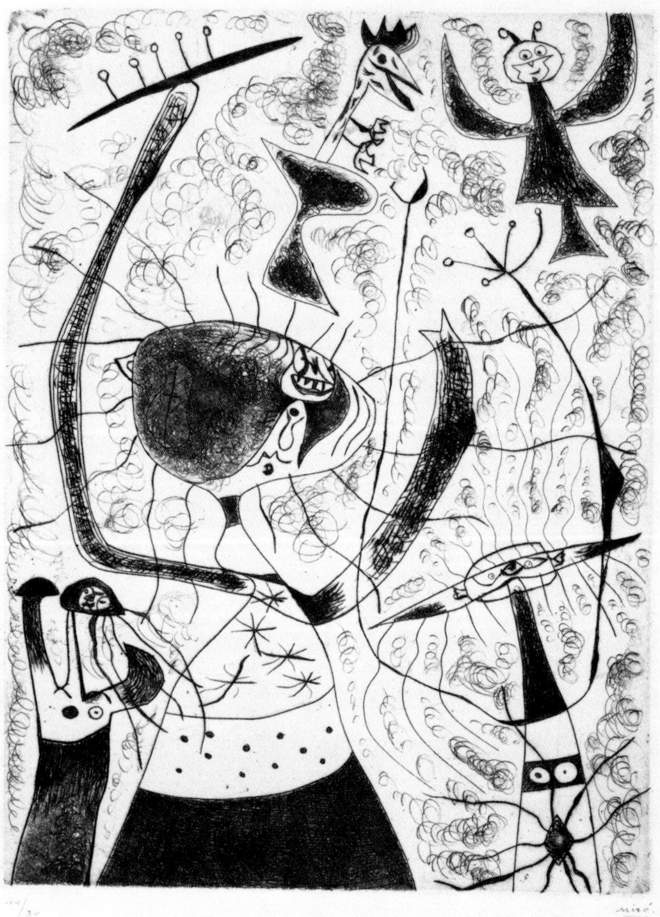

At a certain point Miró visited the print studio of Louis Marcoussis and was impressed with the high quality of his work in the realm of engraving. He commenced to study the intricacies of this art with the masterful Marcoussis, and the eventual result was a succession of nineteen works, each engraved under Marcoussis's watchful eye and printed thereafter at Lacourière's. Most of these prints were copublished by the distinguished dealers Pierre Loeb of Paris and Pierre Matisse (son of Henri), who had established a gallery in New York. This group of etchings constitutes (along with the previously mentioned achievements of Dalí's prints of the 1930s and Tanguy's entire oeuvre) one of the strongest statements of commitment in the history of surrealist printmaking. Of the nineteen plates printed, eleven are single-subject images, and the remaining eight form a group entitled *Série noire et rouge* (figs. 101–8, cat. nos. 92–99). This imaginative group begins with two separate black-and-white plates, followed by six extended subjects evolved from combinations of the two original plates, all six of which were printed with the addition of a vivid red-orange inking to the black-and-white. The results are explosive!

Among the eleven single-image etchings of this group (all of which were engraved in 1938), some are small in size and simple in design, and others are somewhat larger and wonderfully intricate (in Miró's whimsical, storytelling way). Of especial excellence are *La Géante*, *L'Eveil du géant*, and also *Les Trois*

● *Fig. 73*
Joan Miró, *Les Trois Sœurs* (Three sisters), 1938 (cat. no. 87).

Soeurs, with its madcap shenanigans (figs. 1, 100, 73; cat. nos. 87–89). Perhaps the most exciting and tumultuous image of all is the one work that Miró and Marcoussis engraved together, *Portrait de Miró* (fig. 8, cat. no. 91). In the center of the plate is a full-face portrait of Miró (face and hands) engraved by Marcoussis. This is surrounded by a wild, carefree explosion of lines and stars and creatures and words ("Pluie de lyres / CIRQUES DE MELANCHOLIE"), all expressing the wit and imagination of Miró. The plates were engraved at Marcoussis's studio in Clichy, at the foot of the great hill of Montmartre, and then printed at Lacourière's, way up at the top of Montmartre, near Le Sacré-Coeur, and I can only imagine the sight of these two merry rascals dashing up the narrow, sloping streets of Montmartre, freshly engraved plates tucked carefully under their arms, journeying from one atelier to the other.

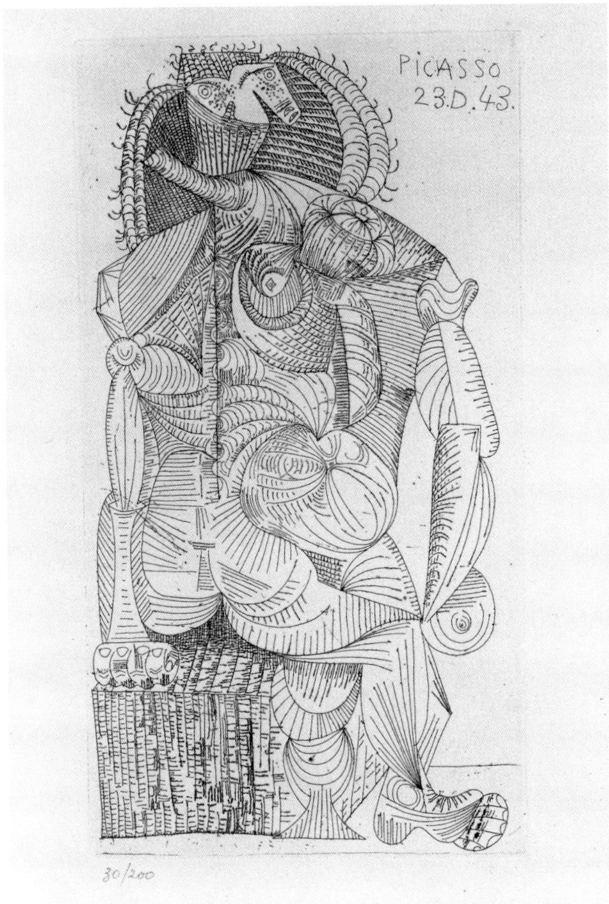

To close out the decade, Miró created small, single prints for books by two special friends, Alice Paalen and Benjamin Péret, and two separate etchings for albums published by other friends, *Solidarité* (1938) and *Fraternity* (1939; fig. 110, cat. no. 100),[12] the former accompanying a poem by Eluard; the latter, one by Stephen Spender. These last two etchings were engraved at Hayter's Atelier 17, and this marked the beginning of a long professional friendship between the two men.

Pablo Picasso was never a formal member of the surrealist group. For the first two decades of the movement's existence he was a strong sympathizer and frequently participated in its group exhibitions. His closer affiliation was with the Communist party, and though this did not interfere with his friendships with many surrealists (some of whom themselves flirted with communism in the 1930s and from whose roster came a handful of staunch party supporters, notably Picasso's close friend Eluard and the ever-important Aragon), it did eventually cause a permanent rupture in his friendship with Breton, but not until shortly after the end of World War II.

The seemingly endless vitality and versatility of Picasso's creative spirit led him inevitably to imagery consecrated by the surrealists. Hardly did he enter this hallowed ground as an intruder, but rather as a welcome and awaited guest. His first especially surrealist image was drawn a year or two prior to the formal

Fig. 74
Pablo Picasso, Untitled (from *Contrée*), 1943 (cat. no. 102).

inauguration of the movement: a charming, small-format plate entitled *Femme*, from 1922–23.[13] By my own criteria the next qualifying image would be the etching *Figures* of 1927.[14] The irregularity of the appearance of these sorts of images correctly informs us that Picasso enjoyed lolling about the edges of the great surrealist terrain but never actually set up camp there.

Next, in 1929, Picasso made a lithograph depicting an especially amusing monument (possibly a project for a monument to Guillaume Apollinaire), then, four years later, a single plate of the one hundred in all making up the suite of etchings published by Ambroise Vollard appeared, bearing the image of a nude female model regarding a prototypical surrealist sculpture (fig. 111, cat. no. 101). Other occasional prints of a surrealist nature followed. Two plates printed from a photosensitive paper called Kodatrice appeared in 1936, one destined to accompany the ten deluxe copies of Eluard's *Les Yeux fertiles*.[15] The most deliberate surrealist prints etched by Picasso in this period were *Figures surréalistes I* and *Figures surréalistes II* of 1933,[16] each printed in a handful of proofs only; both are icons of the purest sort of surrealist imagery. He would close the decade with several distorted portraits of Dora Maar and one of the most dynamic and unforgettable black-and-white prints of the twentieth century, *La Femme qui pleure* of 1937.[17]

Another master of the engraver's art who emerged in Paris in the 1930s was Kurt Seligmann, originally from Basel. Born (like an astounding number of the surrealists) in the year 1900, he made his first recorded print, a harmless landscape, in 1918. He did not enter the domain of surrealist prints until the late 1920s, when he arrived in Paris. By the mid-1930s he had created two exceptional albums of fifteen etchings each: one, *Protubérances cardiaques* (see fig. 122, cat. no. 114), with a text by Jakovski; the other, *Les Vagabondages héraldiques*, with text by his close friend Pierre Courthion.[18] The latter album was printed by Tanneur, as was the etching he drew for the 1935 Jakovski album, *24 Essais*.[19] From that time on, Seligmann printed all of his etchings himself.

When World War II broke out, Seligmann moved to the United States. He set up his presses first in New York City and then on his farm in Sugar Loaf, New York, printing not only his own work but occasional prints for visiting friends as well, including Alexander Calder, Masson, and Tanguy (an estimable large-plate etching that has never, to date, been published). Seligmann's most distinguished print project in America was the haunting series *The Myth of Oedipus* (1944), with text by his friend Meyer Schapiro.[20]

I will return for a moment to the graphic works of Giorgio de Chirico. Following his early efforts in etching and lithography in the 1920s, he returned to printmaking briefly in the 1930s to undertake two separate commissions. The first, in 1930, was a project fit only for an artist of stature: a definitive illustrated edition of Apollinaire's *Calligrammes* to be published by Gallimard.[21] De Chirico complied with relish, producing a suite of sixty-six lithographs—some sketchy, others witty and profound—with which Apollinaire would have been heartily content. Four years later, at the time of de Chirico's last important series of surrealist paintings (the *Bagni misteriosi*), the enterprising publishing group Editions des Quatre Chemins commissioned Jean Cocteau to write a text entitled *Mythologies* and de Chirico to illustrate it with a series of lithographs. De Chirico created ten images based on the *Bagni misteriosi* themes.[22] Curiously, some of the *Bagni* paintings were not produced until a year or so after the completion of the suite of lithographs, suggesting that at least some of these print images were preparatory to the oil paintings. The printer was the pioneer Desjobert; the result, one of the tidiest small-format portfolios of the period. This would be the final, important print statement by de Chirico in his long lifetime. What he produced subsequently were only spiritless rerenderings of his great themes of bygone days.

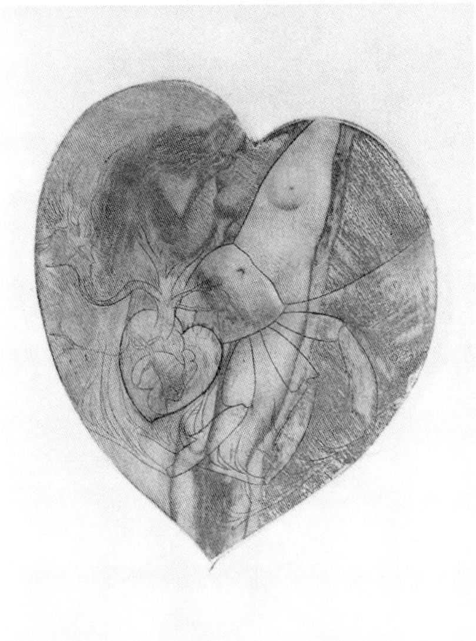

The 1930s were owned by the surrealists, at least in Paris, and the decade ended sadly with the shock of the beginning of another world war. Important International Surrealist Exhibitions were presented all over Europe and in Japan as well: in London, Tenerife, Tokyo, Kyoto, Amsterdam, and finally, in 1938, back in Paris. That same year a small but very professional and dedicated publishing house called G.L.M. (the initials of its proprietor, Guy Lévis-Mano), located in the center of Montparnasse, produced an album that in its way served as a farewell to the wonderful era that was suddenly drawing to a close. The actual purpose of the album was to raise money for orphans of the Spanish Civil War. Prophetically it bespoke the gravity of what would shortly come to pass throughout the European continent. The title of the album was *Solidarité*. The text was a poem by Eluard, perhaps the most deep-feeling of all the poets of his time, entitled *November 1936*. The illustrations were etchings by a strong selection of Atelier 17's all-star roster: Masson, Miró, Picasso, Tanguy, and Hayter himself and his loyal British cohorts John Buckland-Wright and Dalla Husband. The era had come to an unceremonious end.

Another surrealist of the 1930s (and thereafter)—not so well known as some of those already mentioned but extremely adept at coaxing impeccable wonderlands from the shadows of copper and zinc—was Marcel Jean. Always a draftsman, Jean grew increasingly fascinated with the art of engraving, and in

◉ *Fig. 75*
Marcel Jean, Untitled (from *Mnésiques*), 1942; etching, 5½ x 4⅝ in. Courtesy Timothy Baum, New York.

the early 1930s, discovering that the hallowed Lacourière atelier was just a stone's throw from his own Montmartre studio, ventured there, serving a brief apprenticeship under this master. The result was a lifelong fascination with printmaking.

In the 1930s Jean created engravings in all shapes and sizes (one plate was cut in the shape of a heart [fig. 75], another in the profile of an elegant woman). Some of the plates were utilized as illustrations for books of the period; most were simply printed to a couple of proofs, to be passed around among his friends and later coveted by collectors. In 1938, soon after marrying, he went to Budapest to teach at the institute of design there. When the war broke out and the Germans occupied Paris, Jean and his wife decided to remain in Hungary. Seven years later (as excellently described in his autobiography, *Au Galop dans le vent* [1991]) they were finally able to return home.

In 1975, in honor of Jean's approaching seventy-fifth birthday, the Paris publishing group Editions des Grands Jours Surréalistes invited him to assemble all the plates of his early etchings for the printing of a limited-edition, boxed set. Jean conferred with his old friend the master printer Georges Leblanc, then very content in his retirement, and convinced him to return to the atelier for one final project. Together the two old cronies gathered and prepared most of Jean's old plates (a handful could not be located), chose the most desirable paper upon which to print (Vélin d'Auvergne du Moulin Richard-de-Bas), and set to work. The effort took up most of 1974 and resulted in an album entitled *Profil de la mémoire*, containing thirty-six etchings from 1935 to 1942, a miniature retrospective in itself. The covers were designed by the artist, and the spirited bilingual text was written by him as well. Jean continued his sporadic printmaking until shortly before his death in 1993.

The war came to Paris, and the surrealists were forced to scatter. Some remained in France; many, by circuitous routes, reunited in and around New York. Others (like Jean, in Hungary, and Wolfgang Paalen, in Mexico) became completely separated from their cohorts. Of the many who immigrated to America, some (such as Seligmann and Tanguy) never returned to live in Europe again. The severity and protracted duration of the war fractured the spirit of the surrealist group. Almost all survived physically, though one beloved member, Robert Desnos, was arrested by the Gestapo for his activities in the French Resistance in 1944 and transported to Buchenwald and then on to Terezín, in Czechoslovakia. He was found by the liberating force of Russian soldiers and Czech partisans in May of 1945 critically ill with typhus, to which he succumbed a month later.

Some of the artists of the group continued to make prints, if in a sporadic way; for others such activities were curtailed until after the war had ended. The single most important printmaking undertaking during the war years was Miró's group of fifty black-and-white lithographs, the *Barcelona Series*.[23] Horrified by the Spanish Civil War, the artist had remained with his family in exile in France. In the summer of 1939 the Mirós moved from Paris to Varengeville, in Normandy, and remained there until the spring of the following year. At Varengeville Miró began his extraordinary series of gouaches, *Constellations*, which he later completed in Mallorca. In May of 1940 the family returned briefly to Paris, then went to Spain, settling finally in Mallorca. In 1942 they returned by boat to Barcelona and remained there for most of the rest of the decade.

In Barcelona Miró resumed his close relationship with his local dealer, Joan Prats. Prats, a serious admirer of prints as well as paintings, urged him to continue his work on the *Barcelona Series*. The artist approached this endeavor gradually and with care, and in 1944 the series was completed, then published by Prats. The edition size was held to seven copies of each print: five numbered copies and two proof sets for the artist and publisher. These lithographs represent the last great sequence of truly surrealist images drawn by Miró. All of his favorite characters, as previously immortalized in the 1938 etchings and in the *Constellations* gouaches, come to life once again: giants and giantesses, one-eyed creatures with mouthfuls of menacing teeth, odd little family groups standing about, moons and stars and floating fish and flowers—the frivolity and gaiety of earlier, gentler times still intact.

In 1947 Miró journeyed to New York for a visit lasting more than half a year. He reunited with his old friend Hayter and produced a prodigious array of etchings, intaglios, and aquatints, some exquisitely hand-colored. Among them were the eight small plates for Tzara's *L'Antitête*, an etching with a comical little face for the *Laurels Album*, and *Little Girl Skipping Rope* from the first Brunidor portfolio.[24] Miró's printmaking career continued until his death, but the truly surrealist phase came to a close with this fraternal get-together with Hayter.

Hayter remained a tremendous catalyst. The presence of his atelier in New York during the 1940s enabled a number of artists biding their time in exile to continue their printmaking adventures in a relatively uninterrupted fashion. Probably the most important body of work created there was that of Masson, who, like Breton and his family, departed France via Martinique, arriving in New York in the summer of 1941. Between 1941 and 1945 Masson produced eighteen etchings with Hayter. Among this group were several important images, including *Le Génie de l'espèce* (fig. 76, cat. no. 72) and *Petit génie du blé* of 1942,[25] both of which were published by Curt Valentin of the Buchholz Gallery. *Le Génie*, if undeniably influenced by Miró, with flashes of Tanguy as well, remains more Massonian than not and, either in its black printing or the more agreeable variant

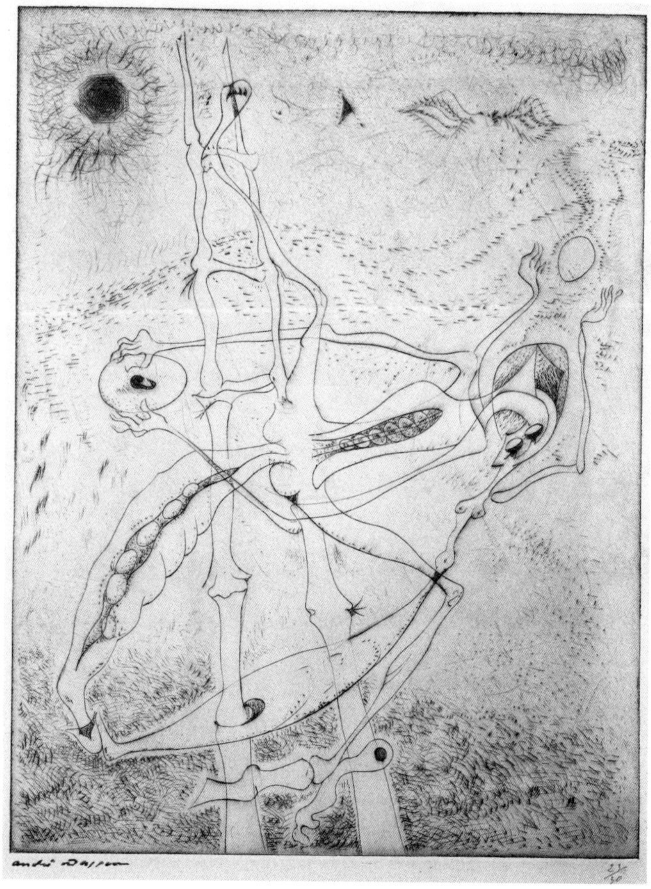

in sanguine, is one of the more fanciful surrealist prints of its time. Later in 1942 Masson produced one of the most overpowering graphic works (a combined-process etching and drypoint) of the century: *Rêve d'un futur désert.*[26] This blockbuster image descries a swath of a fantasy civilization located in some vast and unknown dream-place, its spiraling hillocks enveloped in swirling clouds. The actual plate measures approximately nineteen by twenty-five inches, which for an etching is large in its own right; the power of the image suggests a place so vast that the human mind cannot fully imagine its borders. This etching gives rise to the luxuriously troubling possibility that surrealism is only a fragment of the full, unedited journey outward . . . imagine!

Now we come to Roberto Sebastián Matta Echaurren. Born in 1912 in Chile, Matta came to Paris in the mid-1930s and worked as an apprentice draftsman under Le Corbusier. In 1937 he began to paint, and his body of work in drawing and painting from that time to the mid-1940s was one of the most vital—exemplifying surrealism in its purest form—in the entire history of the movement (comparable in impact to Dalí's work from the 1930s and that of Tanguy from 1926 to 1946). Almost every drawing and oil painting, in fact, from 1936 to 1943 or 1944, succeeded brilliantly in conveying the ultimate power of the marriage of color with spontaneously automatic, morphological imagery. Perhaps it was the intensity of the experience of creating such works that caused Matta, always sharp-minded and strong of body, to recede from the rendering of such masterpieces by the time he was thirty-five.

We who love and champion the graphic arts fervently wish that Matta, such a superior draftsman, had created at least a small handful of mighty renderings with the burin or lithographic crayon comparable to his other work of that early period. Sadly he did not. His one grand effort was a series of eleven drypoints depicting extremely erotic images, presented under the title *The New School* (referring to the New School for Social Research, the site of the printer, Hayter's Atelier 17, at that time), from 1943–44 (see fig. 91, cat. no. 76).[27] The series was apparently destined for a small circle of admiring friends and patrons only, for the edition was to be limited to eleven sets, of which only five or six were ever printed. The only other print of merit from that period was an etching

● *Fig. 76*
André Masson, *Le Genie de l'espèce* (Genius of the species), 1942 (cat. no. 72).

and aquatint of 1944, which accompanied the first twenty-five copies of Breton's book *Arcane 17* (1945).[28]

From 1946 on, Matta remained loyal to the making of prints, both lithographs and etchings. Under the tutelage of Georges Visat in Paris, he mastered the aquatint process and produced many fine albums (*Come detta dentro vo significado*, *Les Voix*, *Les Damnations*, etc.), as well as single prints of equal merit. Unfortunately no print was ever rendered to bear evidence of the mightiness of those magical first half-dozen years.

In France, despite the pall cast by the German occupation, printmaking activity did not cease entirely. In 1940 Victor Brauner, who had taken refuge in the south of France, designed his first etching—three states in all—to illustrate his friend Robert Rius's small volume of poems, *Frappe de l'écho* (figs. 19–21, cat. nos. 5–7), published that year by Editions Surréalistes. Brauner did not create any further prints until after the war, when he was able to return to Paris and the society of his surrealist cohorts.

Picasso, rarely inactive during the seventy-plus years of his printmaking career, created few prints during the early 1940s (save the thirty-one etchings for the *Buffon* series, published in 1942[29]), but two or three dealt with surrealist themes: in particular, the wonderfully contrived creature-personage that illustrates Desnos's *Contrée* (1943; fig. 74, cat. no. 102) and some of the whimsical plates of the same year drawn to illustrate the deluxe copies of Hugnet's *Le Chevre-feuille*.[30]

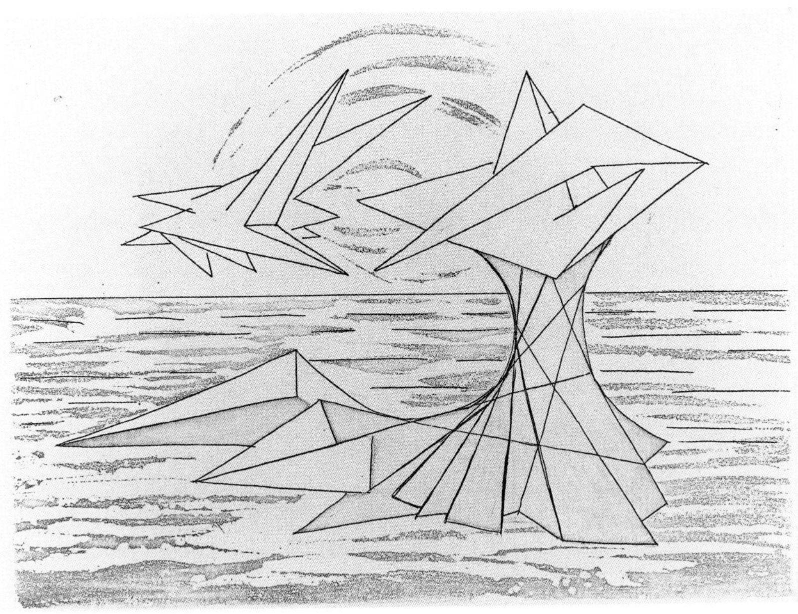

● *Fig. 77*
Oscar Dominguez, Untitled (from *Domaine*), 1942 (cat. no. 41).

Another surrealist who did not terminate his activity during the occupation years was the Spaniard Oscar Dominguez. Dominguez began making prints in the 1930s, first producing two gemlike erotic etchings for the anonymously authored, pocket-size book *Le Feu au cul* and then the truly exquisite drypoint *Femme à la bicyclette* (1935; fig. 47, cat. no. 40), which accompanied Hugnet's *La Hampe de l'imaginaire*, published a year later. Dominguez was not a prolific printmaker, so his next effort of any importance was the series of eight etchings illustrating Robert Ganzo's *Domaine* in 1942 (see fig. 77, cat. no. 41). Finally, in 1945, he etched a very detailed plate to serve as frontispiece for Amy Bakaloff's touching poem-memoir of the occupation,

Sombre est noir (fig. 47, cat. no. 42). This was the last significant print by Dominguez, who died by his own hand in 1957.

Printmaking activity in New York during the war years centered around Hayter's Atelier 17 and, to a lesser extent, the private print studio of Seligmann. In 1943 the literary and art review *VVV*—begun the year before by Breton in association with the young sculptor David Hare, Max Ernst, and later Marcel Duchamp—published a portfolio of works by a group of artists residing in and around New York at that time. The portfolio, unbound and contained in a printed cover and slipcase, consisted of original works by ten artists. The works were the products of various media—etchings (all printed at Seligmann's studio) by Calder, Leonora Carrington (fig. 78, cat. no. 14), Marc Chagall, Masson, Seligmann, and Tanguy; a manipulated, experimental photograph by Hare (printed from an intentionally burned negative); a "poem-collage" by Breton; a pastel frottage by Ernst; and two original painted works by Matta and the young American artist Robert Motherwell. This portfolio, now considered a very rare plum, was announced as an edition of fifty copies, but because of the minuteness of the public responsive to such an offering, only twenty copies were ever assembled.

When the war ended, many of the surrealists regrouped in Paris, but things would never be the same again. Of the prewar surrealist contingent—those who had congregated on a daily basis in cafés, spent holidays together, and

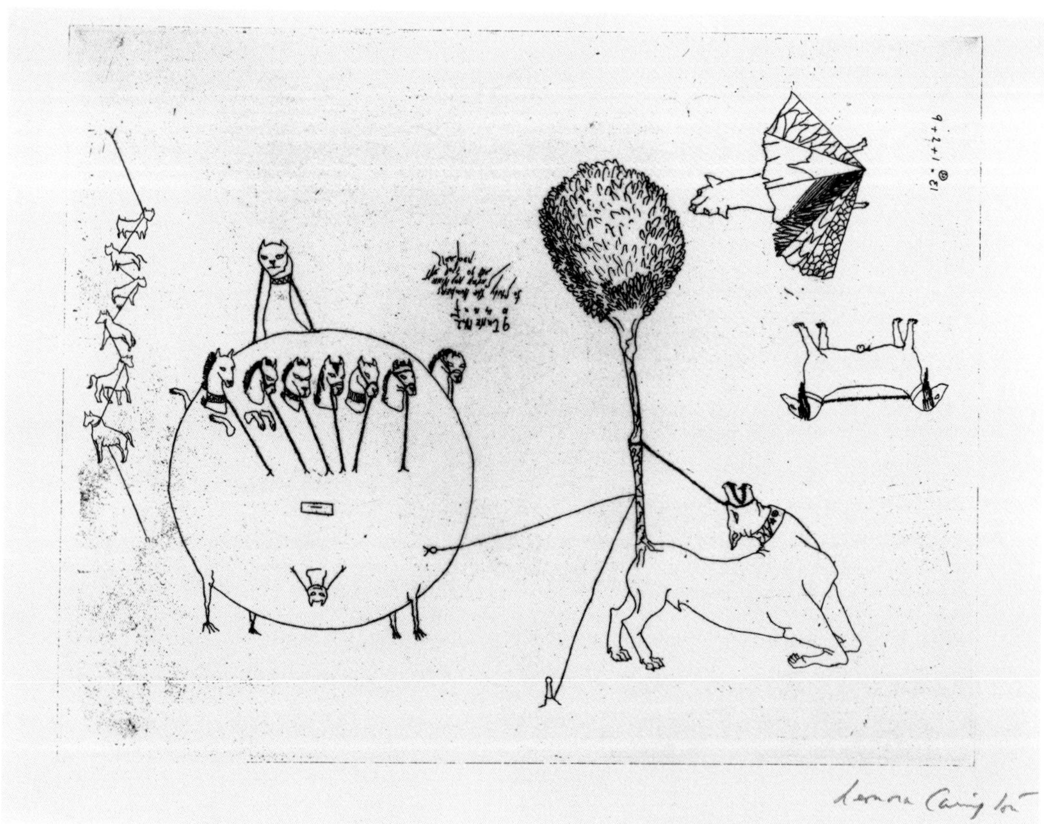

◉ *Fig. 78*
Leonora Carrington,
Untitled, 1942 (cat. no. 14).

commanded the main share of attention in the realms of art and poetry for an uninterrupted decade and a half—many did not return immediately, and others did not return at all. Breton, despite the expulsions and resignations of so many of the surrealists, still remained at the helm and never ceased to explore every possible channel to keep his movement proudly and defiantly afloat. New magazines appeared, manifestoes circulated, fresh volumes of poetry were published, and galleries reopened.

From an ideological standpoint surrealism was momentarily upstaged by the new pet philosophy of the time, existentialism. Breton shrugged it off as "night school." He was accused by some of being a coward for having deserted France during the occupation; others scoffed at him as a has-been. A leader through and through, he disregarded his critics and concentrated on rebuilding his surrealist rock. In 1947, after much serious planning, the first postwar International Surrealist Exhibition, *Le Surréalisme en 1947*, opened in Paris at the Galerie Maeght. Duchamp assisted Breton with the presentation of the show, and a deluxe catalogue, surmounted by a three-dimensional cover by Duchamp, accompanied the exhibition. Works by eighty-seven artists representing twenty-four countries were included, and suddenly surrealism was alive once again.

Surrealist printmaking was similarly resuscitated. The catalogue for the 1947 exhibition included original prints—etchings, lithographs, and a pair of woodcuts (both by Arp)—by more than twenty artists. Represented were Arp, Hans Bellmer, Brauner, Ernst, Hare, Jacques Hérold, Jean, Wifredo Lam, Jacqueline Lamba, Matta, Miró, Man Ray, Kay Sage, Tanguy, Dorothea Tanning, and Toyen, as well as a group of younger or lesser-known new arrivals, welcomed to join the old guard.

With the war over and a new era unfolding, modernization continued as always. In the realm of art original prints gained new popularity as an independent art form. New publishers began to emerge, many in the form of galleries publishing editions of their own coterie of artists (Buchholz in New York, for Masson; Louise Leiris, the continuation of Kahnweiler's old Galerie Simon, in Paris, for Masson and Picasso; Maeght, also in Paris, for Miró, Braque, Giacometti, etc.; small galleries like Marcel Zerbib's Galerie Diderot, publishing Ernst and Tanguy; Nierendorf in New York—before moving back to Berlin—loyal and attentive to Seligmann; and quite a few others).

At one point or another almost every surrealist artist tried his or her hand at printmaking. The only major surrealist who did not create any modern prints was Francis Picabia, who at the outset of the century, while many of his future surrealist cohorts were still mere children, mastered the techniques of engraving and rendered some quite respectable plates of postimpressionist landscapes and the like. Unfortunately, despite the brilliance of his mechanical and subsequent "transparency" drawings and paintings, he never translated any of these images to the graphic media.

One artist who took very naturally to printmaking, in the end becoming one of its most accomplished practitioners, was Hans Bellmer. Bellmer had come to Paris from Germany in 1938, leaving behind most of his belongings and a country that had grown most unsympathetic to his form of art: the creation of life-size erotic doll-sculptures *(poupées)* and photographs of same (in the most compromising postures he could devise). His work was already known to, and greatly admired by, the surrealists. Without his beloved dolls themselves, but with the precious photographs still in his possession, Bellmer commenced to render his images as drawings and later as paintings. In the 1940s, after being released from a French detention camp (one in which Ernst, also a German national, had been incarcerated as well), he remained in France (south of the Vichy line) and survived as best he could. At that time he undertook his first effort in the art of etching, creating a series of six images for Bataille's *Histoire de l'oeil* (still published under the pseudonym Lord Auch). If Bataille was solidly entrenched as the quintessential eroticist in the literature of his time, surely was Bellmer his painterly counterpart.

From 1949 on, Bellmer produced a succession of quality etchings and lithographs. *Transfert des sens* (1949) was his first single-edition lithograph.[31] The image—spiraling faces of languidly reposing ladies, suffocatingly camouflaged in a nebulous web—was wonderfully drawn and printed in a mustard tone. It was the first of a group of most tantalizing lithographs. Among the best of his creations in this medium were three prints from the early 1950s, which he published himself, printing only a few proofs of each. These three prints—his most alluring perhaps—were printed during lunch hours and after closing time at one of the local ateliers (perhaps at Desjobert, the printer of *Transfert des sens*), using whatever scraps of paper happened to be left about the shop. I mention this anecdotally, for in those days Bellmer, like many postwar artists bereft of private funds or permanent galleries, was truly impoverished. His desperation was such that several of the known proofs of these three prize lithographs were printed on the backs of discarded proofs of black-and-white lithographs—images of tugboats hauling barges up the Seine and the like—destined for a contemporary album by the aging postimpressionist Albert Marquet. The three lithographs are *Main articulée*, *Anatomie par l'image*, and *Céphalopode reversible*, a re-creation of the image of one of Bellmer's greatest paintings.[32]

From the mid-1950s on, Bellmer turned more often to engraving, presumably to gain a more precise line for his extremely well executed and detailed compositions. Many memorable plates evolved, including suites for Joyce Mansour's *Jules César*, de Sade's *Petit traité de morale*, and Heinrich von Kleist's *Les Marionettes*.[33] Bellmer—like Ernst, Matta, and others of the time—felt quite at home working alongside Georges Visat at the latter's atelier (from the early 1950s on) and never had to feel impoverished again in regard to his printing projects, for Visat frequently became his publisher as well.

Another luminary of the postwar era of surrealist printmaking was Victor Brauner. Brauner, one of the Romanian transplants to the Paris surrealist group in the early 1930s (like Tzara, via Dada and Zurich, much earlier on, and Brauner's close pal Jacques Hérold), made his first print in 1940 (as mentioned earlier), then resumed his printmaking activity in the second half of the decade. From then to his death, in 1966, he created a modest body of graphic works, not much in excess of thirty images, but as with Tanguy, quality won out over quantity, and many of the works are unforgettable. Brauner's specialty was hand-coloring. His contribution to the Brunidor *Portfolio Number 2*, published under the direction of Robert Altmann in Paris in 1952 (a sequel to the first Brunidor portfolio, published in New York in 1947), was a pair of etchings printed on a single sheet, with each of the 110 copies hand-colored in watercolor (see fig. 79, cat. no. 8). The result: 110 superb gems! Only the first six copies of the deluxe edition of his good friend (and compatriot) Gherasim Luca's poem *Ce Château pressenti* of 1958 boast the accompanying etching in a hand-colored state (fig. 25, cat. no. 12)—with the perfect coloration for a sunlit Orthodox Easter! To celebrate the limited-edition monograph written on his work by yet another close friend, Sarane Alexandrian (titled *Brauner l'illuminateur*, 1954), Brauner hand-colored all thirty-five of the etchings allotted for the deluxe edition, painting each image entirely differently from the others. Brauner loved the magic of bright color. He also delighted in designing original silkscreen posters for his own exhibitions, the most striking of which presents a central image coated with sumptuous gold leaf, applied by hand.

Max Ernst spent most of the 1940s living on a remote mountaintop in Arizona, where he painted and sculpted but had no printmaking facilities. As a consequence he made no prints again until after 1945, and even in the first years after the war he made prints only when traveling to places where the necessary facilities were available. In 1946 a definitive, limited edition of Tzara's epic Dada play *Le Coeur à gaz* was published, and the frontispiece was an aquatint etching by Ernst,[34] engraved at Hayter's studio in New York during an earlier visit. Also engraved at Hayter's was the haunting and wonderfully intricate drypoint *Correspondences dangereuses* (fig. 55, cat. no. 53), destined for inclusion in Altmann's first Brunidor portfolio. In 1948, while in Los Angeles preparing for his major exhibition (in January 1949) at the Copley Galleries, Ernst made the acquaintance of an amiable local printer named Lynton Kistler and took advantage of that gentleman's hospitality to work briefly in his studio. The results were quite gratifying: a tiny but decisive etching entitled *Sun and Sea* and another intricate black-and-white image that would be offered with the deluxe copies of the Copley Galleries catalogue.[35] The final project fulfilled under Kistler's admiring eye was a plate containing eight amusing vignettes (mostly masklike, floating heads), from which only two or three proofs were printed. The plate was later shipped to Lacourière's atelier in Paris, where it was cut into eight separate plates for one of the three volumes of Tzara's *L'Antitête*,[36] published in 1949 (the other two volumes were illustrated with etchings by, respectively, Miró and Tanguy).

In 1949, following his return to France with his wife, the American artist Dorothea Tanning, Ernst began a new and enjoyable era in the realm of printmaking. The catalyst was the comparatively new print atelier of Georges Visat—a man of technical prowess and personal exuberance—who was honored by the opportunity to work with Max Ernst. For Ernst, Visat's place became a studio-away-from-home (most of his life in France, after his return from America, was spent a good distance from Paris). That same year he made his first etchings chez Visat: a title page and two succeeding images for Benjamin Péret's *La Brebis galante*.[37] That was followed, in short order, by illustrations for a French-language edition of Lewis Carroll's *The Hunting of the Snark*, Henri Michaux's *Tranches de savoir*, and a second Péret volume, *Mort aux vaches et au champ d'honneur*.[38] In 1950 Ernst began to make lithographs as well, at the famous Desjobert atelier. The first lithograph printed there was designed to illustrate the deluxe copies of the *Almanach surréaliste du demi-siècle*, edited by Breton, including more than thirty texts by surrealists of the old guard and the new.[39]

For Ernst 1950 was an especially active year, for that was the year he mastered the art of aquatint as well, again guided by Visat, and his first efforts were exceptional, in particular the two plates entitled *Figure* and *Oiseaux*.[40] These aquatints were published in comfortably small editions by Marcel Zerbib, a dealer and publisher who was one of the first members of the art community to assist Ernst upon his return to Paris. Also in 1950 Ernst (working chez Desjobert) produced a series of witty and colorful lithographs for the publisher Guilde de la Gravure (based in Paris and Geneva): *Danseuses* (fig. 56, cat. no. 54; printed only in black-and-white), *Etoile de mer*,[41] *Rhythmes* (fig. 57, cat. no. 55), and *Masques* (fig. 58, cat. no. 56).

For Ernst 1953 saw the publication of *Das Schnabelpaar*—eight etching-aquatints printed in color, published by Galerie Beyeler in Basel—and 1955, Antonin Artaud's *Galapagos*, with eleven kaleidoscopic etchings of varying sizes,

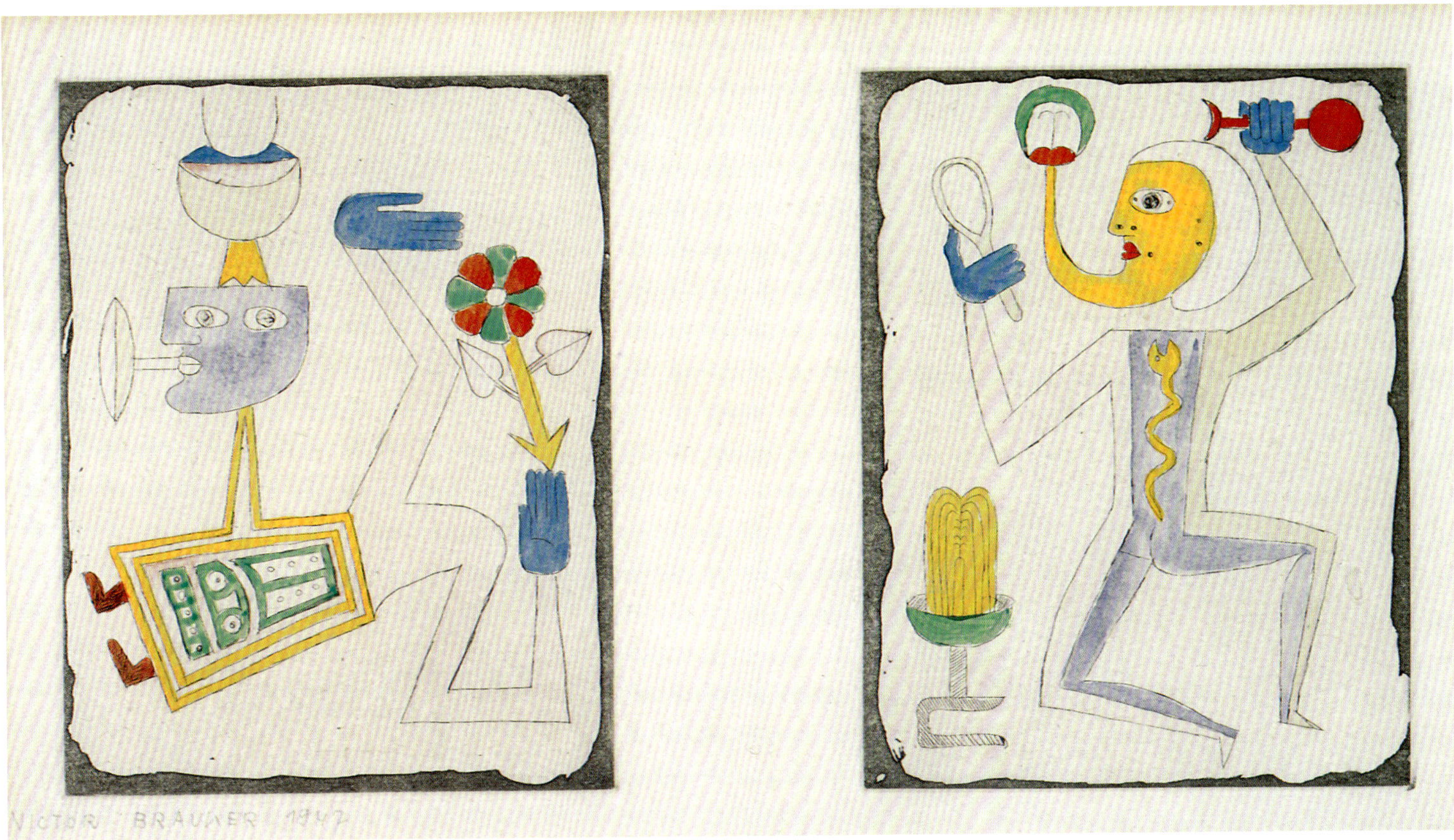

published by the enterprising new Paris publisher Louis Broder.[42]

I cannot mention all the significant prints created by Ernst in these last two decades of his life, for there are far too many (a few hundred prints compose his entire graphic work). I will speak briefly of *Hibou* and *Hibou-Arlequin*, which finalize the series of lithographs drawn at Desjobert (the *Hibou*, squatting contentedly and staring sharply at the viewer's eye, adorns the cover of the Penguin Books edition of Franz Kafka's short stories); the images of embryonic nebulae designed to illustrate the poems of Friedrich Hölderlin (1961); and the nervous, jumpy, cosmic creatures resplendent in the etchings for Léna Leclerc's *La Rose est nue*, also of 1961.[43] I will complete my discussion of Ernst with a brief mention of a very large, resounding masterwork from 1964, *Maximiliana ou l'exercise illégal de l'astronomie*.[44] This imposing, beautifully printed, handsomely boxed tome presents a series of thirty-four etchings, some with aquatint, all in color, assembled amid wondrous adventures in interplanetary typography. The printer was, as was usual by this point, Visat; the publisher, the great Iliazd. *Maximiliana* was published in an edition of seventy-five numbered sets.

Dorothea Tanning, Ernst's wife and unwavering great friend during more than thirty exciting years together, was also one of the most talented printmakers among the surrealists in the postwar era. Like Ernst, she made her litho-

● *Fig. 79*
Victor Brauner, Untitled, 1947 (cat. no. 8).

graphs at Desjobert and pursued her experiments in the myriad alternative methods of etching at Visat's studio.

Tanning's first encounter with etching was in a class in New York in 1942, and both of the unique proofs produced are entirely creditable. Her next consequential efforts were an etching contributed to the exhibition catalogue *Le Surréalisme en 1947* and two lovely color lithographs, *Métamorphoses* and *Bateau bleu* (1950; fig. 132, cat. no. 125), published by Guilde de la Gravure.[45] Next was an album of seven color lithographs of explosive surrealist fantasies: *Les 7 Périls spectraux*.[46]

In 1953 Tanning began making etchings with Visat, and many surprises resulted from that professional union. Beginning in 1965, more lithographs were evolved, this time in Vence, at the atelier of Pierre Chave, a neighbor of Tanning and Ernst's in the south of France. This involvement with lithography continued at the Paris atelier of Mourlot Frères. Since 1985 Tanning has lived in New York, and her printmaking activity has continued, first with an atelier in California and then at the fine atelier of Maurice Sanchez in New York City. Through the artist's personal generosity a virtually complete collection of her graphic work resides permanently in the print room of the New York Public Library.

Some of the surrealist artists, including a few of the most famous, approached the challenge of printmaking late in their careers, and the results were variable. René Magritte, who died in 1967, did not make his first prints—two etchings pulled at the Atelier Georges Leblanc in Paris—until 1962. These were linear works, drawn without any fancy frills, but both presented important images from the artist's repertoire: *Ceci n'est pas une pipe* and *Les Travaux d'Alexandre* (figs. 64–65, cat. nos. 62–63). In 1963, at Mourlot, Magritte produced his first lithograph, related to a painting of the same year, *Les Bijoux indiscrets* (fig. 80, cat. no. 64). This especially surrealist image was published both as a separate edition and as a lithographic plate in the Christmas 1963 issue of the famous French art publication *XXe Siècle*. His only other lithograph (his entire graphic oeuvre numbers only twenty images) was also printed in a limited edition and then used separately, this time as the poster for the *Salon de mai* of 1965 (fig. 66, cat. no. 65). The following year he made his third and perhaps most successful etching, *Paysage de Baucis* (fig. 67, cat. no. 66). The next group of prints, etched after a series of preparatory ink drawings, allow us an entire playground of Magrittean iconography. They compose a portfolio entitled *Aube à l'antipode* and were printed at the atelier of J. J. J. Rigal. That completed the lifetime graphic work of the artist. The final eight images were printed and published posthumously by Visat, with the artist's widow's consent, each a relatively small-format work, seven of the eight printed in color.

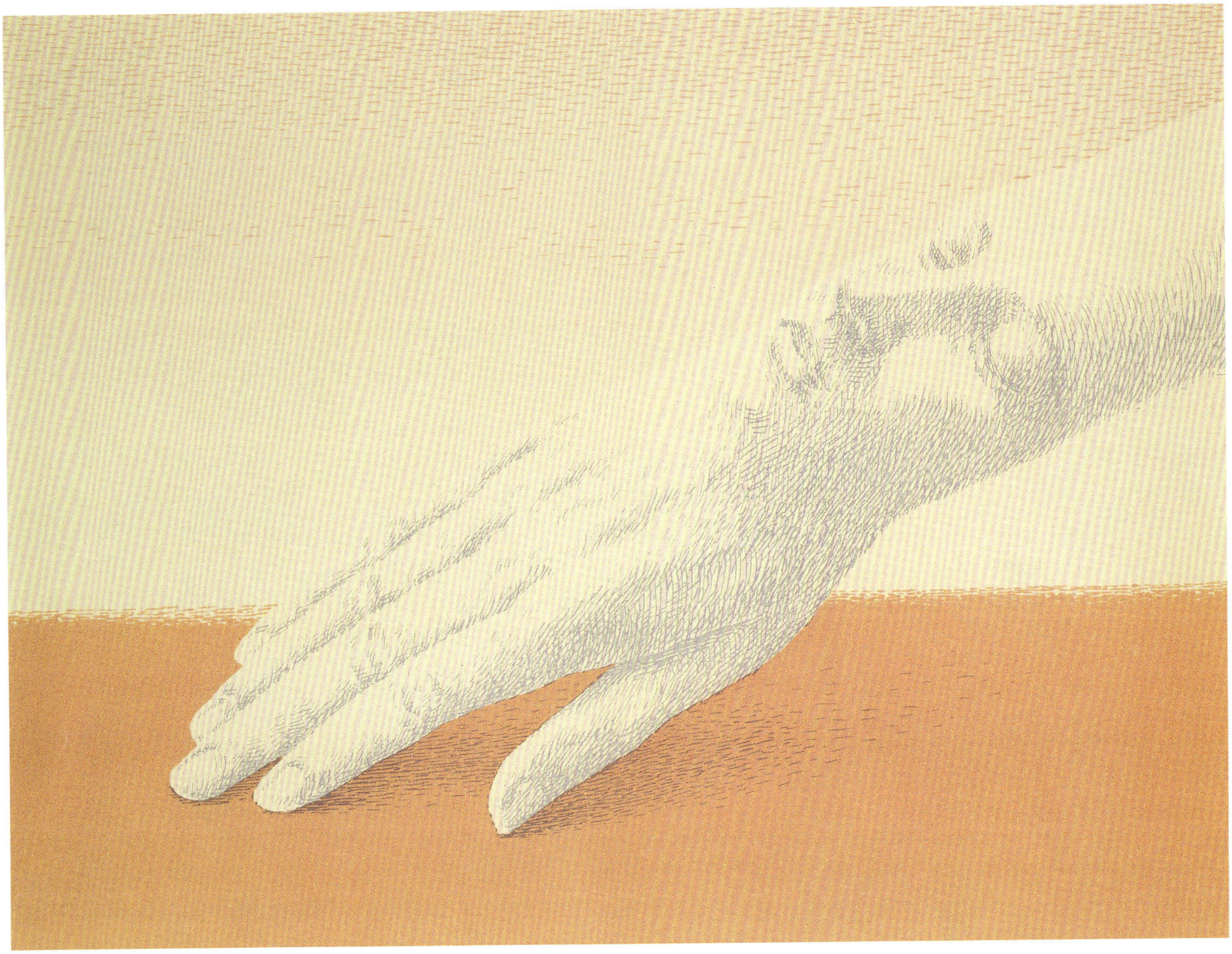

The other major surrealist from Belgium, Paul Delvaux, also began his printmaking career rather late in life. His medium of choice was lithography, though his first efforts were in etching: one single print in 1947, four more in 1960 (see fig. 81, cat. no. 33), and then a sprinkling throughout the rest of his career. The lithographs, the earliest of which date to 1966, are all full, complete images, not dissimilar to the artist's panoramic paintings. Almost every example portrays women, ranging from puberty to middle age, in every sort of setting and pose: indoors, outdoors, in daylight, beneath a full moon, reclining, walking about aimlessly in a garden, and so on. Some of the lithographs are in color, but except for one or two of the color works, the black-and-white images are equally powerful. Delvaux's graphic oeuvre numbers about one hundred prints in all.

One of the original members of the surrealist group—and, like Arp and Ernst, a graduate of Dada—was the American expatriate Man Ray. The quin-

◉ *Fig. 80*
René Magritte, *Les Bijoux indiscrets* (The talkative jewels), 1963 (cat. no. 64).

tessential man-for-all-seasons, Man Ray excelled in every area of visual art expression. One of the greatest photographers of the century, he also painted, drew, collaged, and created objects, always in the most interesting and imaginative ways. Perhaps because of his facility with the camera and his superb drawing skills, he devoted little time to printmaking. He did make some excellent *cliché verre* prints in the early 1920s, and in 1926 he found a superior pochoir (silkscreen) printer in Paris. The result was the *Revolving Doors* portfolio: a remaking of the ten images that he had originally rendered as collages in New York a decade earlier, with blazing, pure primary colors replacing the more somber tones of the collages (figs. 112–21, cat. nos. 103–12). Man Ray made his next print twenty-two years later, while living out his decade of "exile" in Los Angeles. The print, a color lithograph entitled *Roman Noir* (c. 1948),[47] is a sophisticated work, with each of the fifty examples uniquely colored. That was the artist's only printmaking effort during his stay in California.

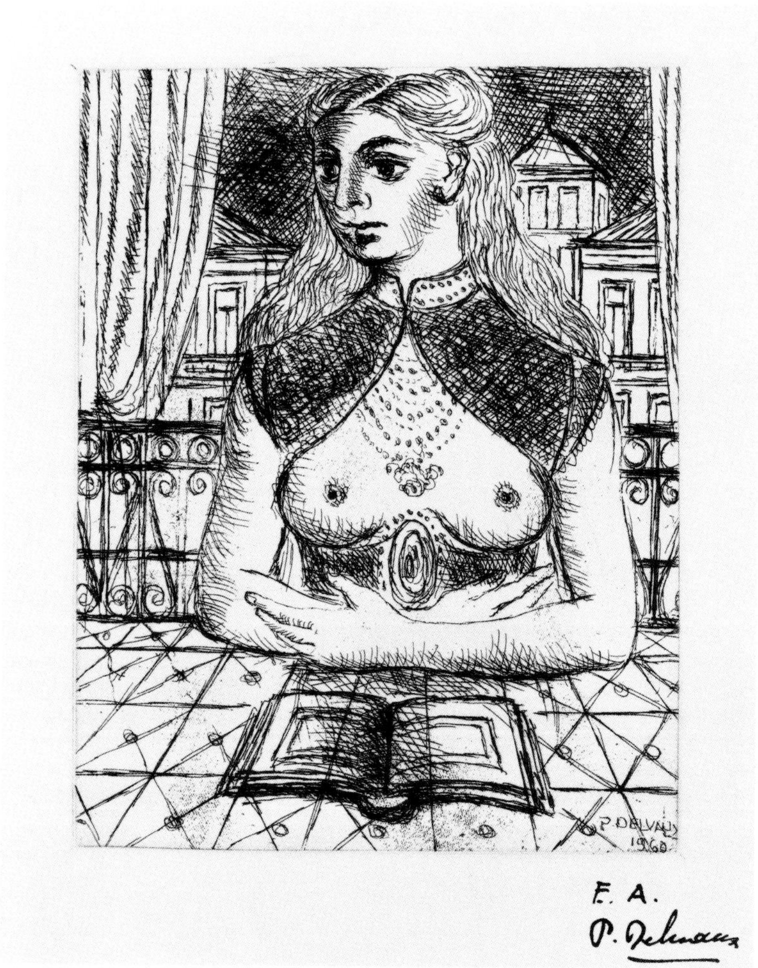

Upon his return to Paris Man Ray made a lithograph for Guilde de la Gravure: an abstract color image whose title is more interesting than the work itself: *Post-Columbian Object*.[48] From 1960 to the year of his death (1976), he signed his name or initials to approximately 150 different graphic images. Some were original prints, etchings and lithographs alike; others were limited editions of photolithographs, many after the artist's most celebrated images in other media (paintings, watercolors, drawings, even "rayographs"). Man Ray frowned when questioned too academically about the difference between his original prints and those that reproduced works from other media. "What difference does it make?" he would argue. "They're all works by me, aren't they?" From the public's point of view he was not incorrect, for in the end it is the popularity of the image that reigns. Man Ray's most celebrated painted work is assuredly his oil of 1932–34 *A l'heure de l'observatoire—les amoureux*, which was published as a

● *Fig. 81*
Paul Delvaux, *Buste de femme III* (Half-length portrait of a woman III), 1960 (cat. no. 33). © Estate of Paul Delvaux/ Licensed by VAGA, New York, NY.

photolithograph in 1967 in an edition of 150 and is continually much in demand and generally unfindable (fig. 83, cat. no. 113). This print fetches five to ten times the price of most other graphic works associated with Man Ray. He is recalled by many as the first "pop" (as in "popular") artist.

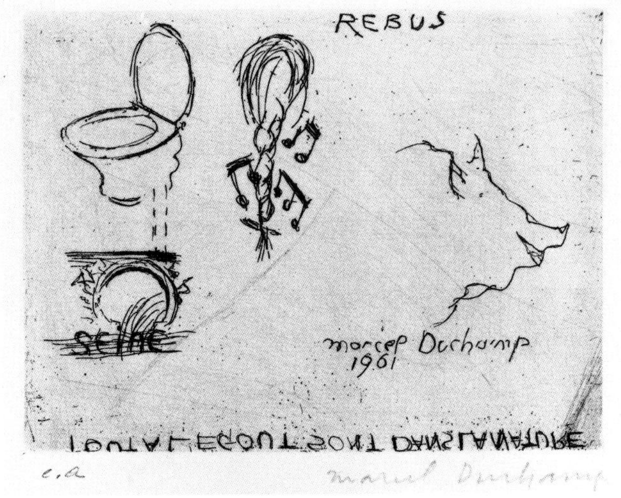

● *Fig. 82*
Marcel Duchamp, *Rebus*, 1961; etching, 4½ x 5¾ in. Courtesy of Timothy Baum, New York.

Similarly to Man Ray, his good friend Marcel Duchamp, the other dean of multimedia art creation, did not initially adopt printmaking as a means of expression. Duchamp lived a good portion of his life as a non-printmaking print-maker in a way, for the greatest monument he left behind was surely *The Large Glass* (1915–23), and what greater, more imposing intaglio work could there be than that? But, to travel from one extreme of size to another, in 1941 the first print by Duchamp did finally appear and was nothing but a minuscule, silkscreened rendering of a small moustache and matching goatee, those once affixed to the hallowed visage of Leonardo's Mona Lisa, now isolated and tipped into a small, limited-edition pamphlet written by Georges Hugnet, entitled *Marcel Duchamp*.[49]

In 1958 came a drypoint, *L'Equilibre*—which simply presented the word itself in the artist's scrawl, broken into three parts and printed backward—followed a year later by the wonderful etching *NON*, illustrating exactly that.[50] Each was printed in an edition of forty examples. Also in 1959 came a silkscreen of Duchamp's face in profile (fig. 84, cat. no. 44), which was printed in two separate color editions: blue or orange (both against the same black background). More small etchings followed: one a "rebus," in 1961 (fig. 82), another a charming sketch of the artist's famous *Fountain* (an ordinary urinal), entitled *Mirrorical Return* and adorned with an amusing letterpress text.[51] In 1965 came *The Chess Players*, with one state in black-and-white and a second in bistre, as well as the series of nine etchings re-creating various elements of *The Large Glass*, all engraved in Cadaqués, Spain, during the artist's summer holiday.[52] The final series of works engraved by Duchamp (and by this time he was truly warming up to the pleasures of etching) was made in New York between the winter and spring of 1967 and 1968. The general theme of this group is *The Lovers*, and each plate is witty and lively.[53] A few months after the completion of the final plate of this series, its ever-youthful creator passed away, at the age of eighty-one.

As I mentioned earlier, almost every surrealist artist produced a body of graphic work of some sort. I have tried to single out the more vigorous and historically important moments of printmaking during the surrealist era: the artists,

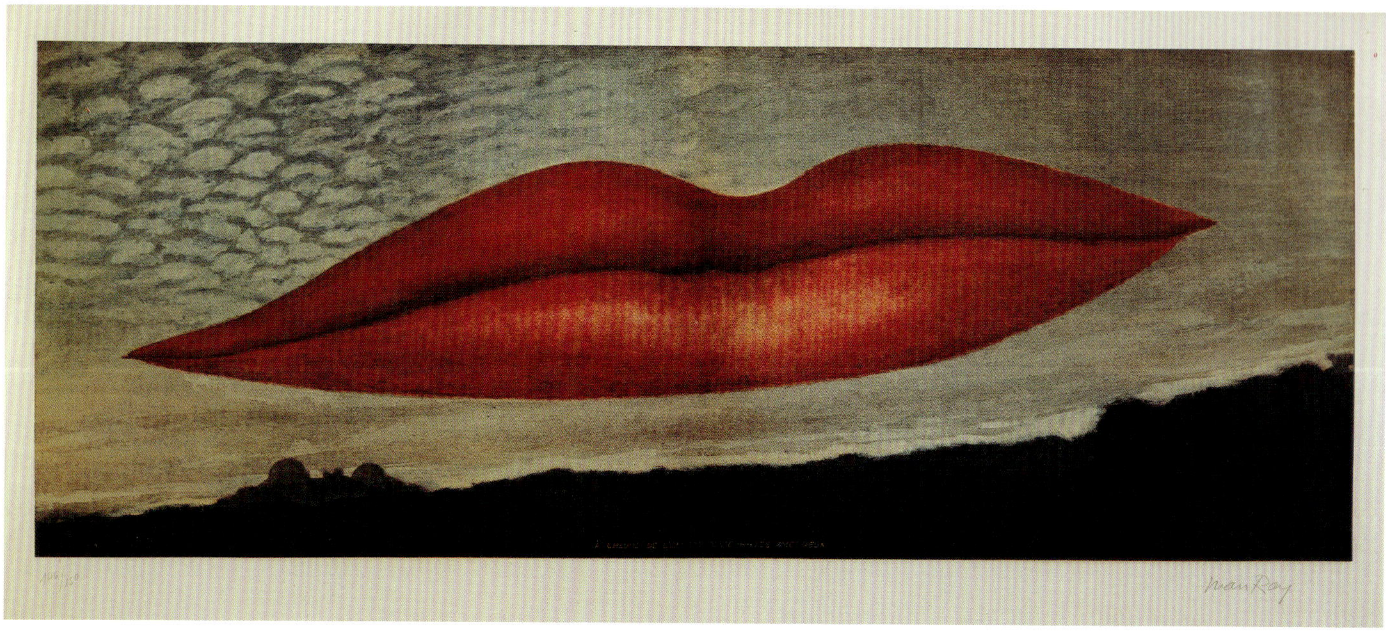
Man Ray

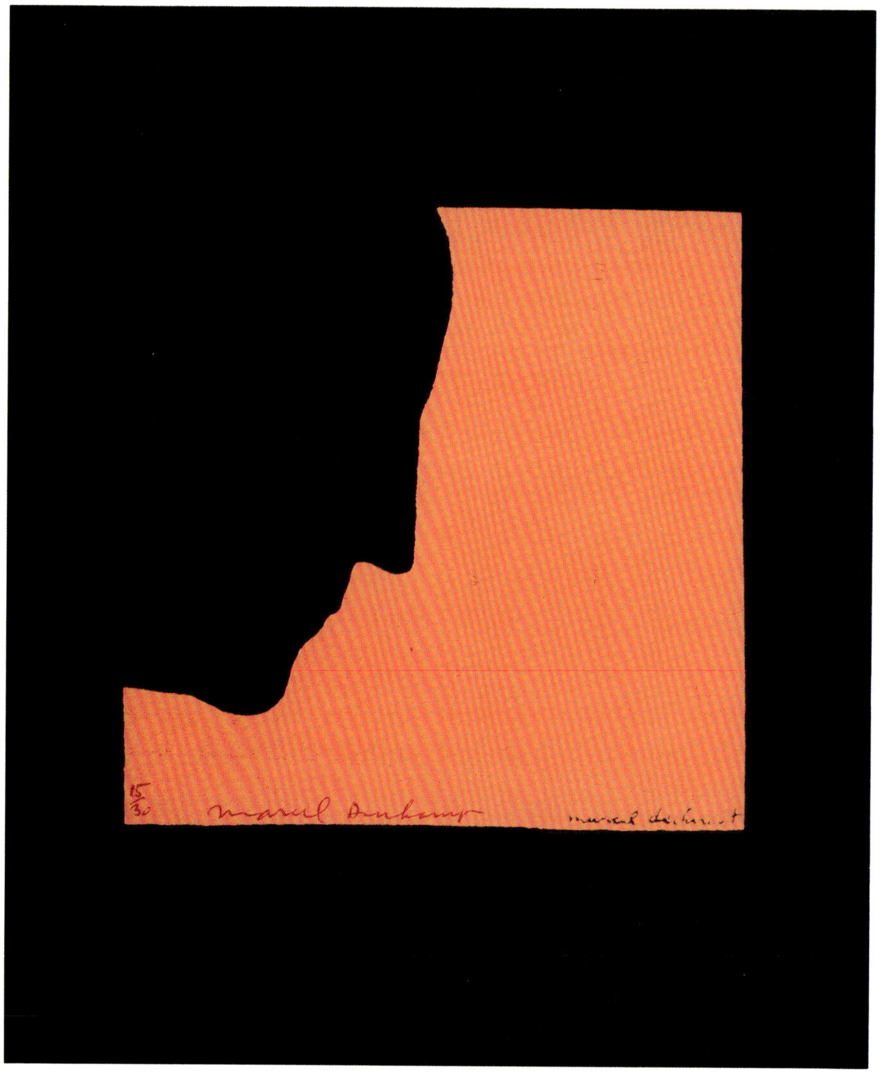
15/30
marcel duchamp

the ateliers, the projects themselves, the occasional exceptional print or print series. There are still a few more surrealists whose work in the print media merits mention, however, so I will attend to them now. Most of these artists created prints bearing images quite akin to their paintings and drawings. Nonetheless, the extension to etching or lithography enables us to learn more about each artist's subject matter and aesthetic intent.

Leonora Carrington's first published etching (fig. 78, cat. no. 14) appeared, as already mentioned, in the *VVV* portfolio of 1943. Subsequent to that she moved to Mexico, where she later developed a true interest in printmaking. Her subject matter always remained in the realms of personal mythology and related fantasy, and many of her lithographs venture further afield than the remotest of her paintings and drawings.

◉ *Fig. 83*
Man Ray, *A l'heure de l'observatoire—les amoureux* (Observatory time—the lovers), 1967 (cat. no. 113).

Wifredo Lam, who figured in the first Brunidor portfolio alongside Ernst, Hayter, Matta, Miró, Seligmann, and Tanguy, continued his printmaking career on a regular basis and, similarly to Brauner, became quite diligent at the art of hand-coloring. One of his truly lovely series of hand-colored works was for the deluxe copies of René Char's *Le Rempert de brindelles*, published by Louis Broder in 1953, for which he delicately colored all of the etchings as well as certain highlighted details of the cover.[54]

Valentine Hugo was both an artistic and spiritual force among the surrealists, from the 1920s until her death in 1968. Her portraits of the other artists and poets of the group are integral to the surrealist art of the 1930s, as were the images depicting her dreams. Among her outstanding achievements in printmaking are the twenty-two drypoints illustrating Eluard's *Les Animaux et leurs hommes/Les Hommes et leurs animaux* of 1937. The first eight copies of this very rare book present the etchings in various color states as well as the primary black-and-white. Another special achievement by Hugo is the series of eight drypoints engraved and printed by her to illustrate de Sade's novel *Eugénie de Franval* (1948). Incredibly, these images reach the same level of erotic exquisiteness as the text itself, and never in an indecorous way.

Another prolific printmaker, but not one who illustrated as many books as her peers, was Leonor Fini. A fine draftsman, Fini produced a mass of lithographs depicting sylphlike ladies floating or dancing about and mysterious faces partially obscured by cloudlike coverings which tease, then haunt you. She also produced several fantasy genre images of women in intimate environments—boudoirs, private train cars, window seats, or tea tables set for two only—where no man seems to be allowed. Fini's was a personal as well as private inner world, and nobody else's keys would ever rattle or disturb her hidden doors.

◉ *Fig. 84*
Marcel Duchamp, *Self-Portrait in Profile* (cat. no. 44).

The last two artists who come to mind were both visitors from other lands. Jacques Hérold came from Romania about the same time as Brauner, and his early imagery was not so distant from the folk figures of his homeland. Hérold was fascinated by the spectral side of things, and many of his prints portray wondrous, starry creatures, floating or walking quietly about, hovering between deepest sleep and blinding-light wakefulness. Later his figures turned to fluttering, flickering abstract shapes and patterns.

I will close with Toyen (Marie Cerminová), who was born in Prague and died in Paris. She was considered by many one of the most pure (as in untainted) of the surrealists. Her graphic work was not at all prolific, but was isolated and always very specific. Her etchings served as frontispieces to certain special, precious books, and her focused exactitude would invariably produce the ideal image for each text. Memorable are her lovers kissing with birds in place of lips, eyes staring down from forest trees. Toyen, more than anyone perhaps, knew exactly the nuances of hand coloring, applying it almost like a ballerina's makeup. This is the real source of surrealist enchantment: the delicacy of the hands in motion, not just the embroidery itself.

Notes

1. Arntz 3–10, 16–25, 59–77.
2. Spies-Leppien 8, 9.
3. Saphire 1–4; Saphire-Cramer 1.
4. Saphire 5–11.
5. Saphire 22–26.
6. Saphire 27–34.
7. Saphire 35–37.
8. Dupin 1–8.
9. Mourlot 2–5; Cramer 1.
10. Michler-Löpsinger 7.
11. Dupin 18, 17.
12. Dupin 42–43.
13. Bloch 56.
14. Bloch 81.
15. Bloch 289.
16. Bloch 1323–25, 1326.
17. Bloch 1333.
18. Mason 20–34, 37–52.
19. Mason 54.
20. Mason 117, I-122.
21. Ciranna 17–82.
22. Ciranna 83–92.
23. Mourlot 6–55.
24. Dupin 53–60, 51, 52.
25. Saphire 86.
26. Saphire 90.
27. Sabatier 1–7.
28. Sabatier 8.
29. Bloch 328–58.
30. Bloch 361.
31. Denoël 20.
32. Denoël 24, 27, 35.
33. Denoël 31–33, 78–87, 97–105.
34. Spies-Leppien 23.
35. Spies-Leppien 26, 30.
36. Spies-Leppien 27.
37. Spies-Leppien 28.
38. Spies-Leppien 32–34.
39. Spies-Leppien 35.
40. Spies-Leppien 37, 39.
41. Spies-Leppien 47.
42. Spies-Leppien 56, 59.
43. Spies-Leppien 64, 67, 77, 78.
44. Spies-Leppien 95.
45. Waddell-Ruby 3–5.
46. Waddell-Ruby 6.
47. Pilat 32.
48. Pilat 12.
49. Schwarz 310.
50. Schwarz 346, 352.
51. Schwarz 360, 370.
52. Schwarz 380, 382–90.
53. Schwarz 398–402.
54. Tonneau-Ryckelynck 5307–10.

Plates

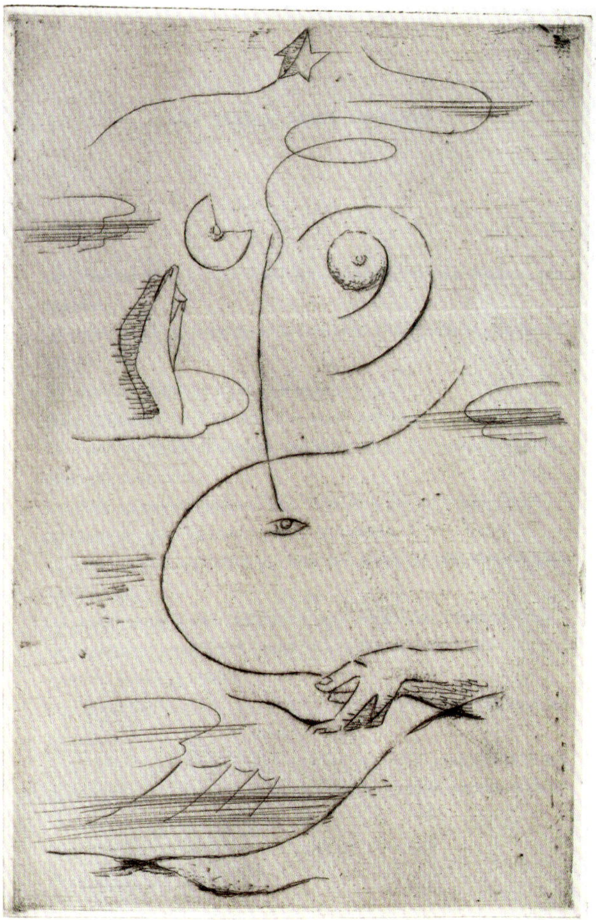

● *Fig. 85 (above)*
André Masson, Untitled (from *C'est les bottes de 7 lieues . . .*), 1926 (cat. no. 69).

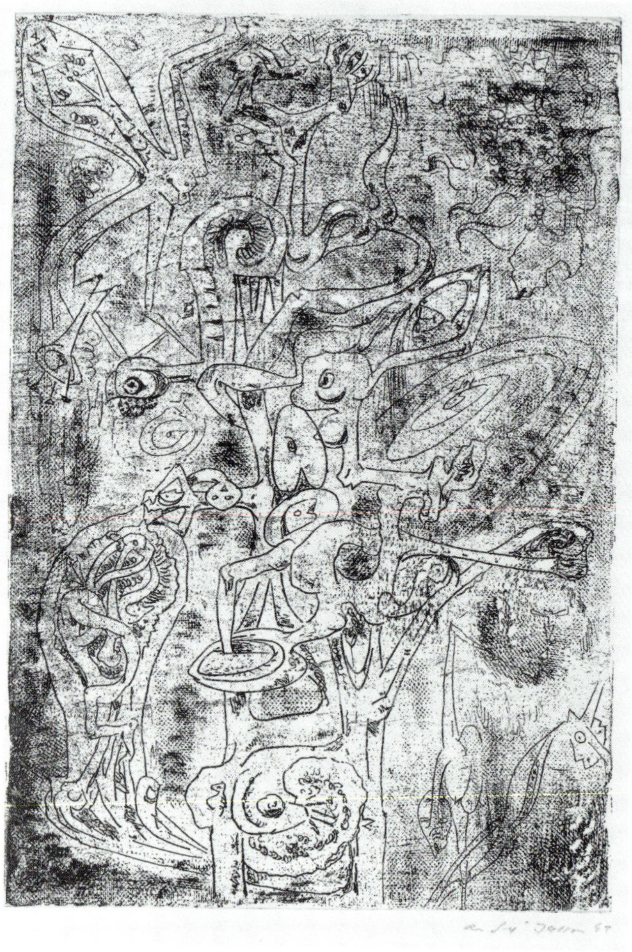

● *Fig. 86 (right)*
André Masson, *Les Fruits de l'abîme* (Fruits of the abyss), 1942 (cat. no. 73).

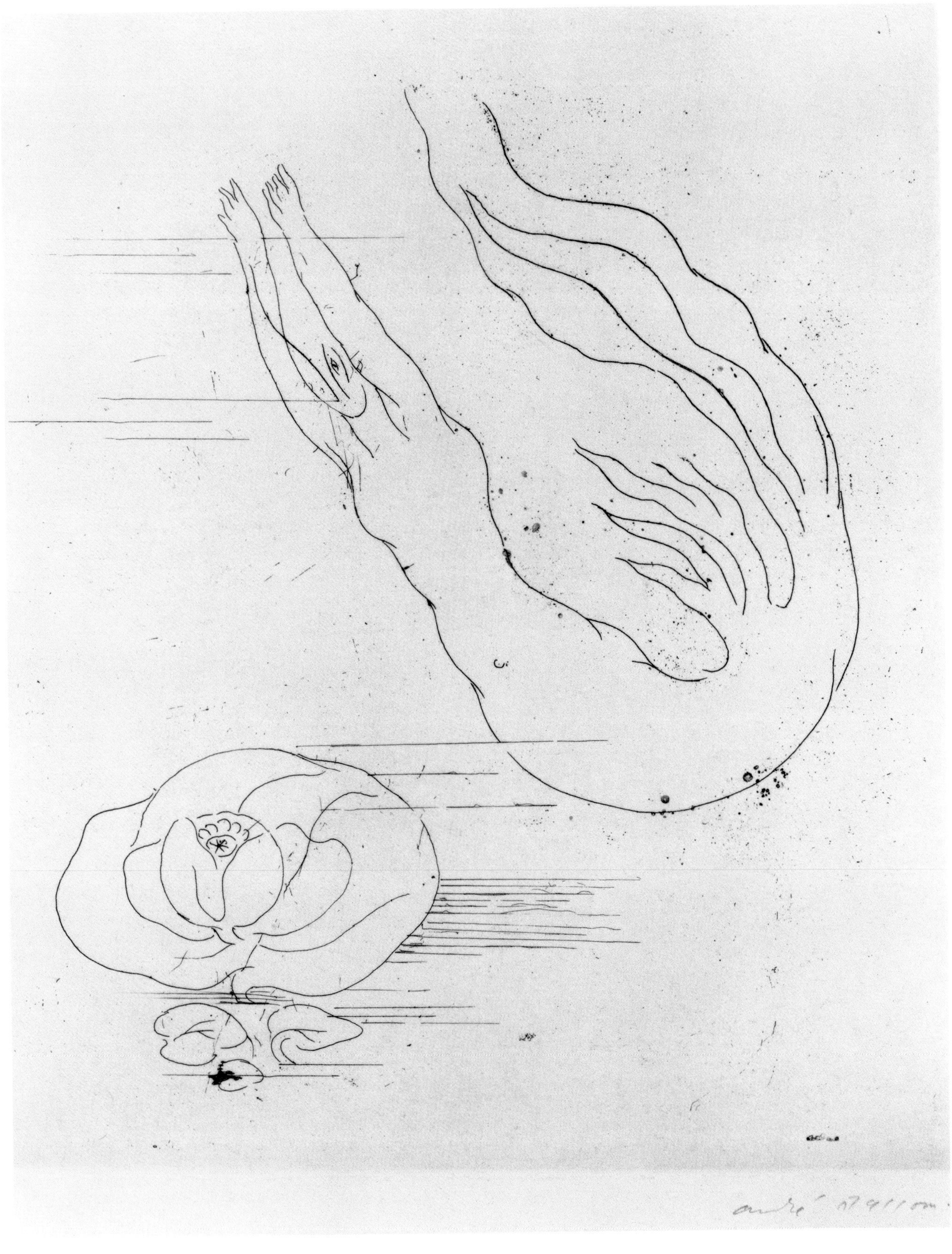

● *Fig. 87*
André Masson, *Ondine*, 1933
(cat. no. 70).

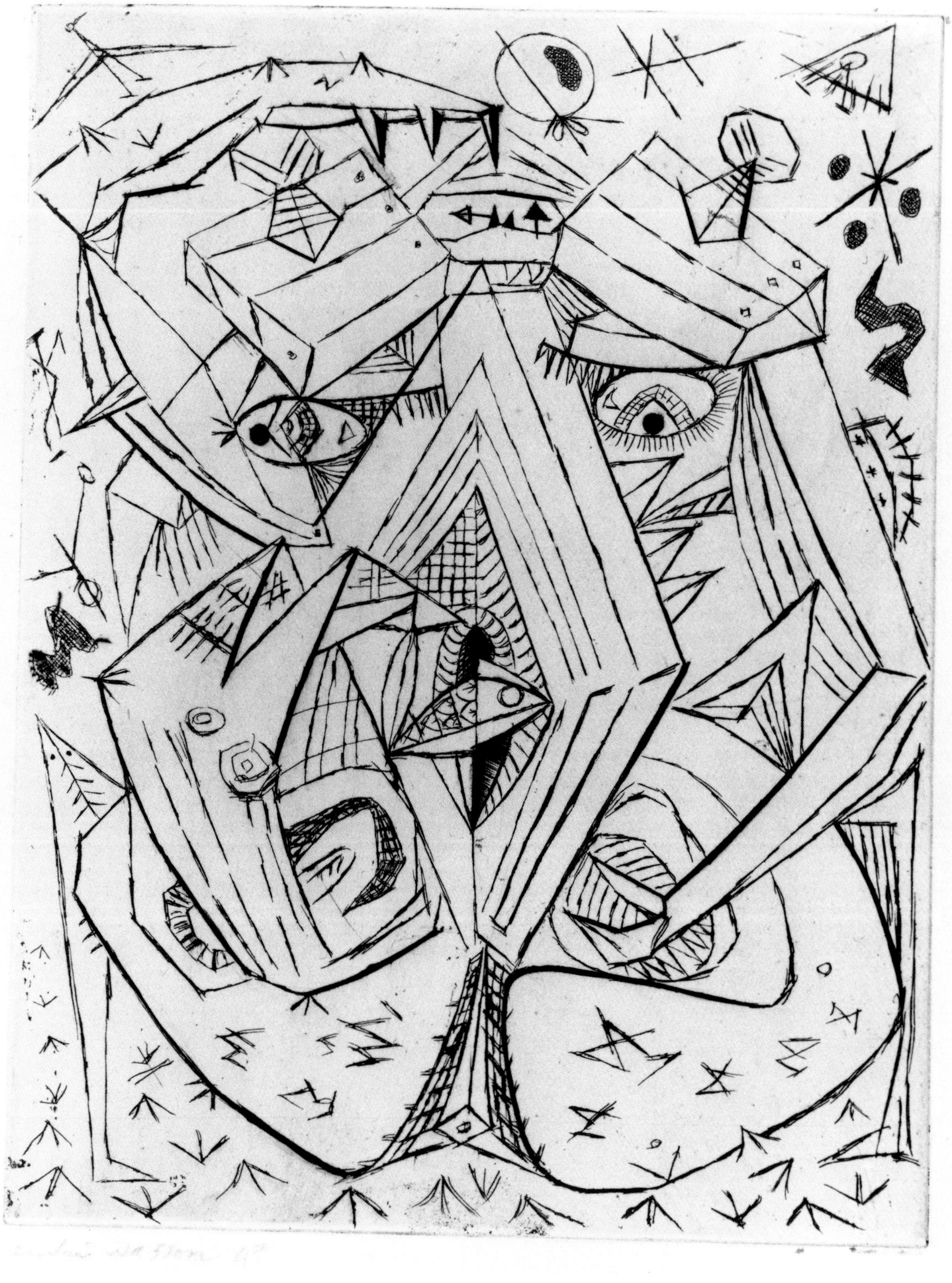

● *Fig. 88*
André Masson, *Le Crabe de terre*
(Sand crab), 1942 (cat. no. 71).

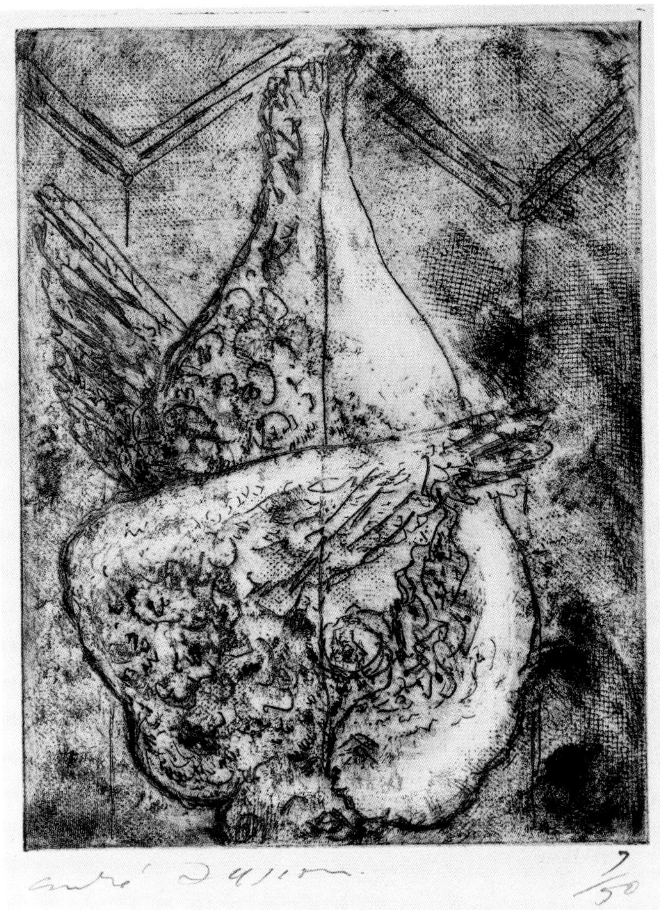

● *Fig. 89*
André Masson, *Nocturne*, 1944 (cat. no. 74).

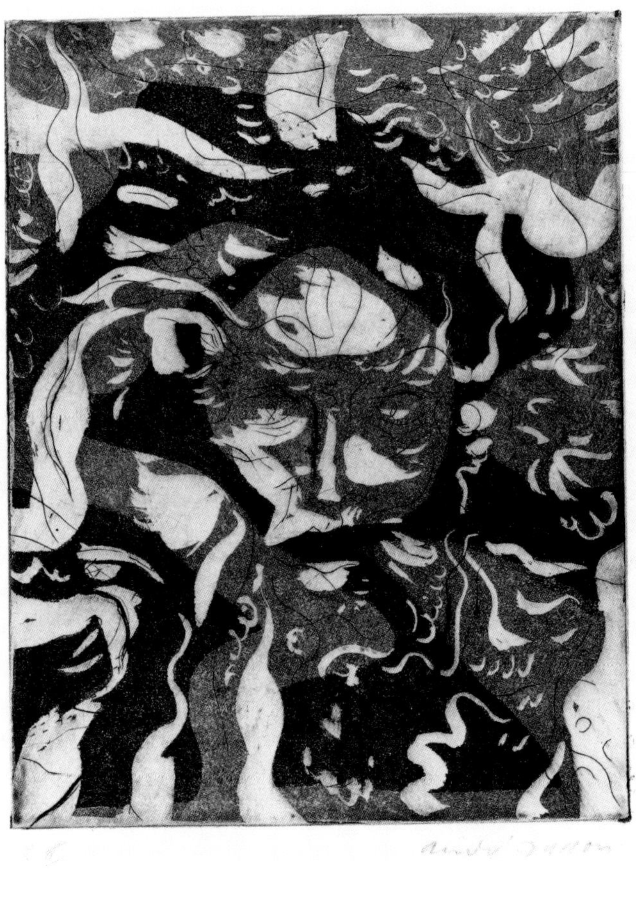

● *Fig. 90*
André Masson, *Improvisation*, 1945 (cat. no. 75).

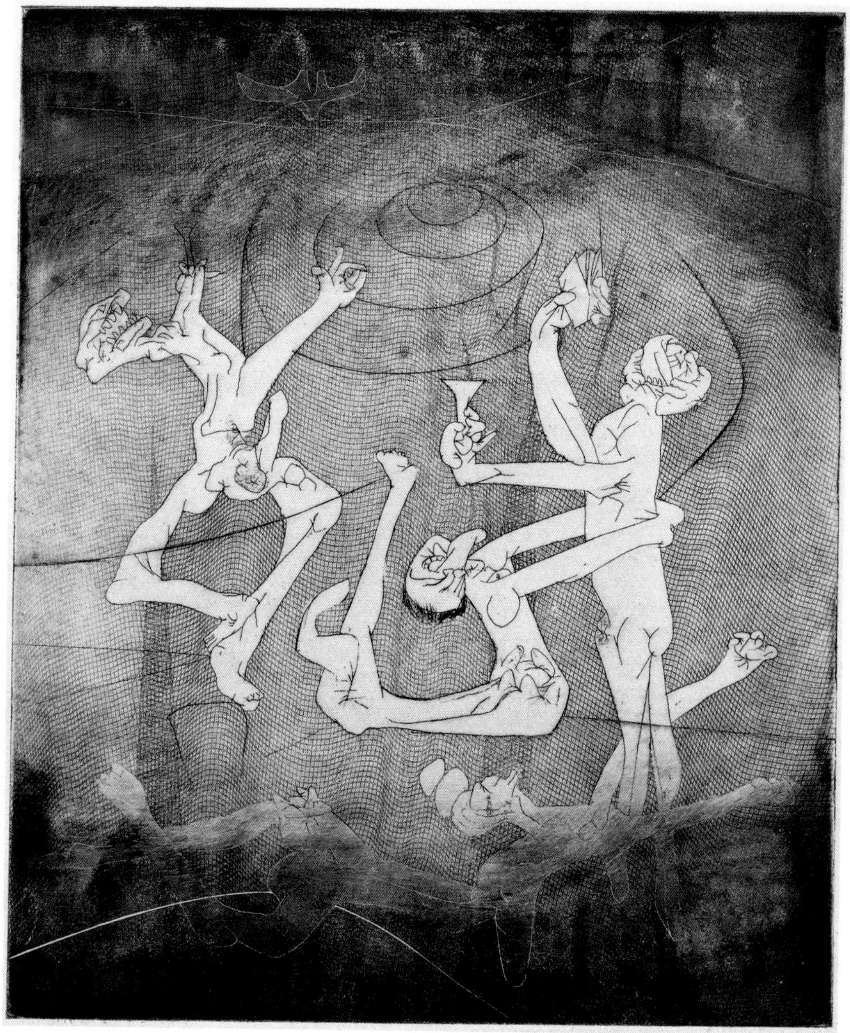

● *Fig. 91*
Roberto Sebastián Matta Echaurren, Untitled (from *The New School*), 1943 (cat. no. 76).

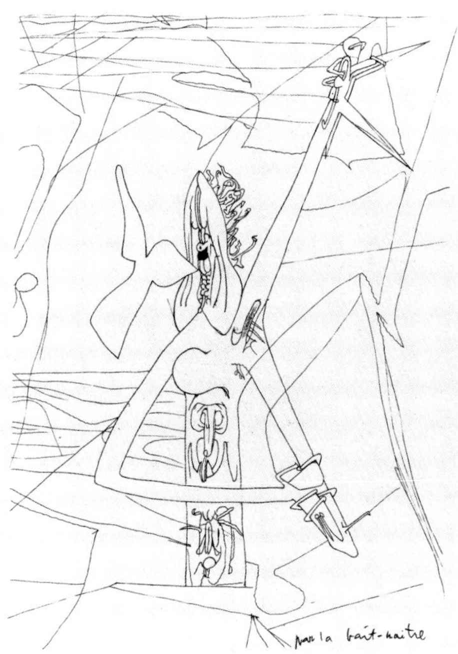

● *Fig. 92*
Roberto Sebastián Matta Echaurren, *Par la bait naître*, 1946 (cat. no. 77).

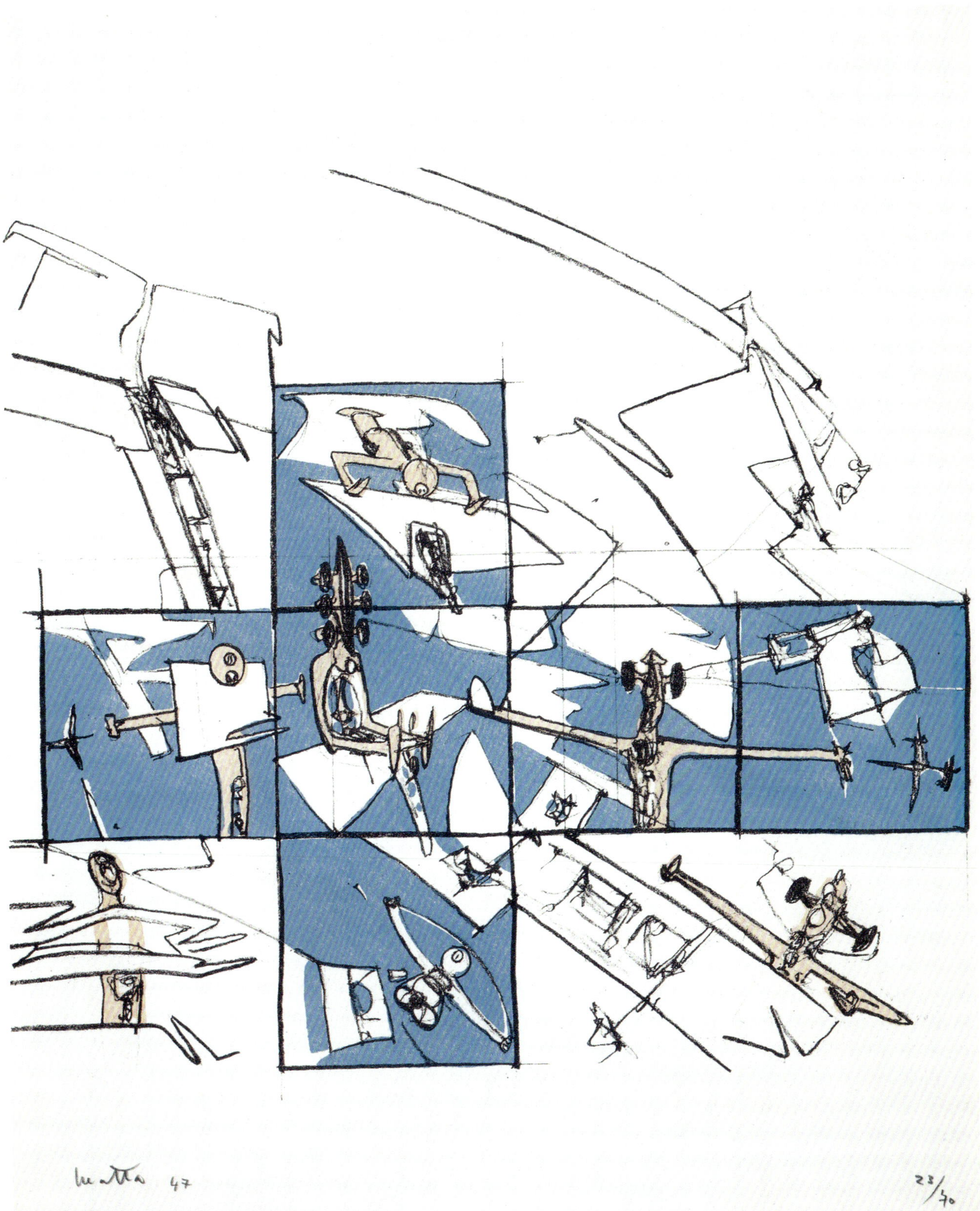

● *Fig. 93*
Roberto Sebastián Matta Echaurren, *I Want to See It to Believe It*, 1947 (cat. no. 78).

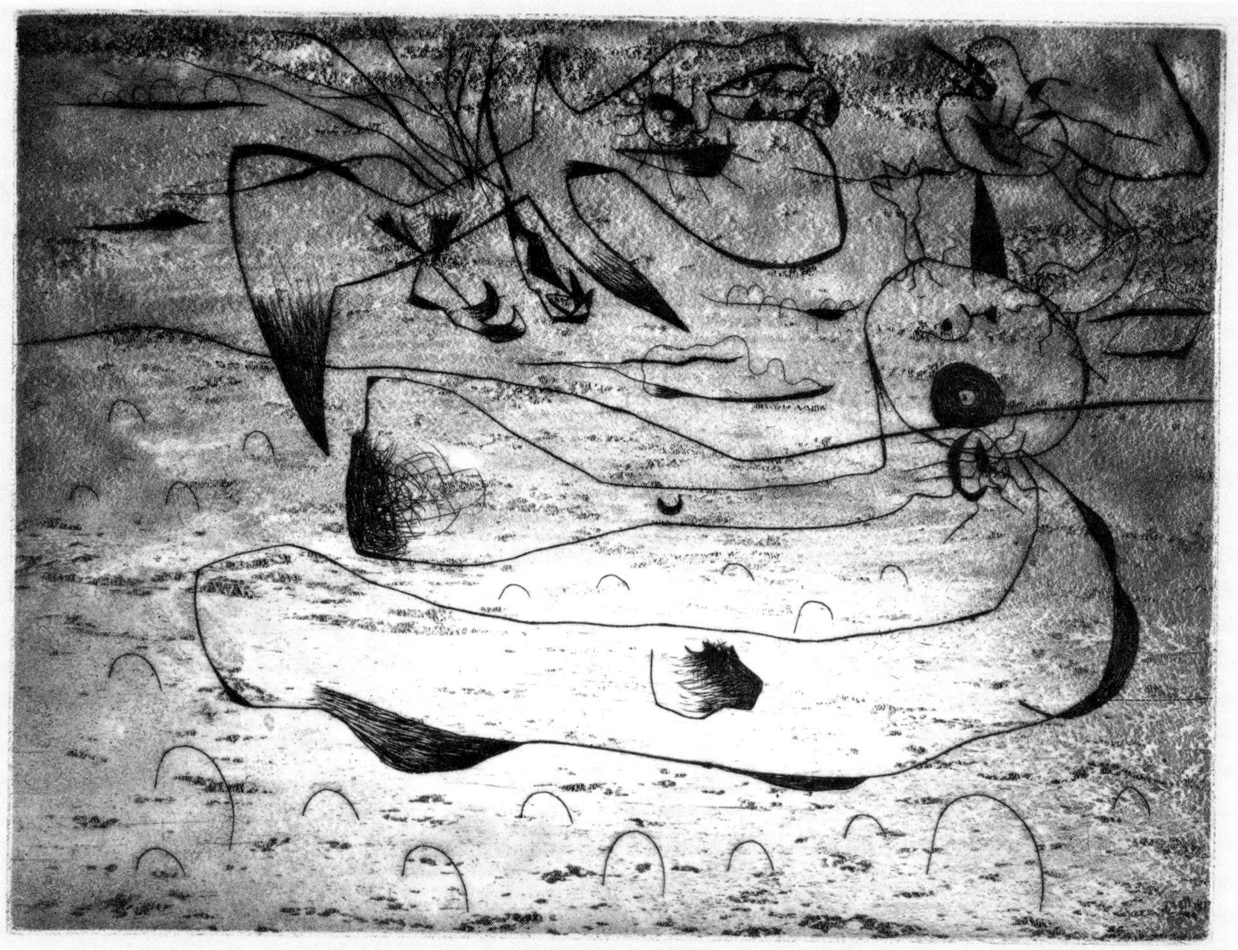

● *Fig. 94*
Joan Miró, *L'Aigle et la femme la nuit* (Eagle and woman at night), 1938 (cat. no. 84).

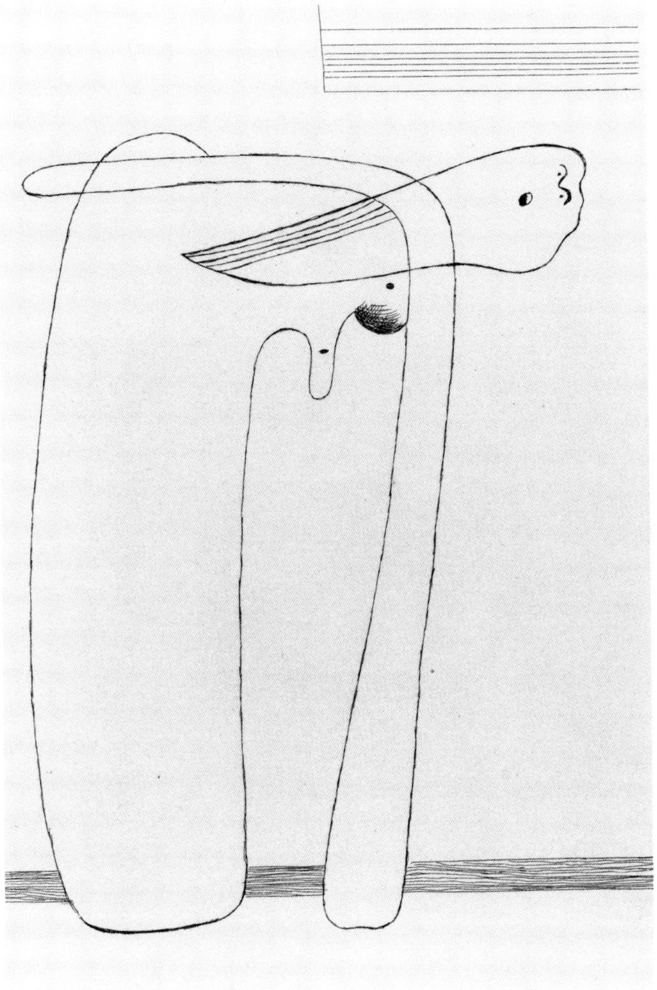

◉ *Fig. 95*
Joan Miró, Untitled (from *Enfances*), 1933 (cat. no. 80).

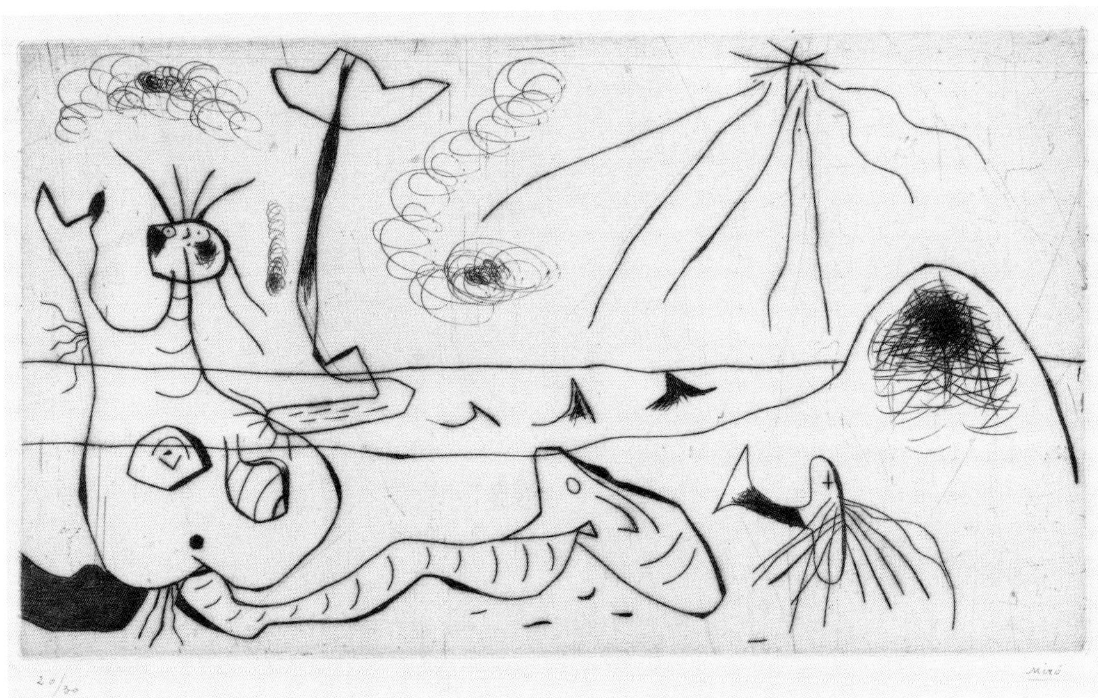

◉ *Fig. 96*
Joan Miró, *La Baigneuse* (The bather), 1938 (cat. no. 85).

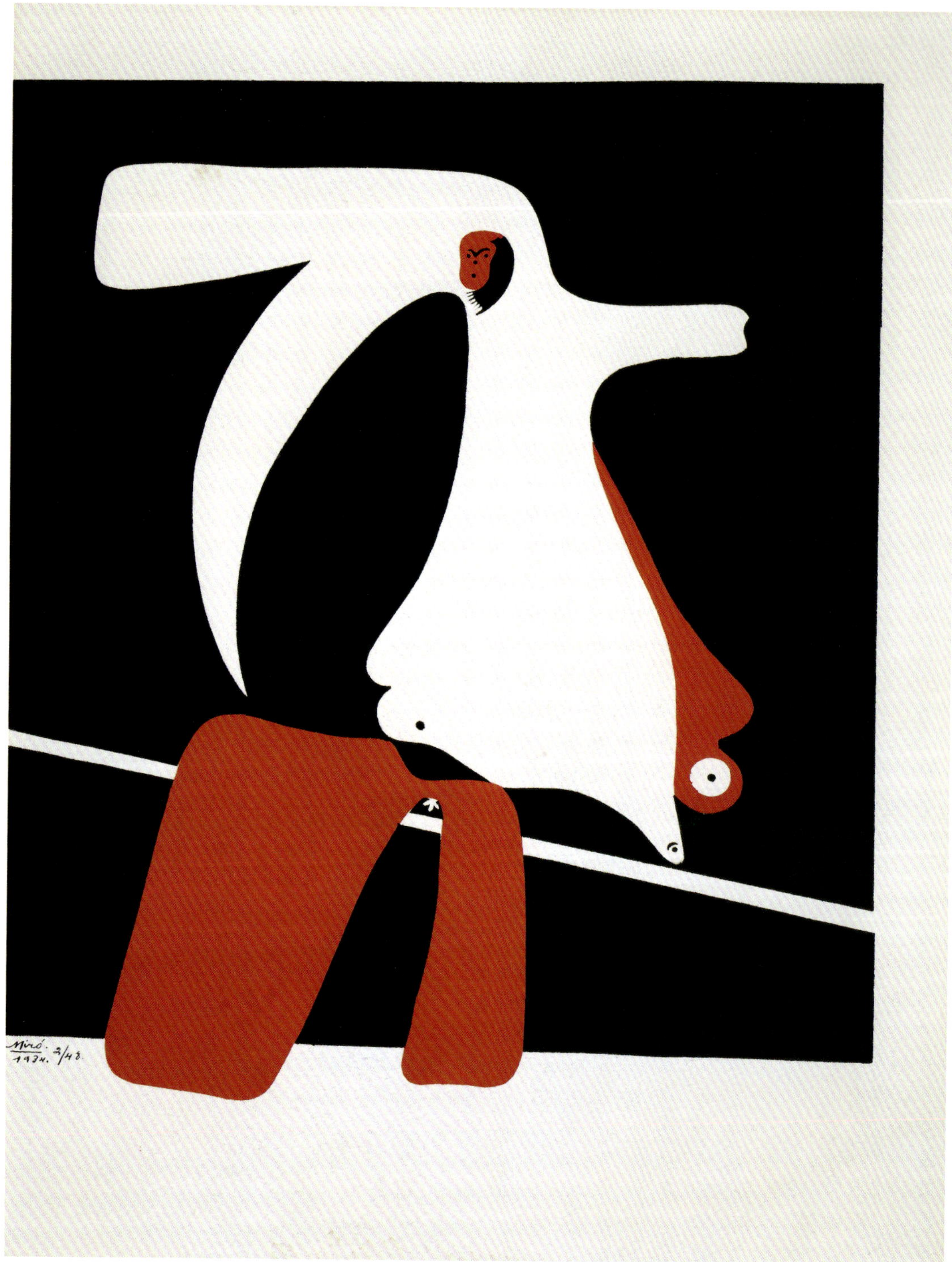

● *Fig. 97*
Joan Miró, Untitled (from *Cahiers d'art*), 1934 (cat. no. 81).

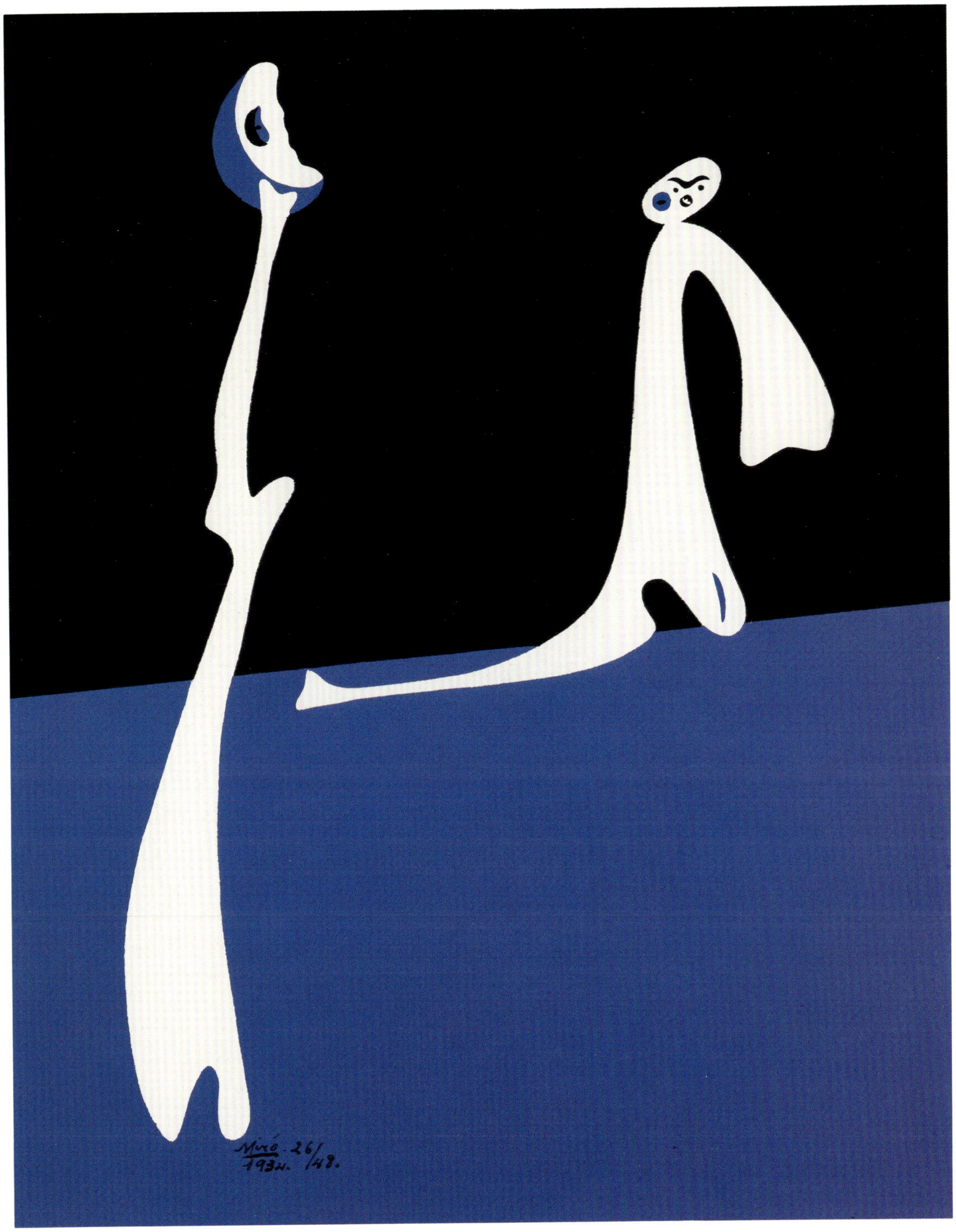

● *Fig. 98*
Joan Miró, Untitled (from *Cahiers d'art*), 1934 (cat. no. 82).

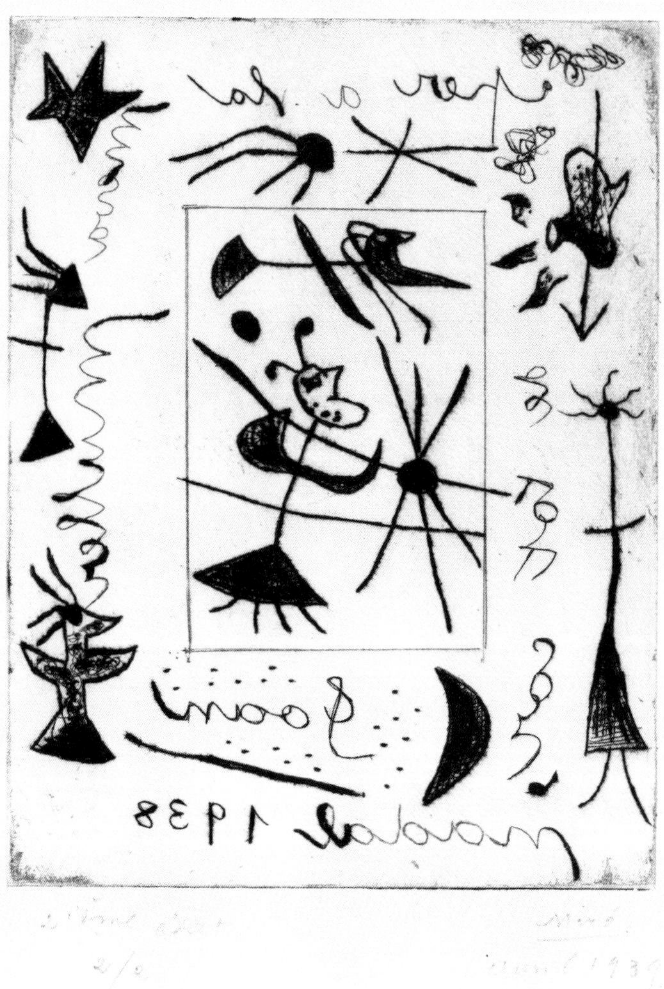

◉ *Fig. 99*
Joan Miró, *Bijou et cadre* (Jewel and frame), 1938 (cat. no. 86).

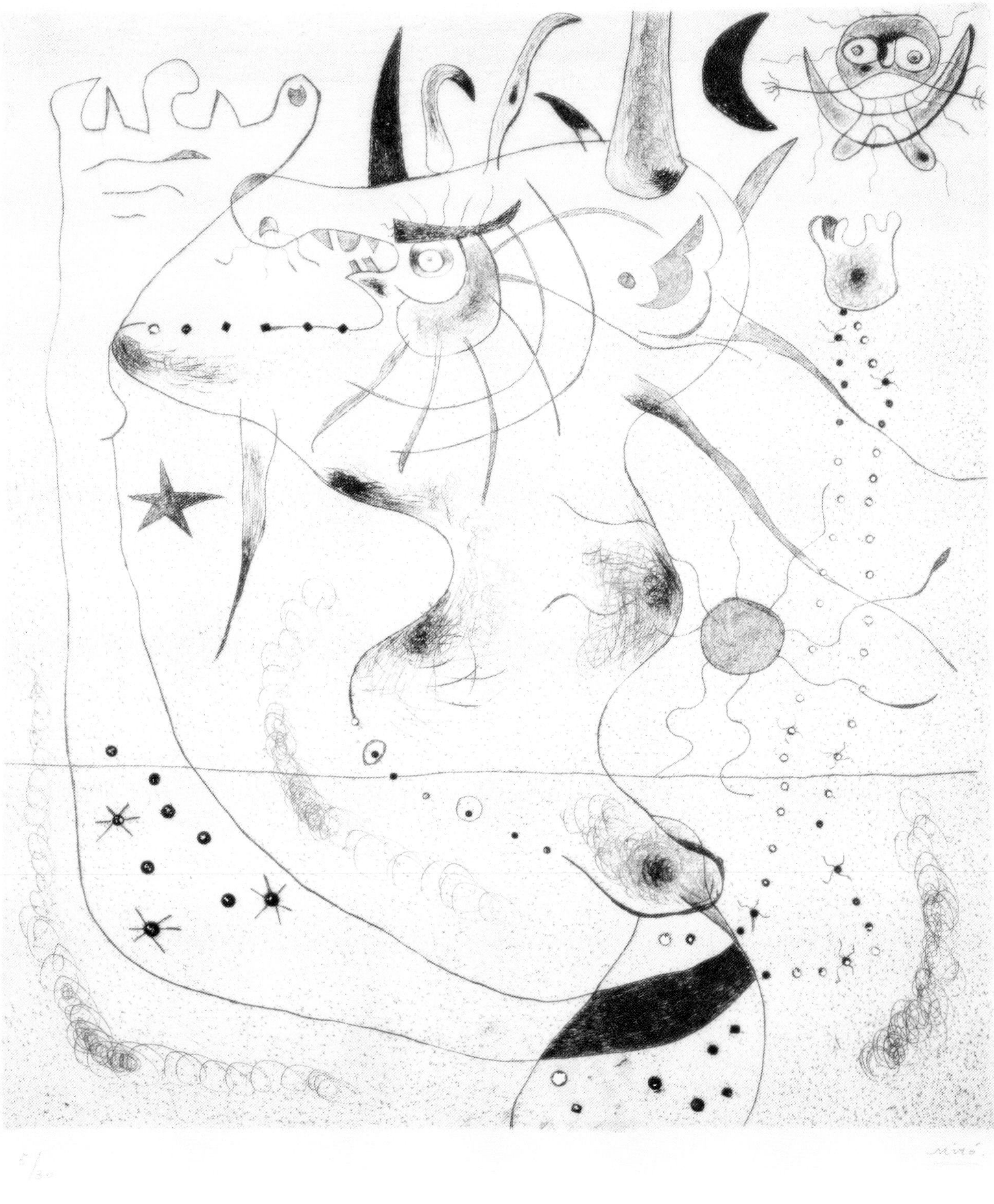

Fig. 100
Joan Miró, *L'Eveil du géant* (Awakening of the giant), 1938 (cat. no. 88).

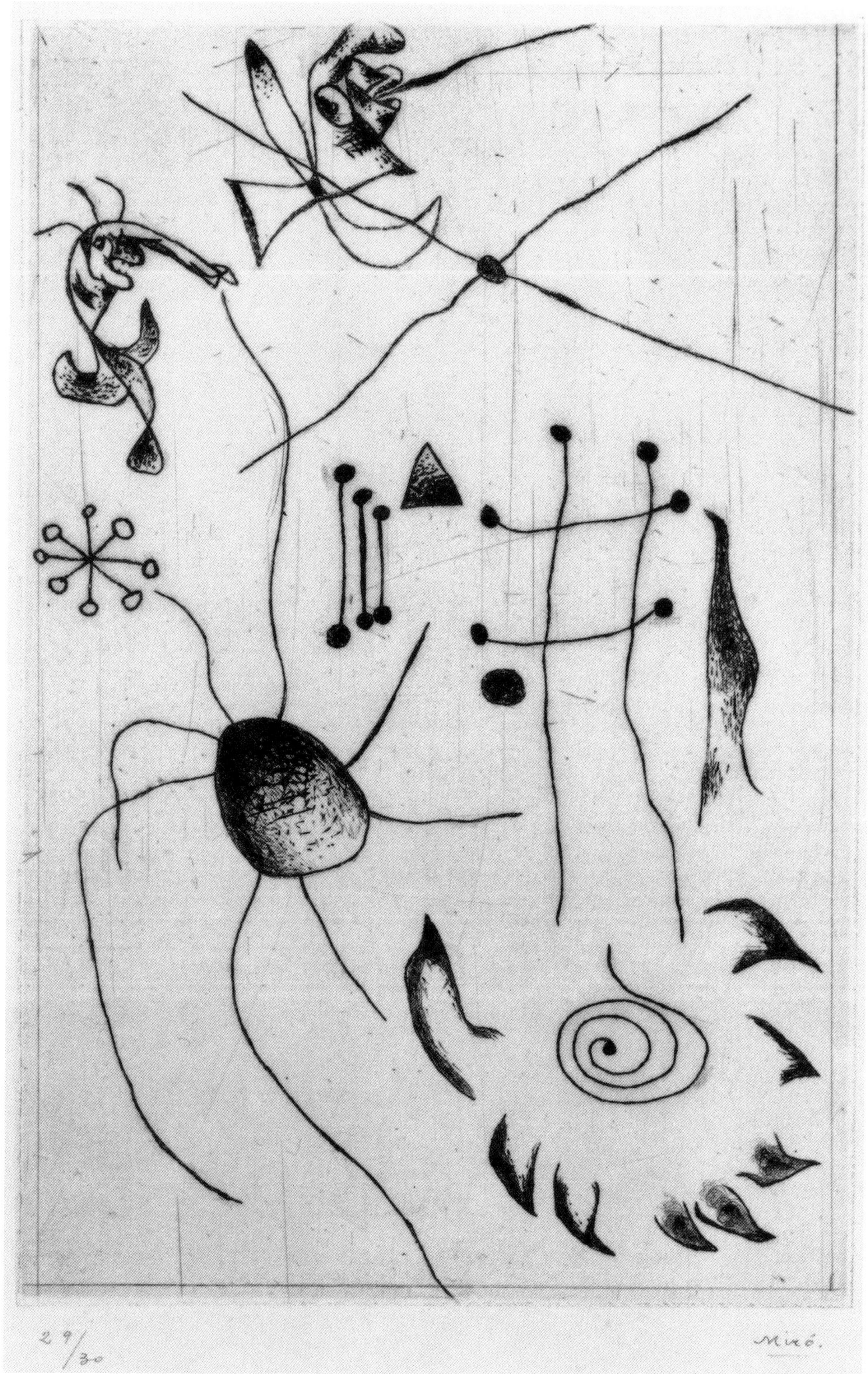

Fig. 101
Joan Miró, Untitled (from *Série noire et rouge*), 1938 (cat. no. 92).

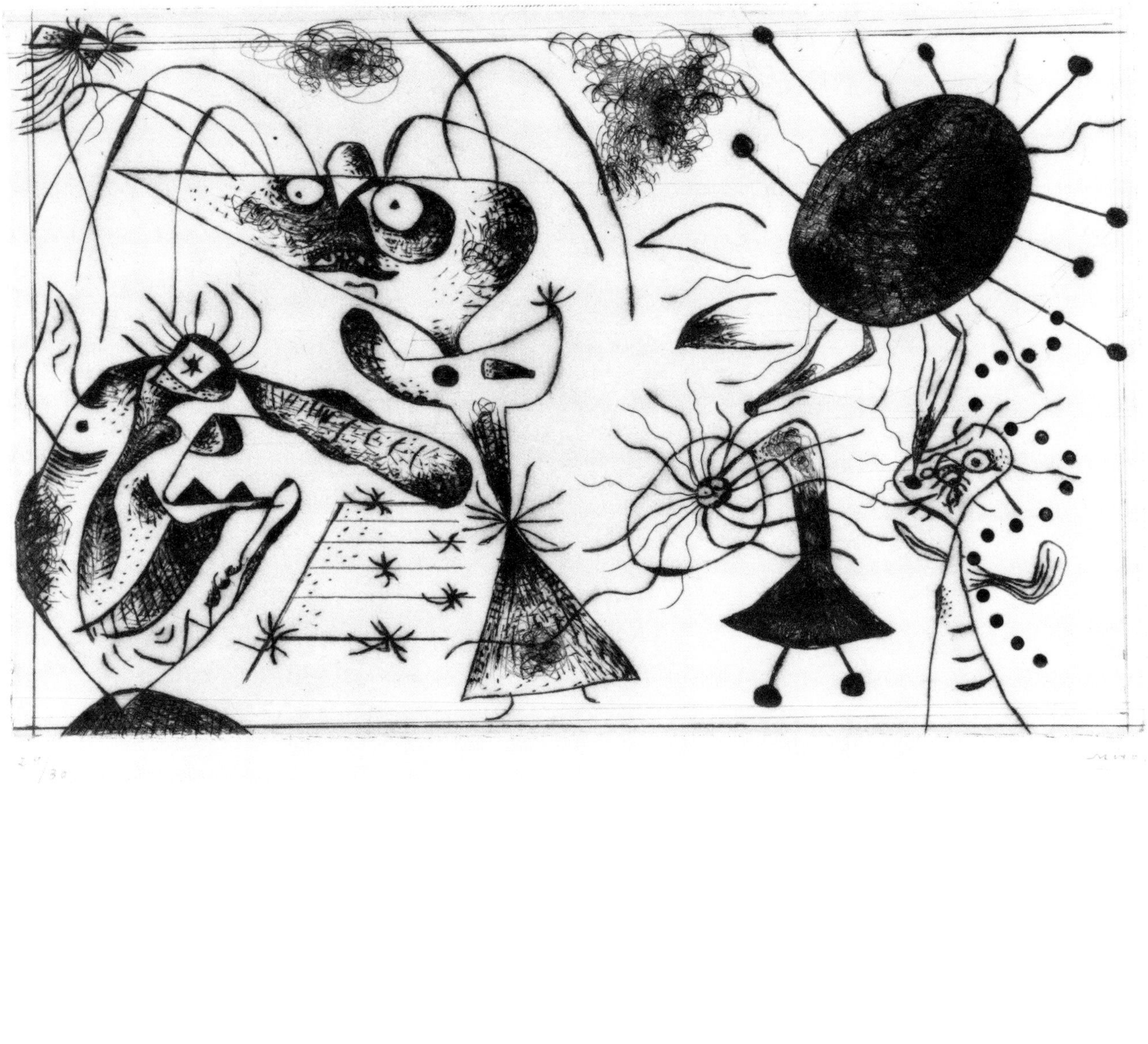

● *Fig. 102*
Joan Miró, Untitled (from *Série noire et rouge*), 1938 (cat. no. 93).

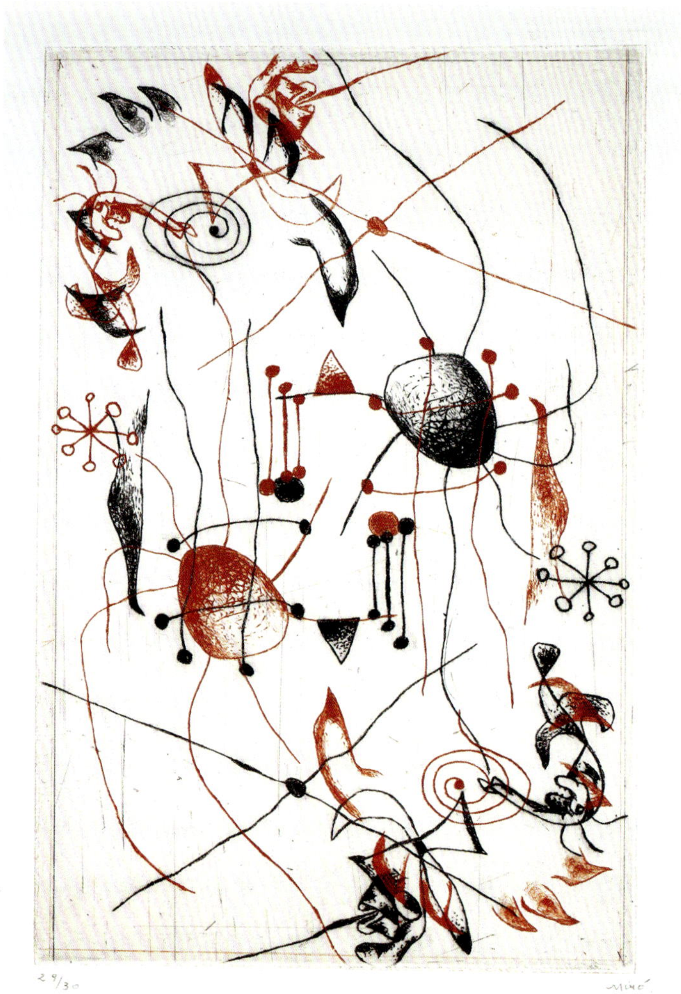

◉ *Fig. 103*
Joan Miró, Untitled (from *Série noire et rouge*), 1938 (cat. no. 94).

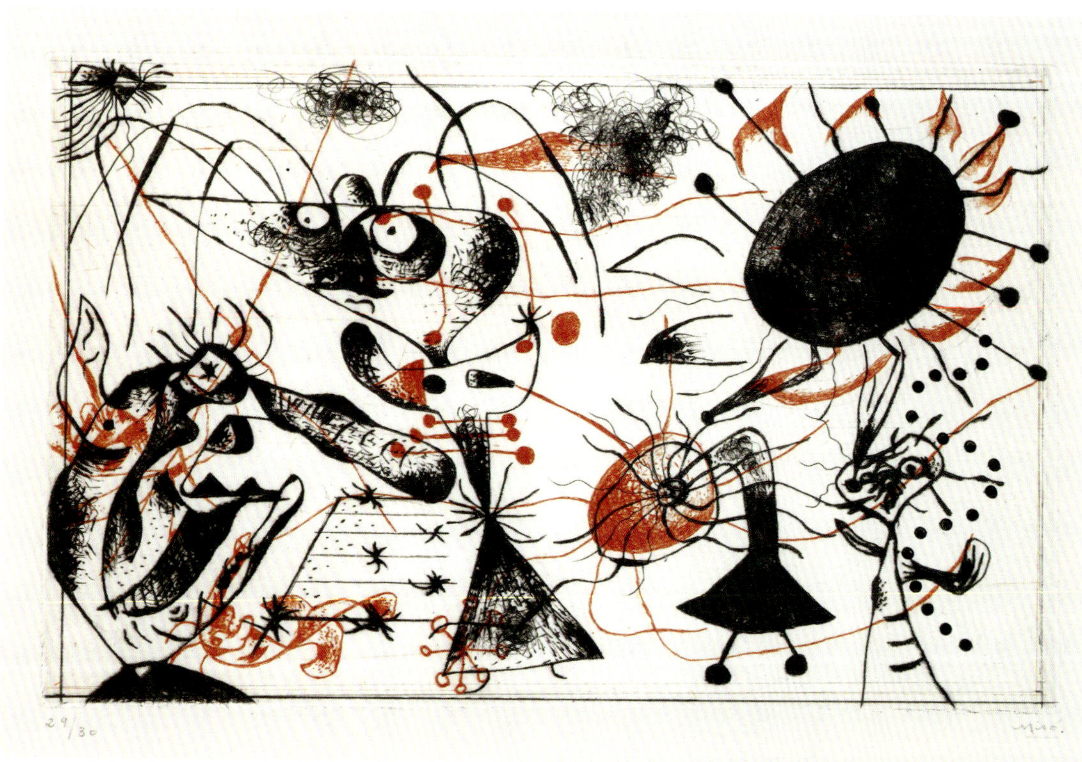

◉ *Fig. 104*
Joan Miró, Untitled (from *Série noire et rouge*), 1938 (cat. no. 95).

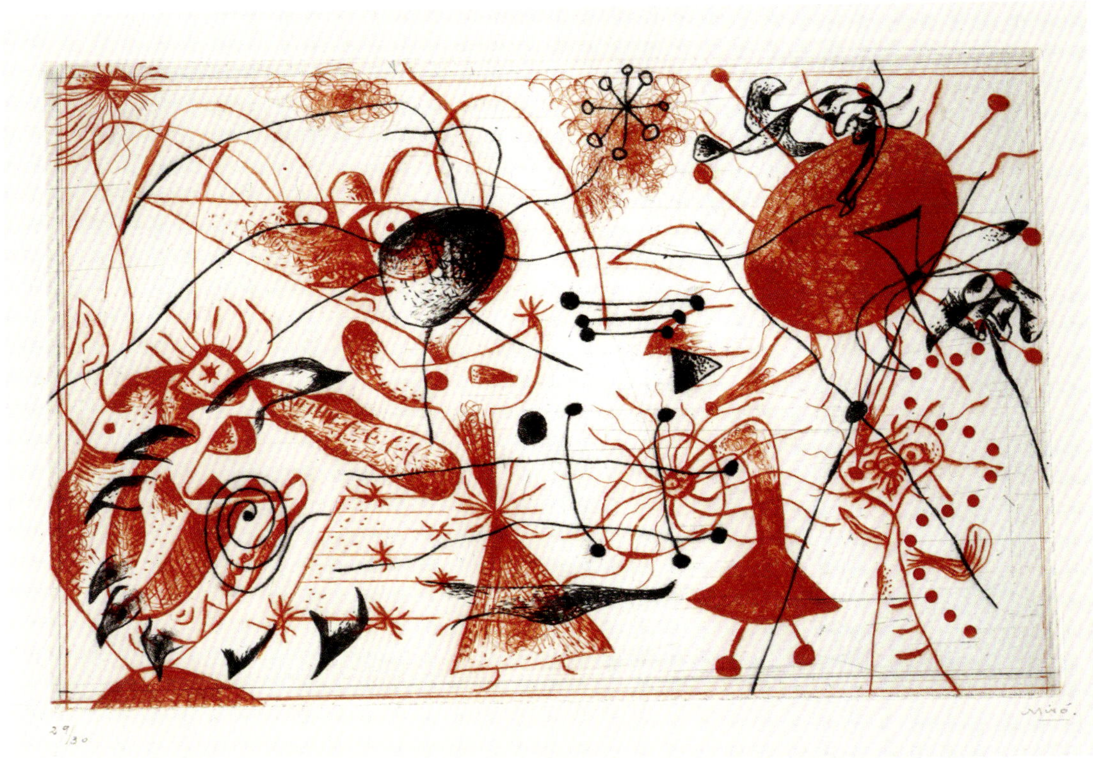

● *Fig. 105*
Joan Miró,
Untitled (from *Série noire et rouge*), 1938 (cat. no. 96).

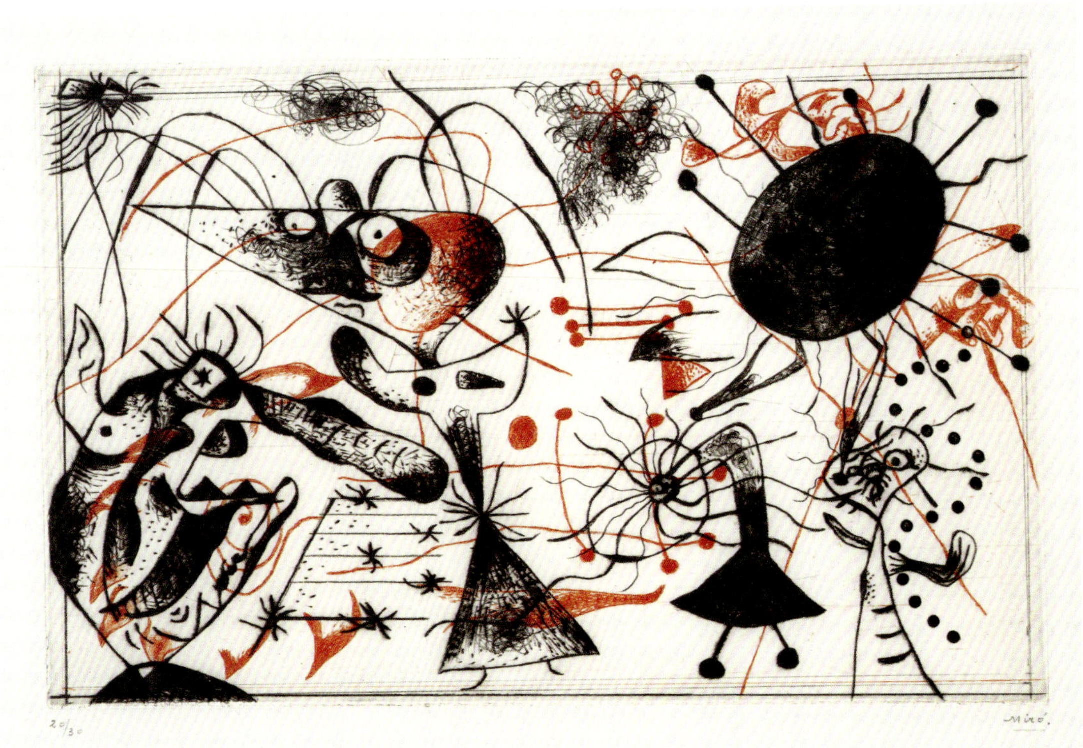

● *Fig. 106*
Joan Miró,
Untitled (from *Série noire et rouge*), 1938 (cat. no. 97).

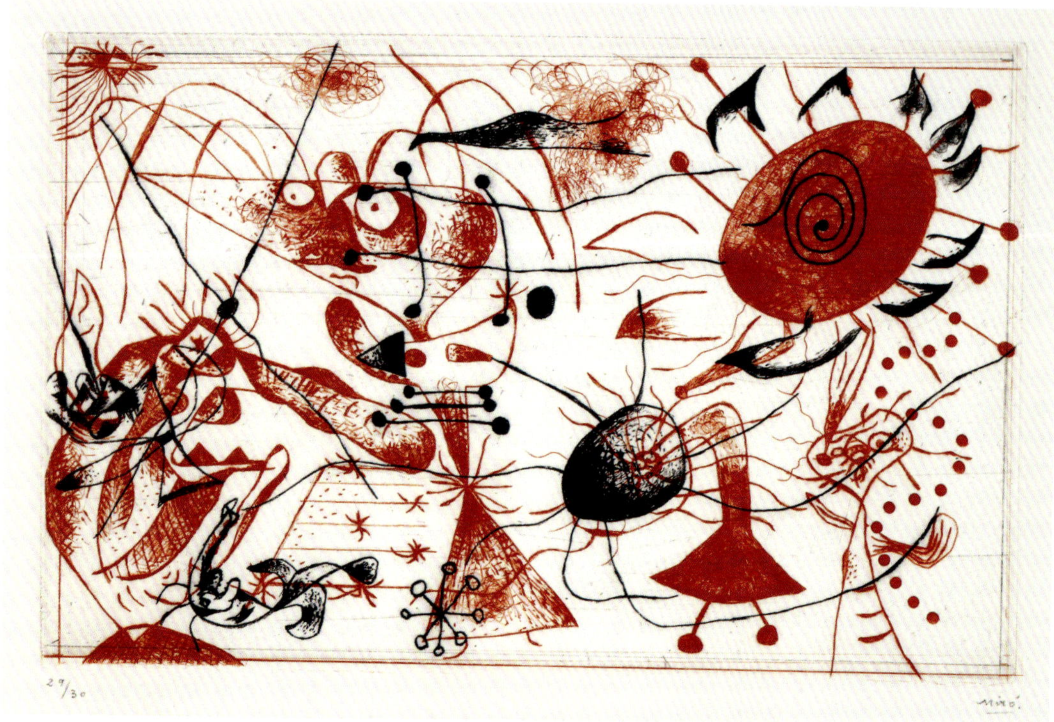

◉ *Fig. 107*
Joan Miró,
Untitled (from *Série noire et rouge*), 1938
(cat. no. 98).

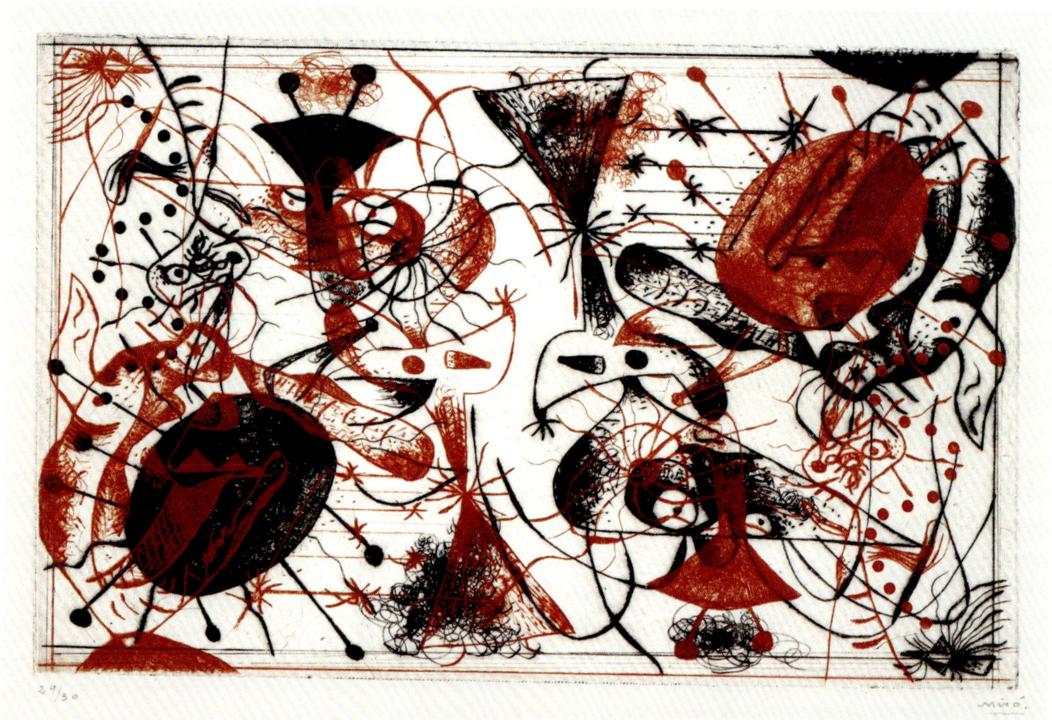

◉ *Fig. 108*
Joan Miró,
Untitled (from *Série noire et rouge*), 1938
(cat. no. 99).

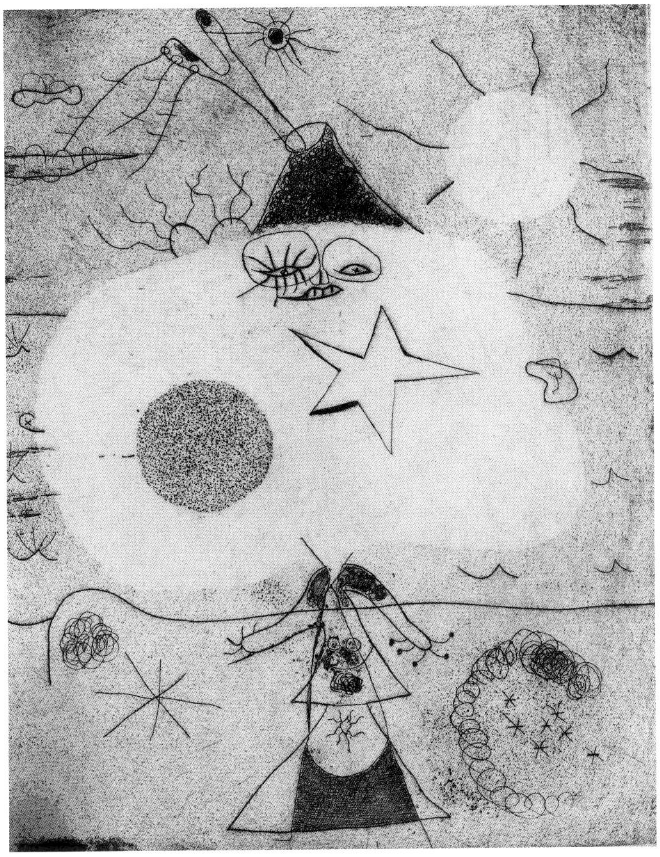

◉ *Fig. 109 (top)*
Joan Miró, *Femme et volcan* (Woman and volcano), 1938 (cat. no. 90).

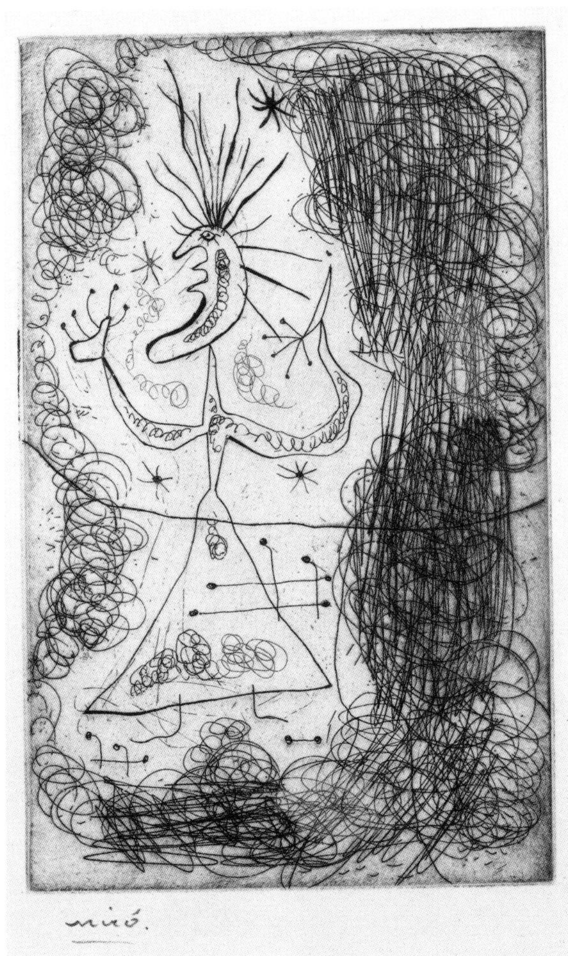

◉ *Fig. 110 (below)*
Joan Miró, Untitled (from *Fraternity*), 1939 (cat. no. 100).

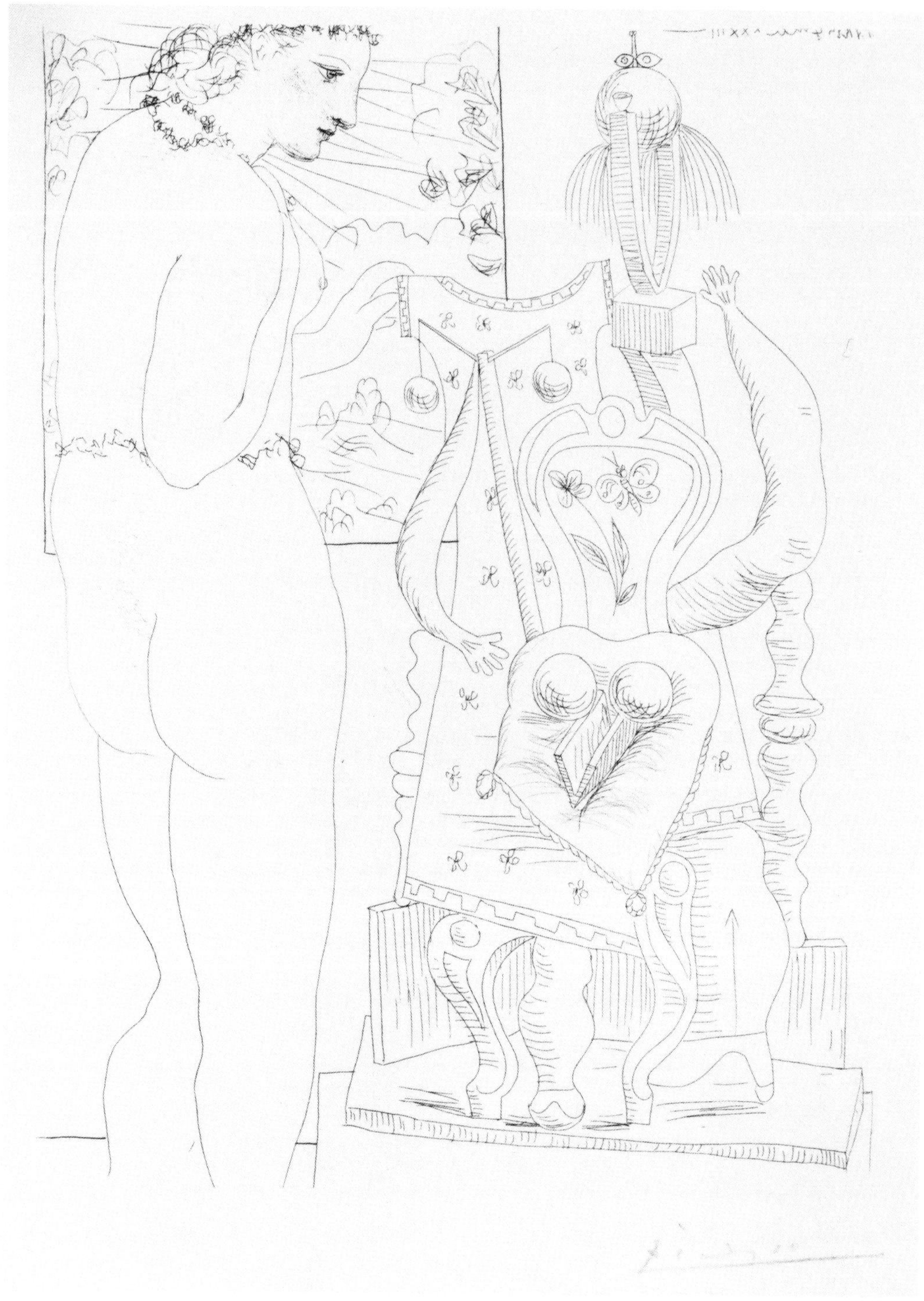

● *Fig. 111*
Pablo Picasso, *Modèle et sculpture surréaliste* (Model and surrealist sculpture), 1933 (cat. no. 101).

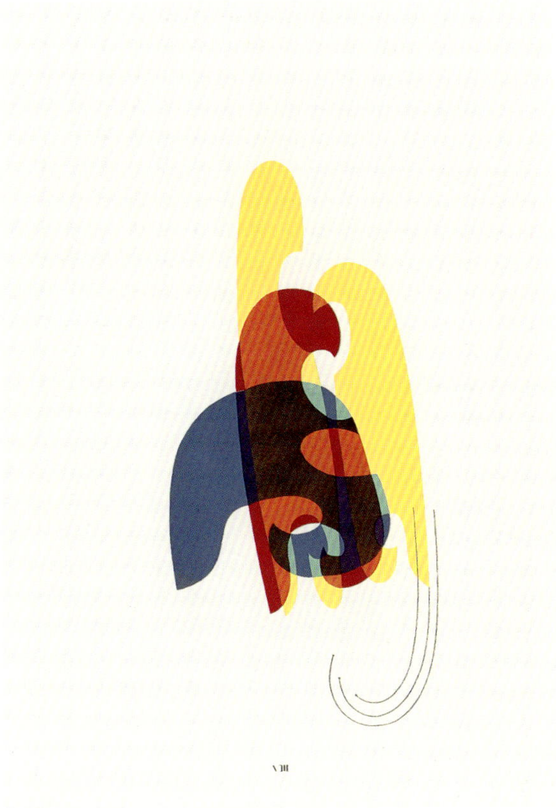

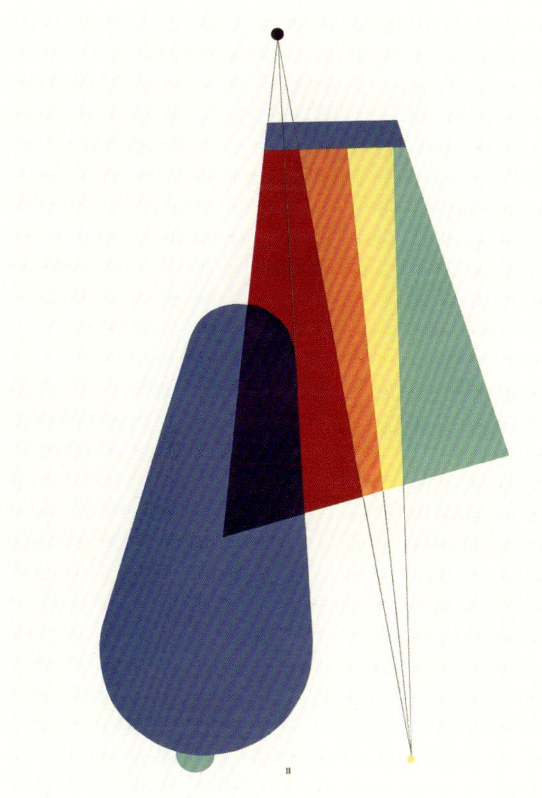

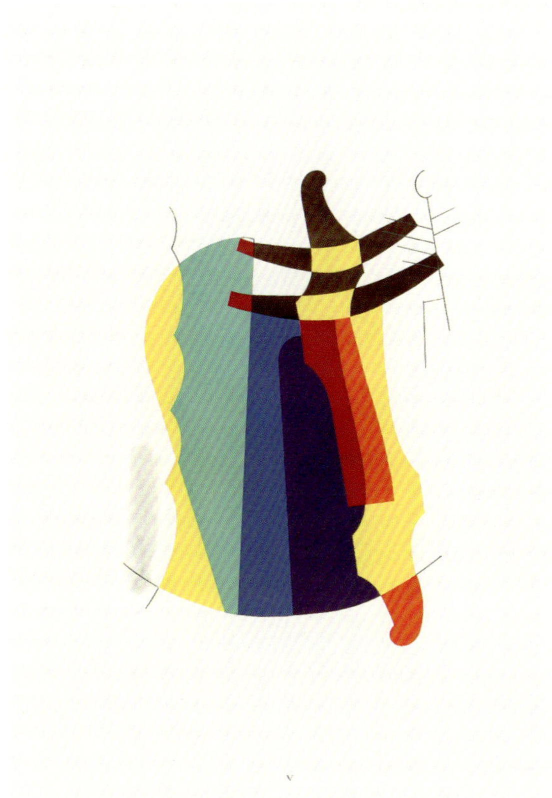

◉ *Fig. 112 (top, left)*
Man Ray, *Shadows*, from the series *Revolving Doors*, 1926 (cat. no. 103).

◉ *Fig. 113 (top, right)*
Man Ray, *Long Distance*, from the series *Revolving Doors*, 1926 (cat. no. 104).

◉ *Fig. 114 (left)*
Man Ray, *Legend*, from the series *Revolving Doors*, 1926 (cat. no. 105).

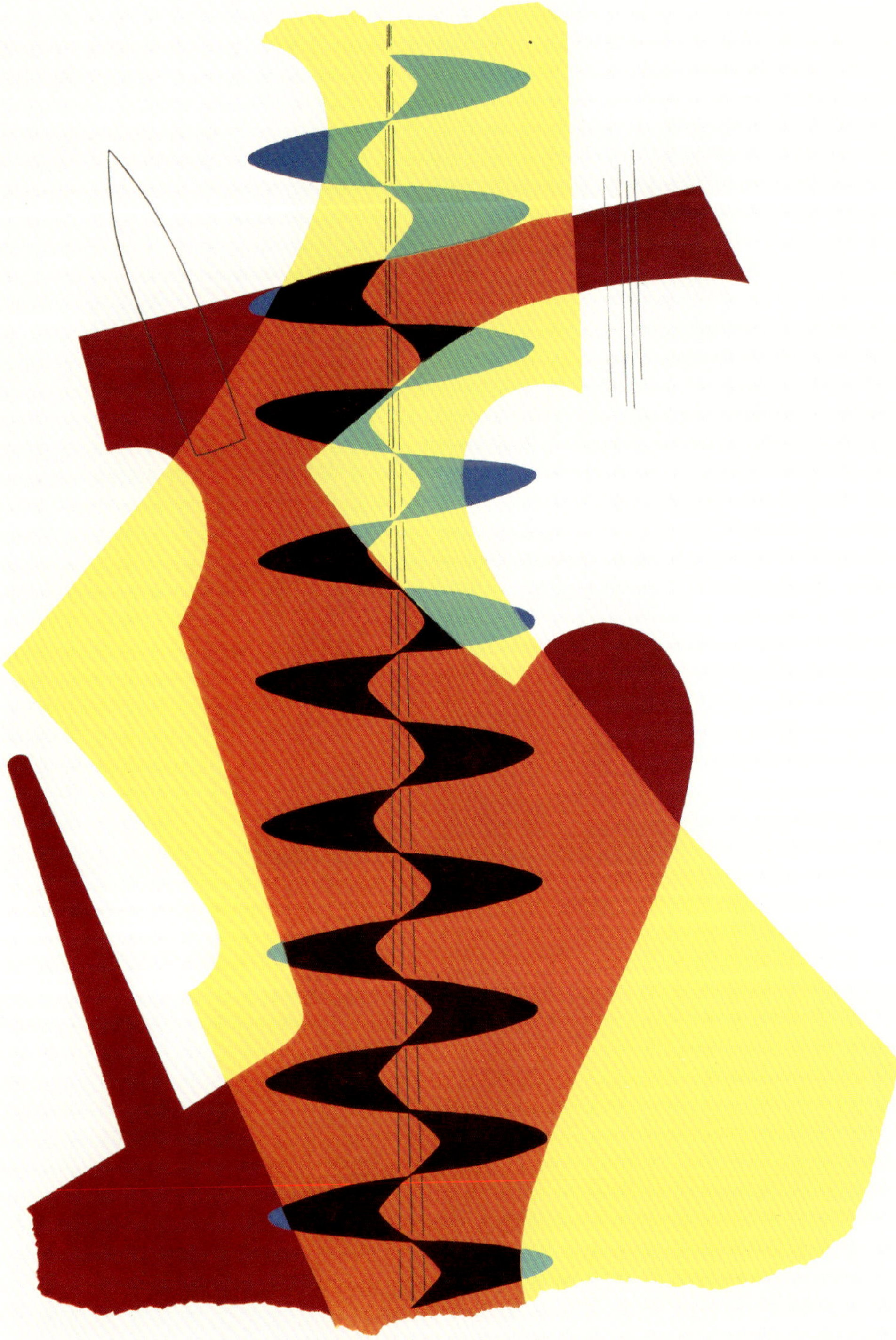

IV

● *Fig. 115*
Man Ray, *The Meeting*, from the series *Revolving Doors*, 1926 (cat. no. 107).

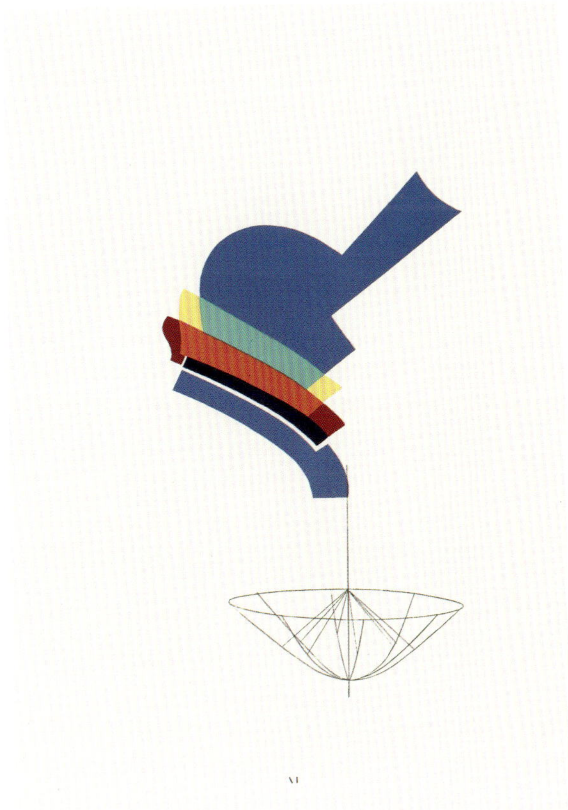

◉ *Fig. 116*
Man Ray, *Decanter*, from the series *Revolving Doors*, 1926 (cat. no. 106).

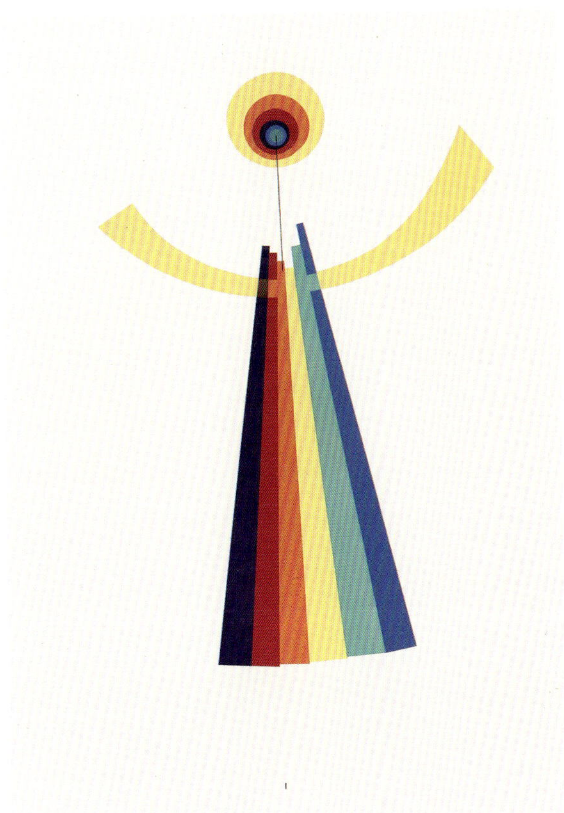

◉ *Fig. 117 (below left)*
Man Ray, *Mime*, from the series *Revolving Doors*, 1926 (cat. no. 108).

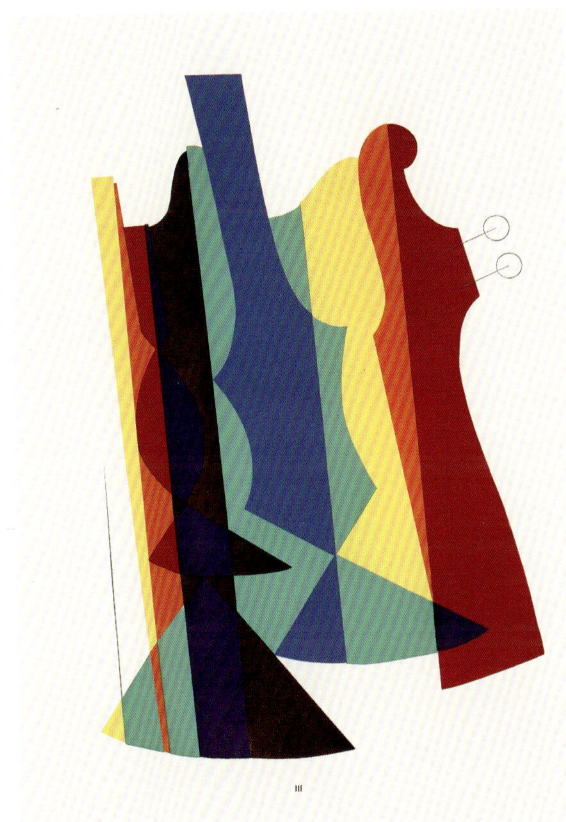

◉ *Fig. 118 (above)*
Man Ray, *Orchestra*, from the series *Revolving Doors*, 1926 (cat. no. 109).

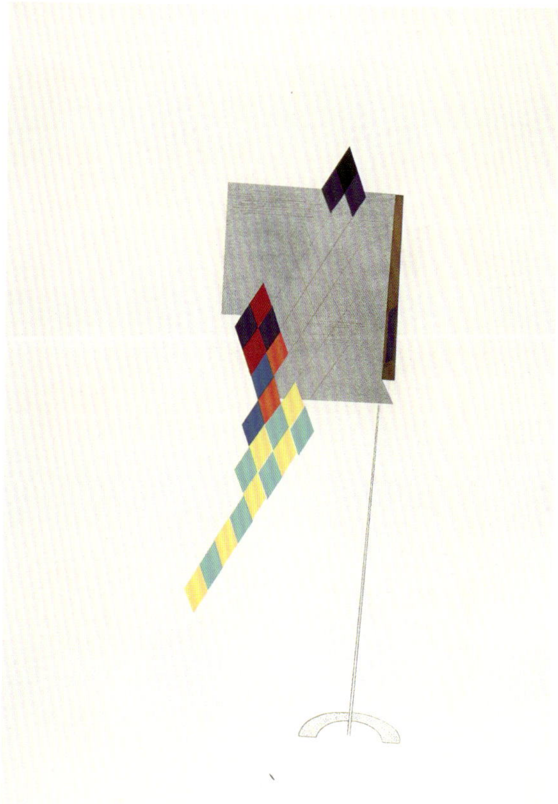

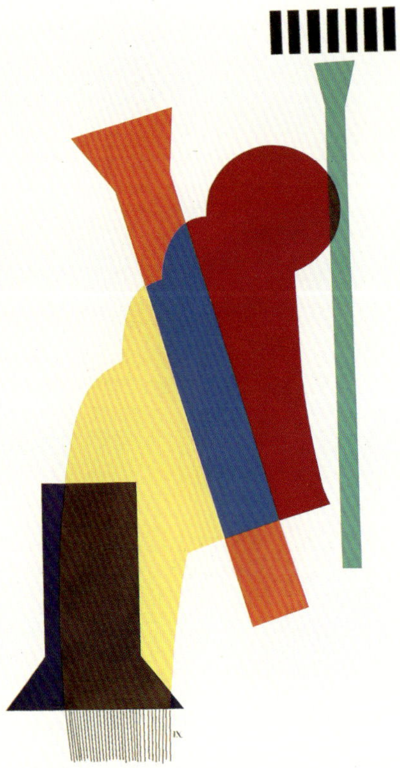

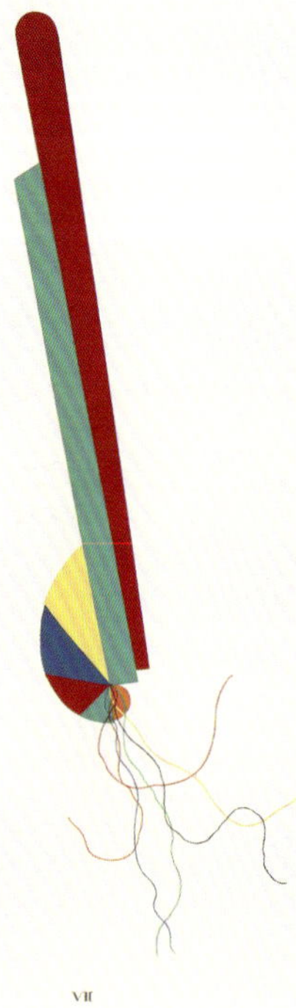

● *Fig. 119 (top, left)*
Man Ray, *Dragon Fly*, from the series *Revolving Doors*, 1926 (cat. no. 110).

● *Fig. 120 (top, right)*
Man Ray, *Concrete Mixer*, from the series *Revolving Doors*, 1926 (cat. no. 111).

● *Fig. 121 (right)*
Man Ray, *Jeune Fille* (Young girl), from the series *Revolving Doors*, 1926 (cat. no. 112).

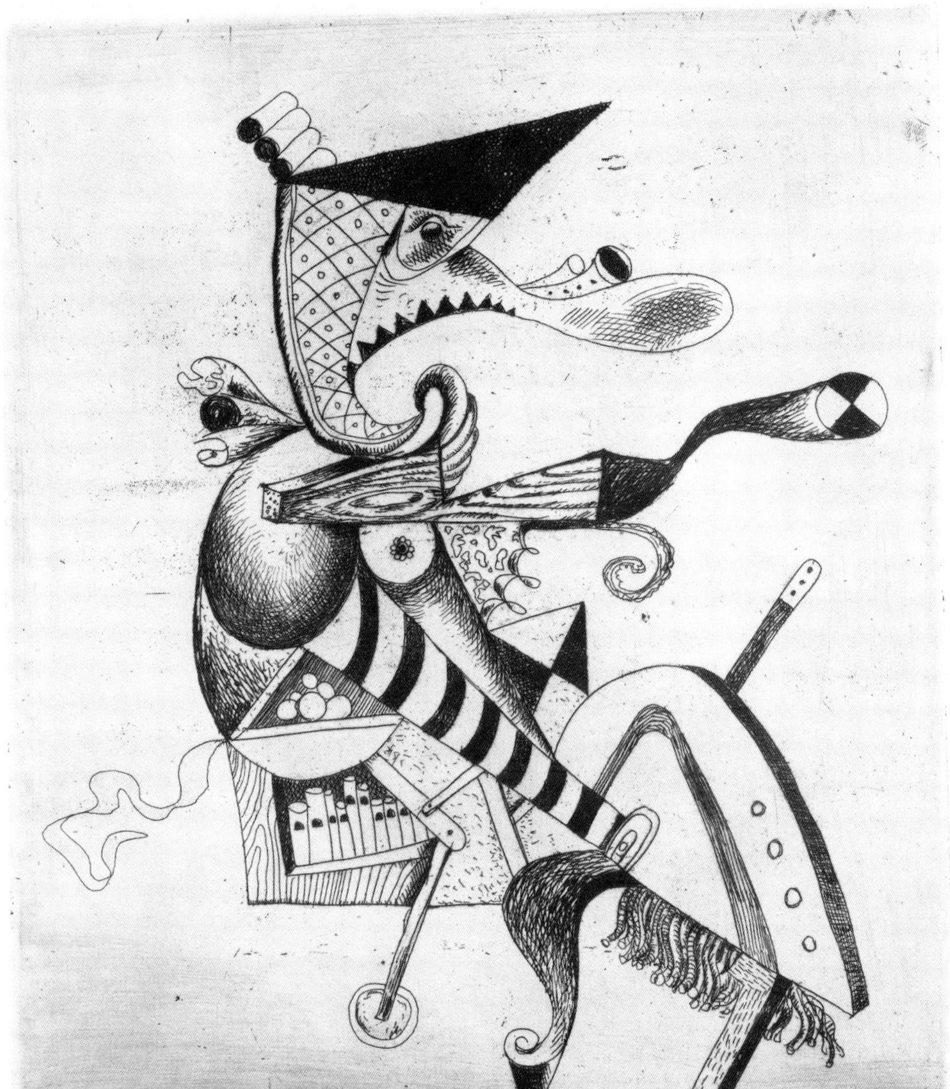

● *Fig. 122*
Kurt Seligmann, *Corsaire*, 1930 (cat. no. 114).

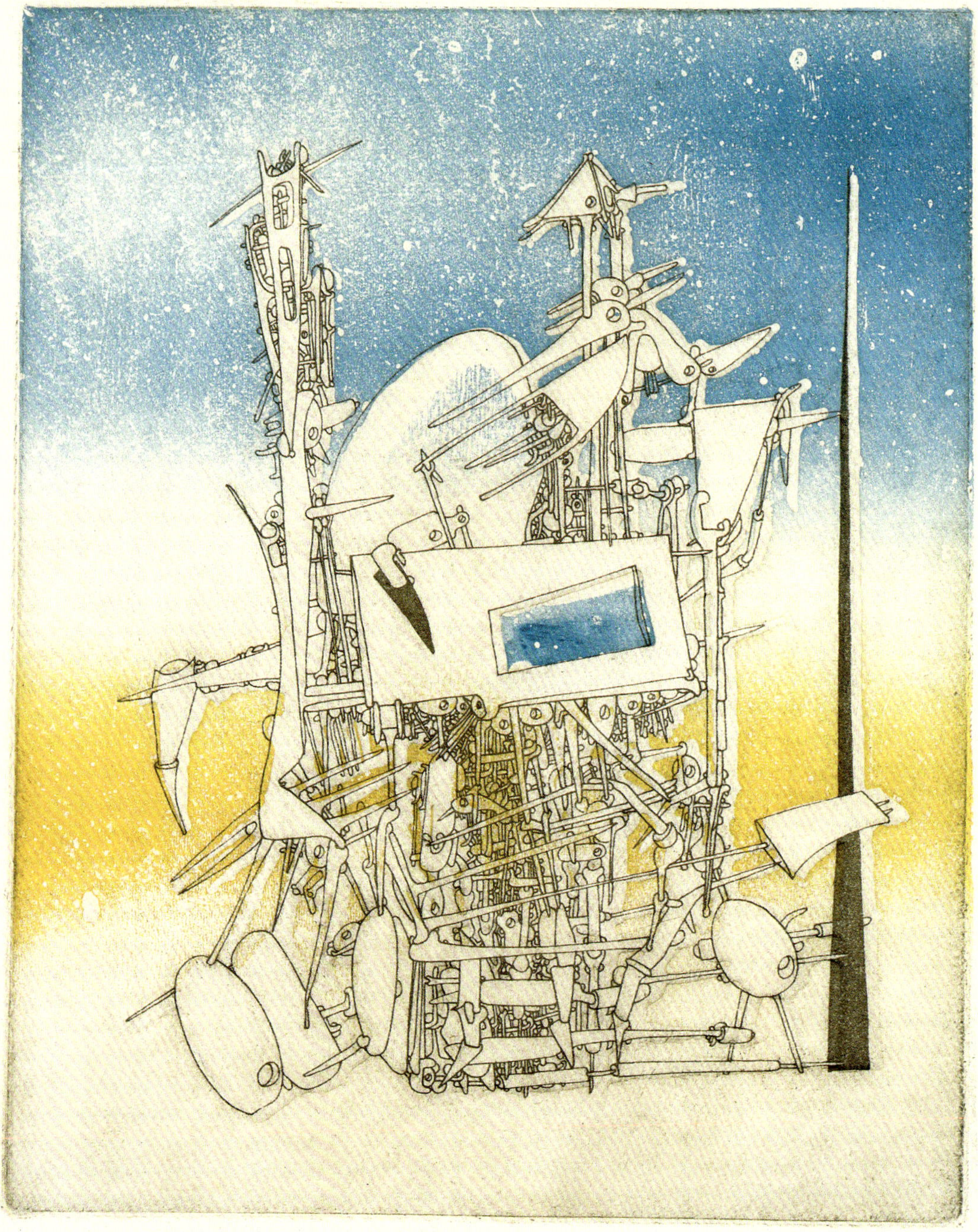

● *Fig. 123*
Yves Tanguy, Untitled (from *Le Grand Passage*), 1954 (cat. no. 122).

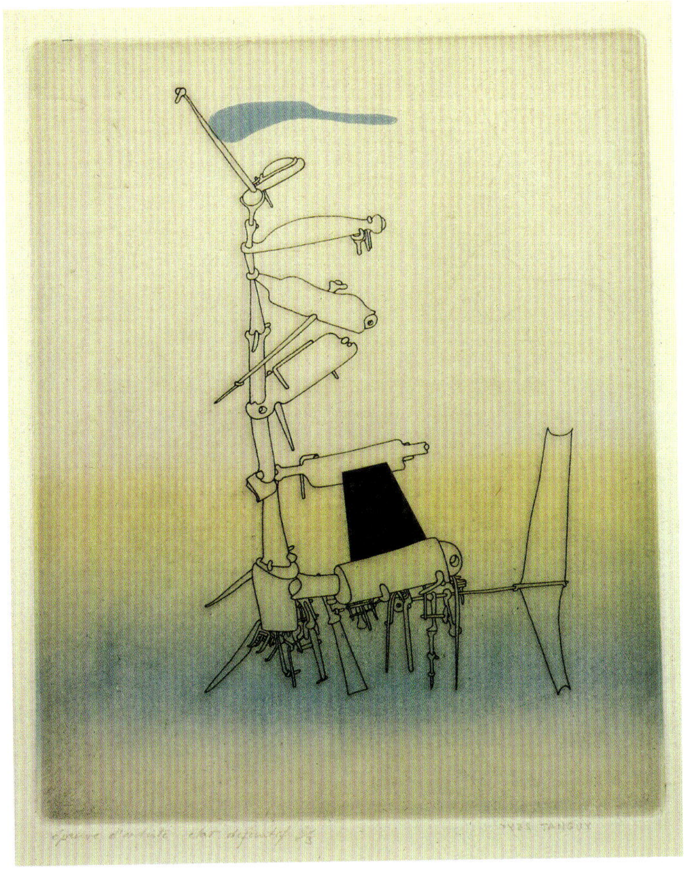

◉ *Fig. 124*
Yves Tanguy, Untitled (from *Le Grand Passage*), 1954 (cat. no. 123).

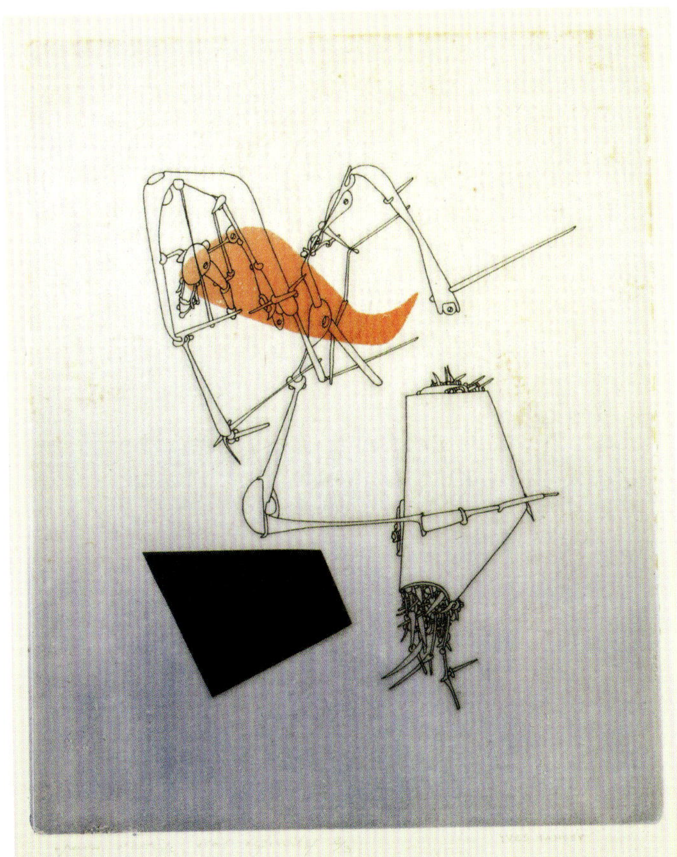

◉ *Fig. 125*
Yves Tanguy, Untitled (from *Le Grand Passage*), 1954 (cat. no. 124).

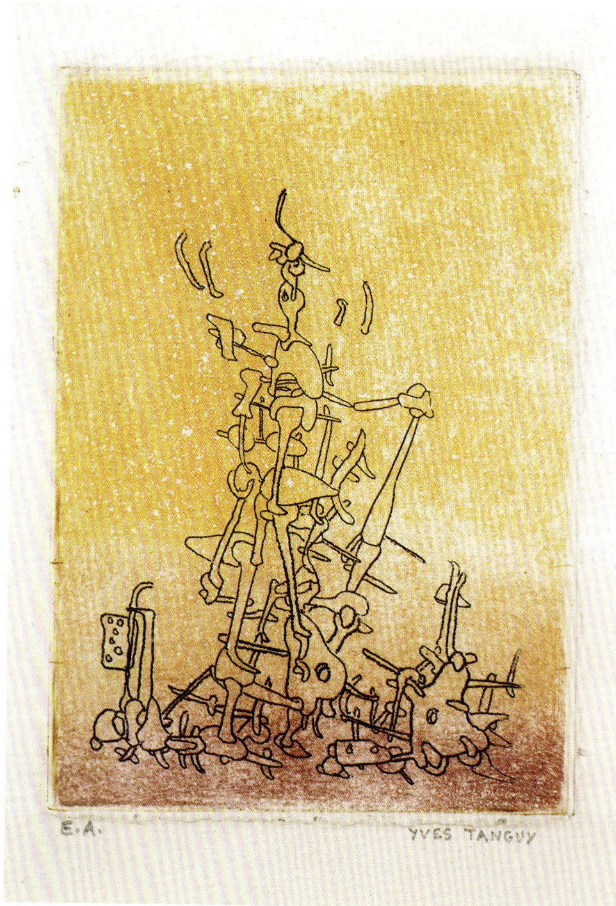

● *Fig. 126*
Yves Tanguy, Untitled (from *Sept Microbes vus à travers un tempérament*), 1953 (cat. no. 121).

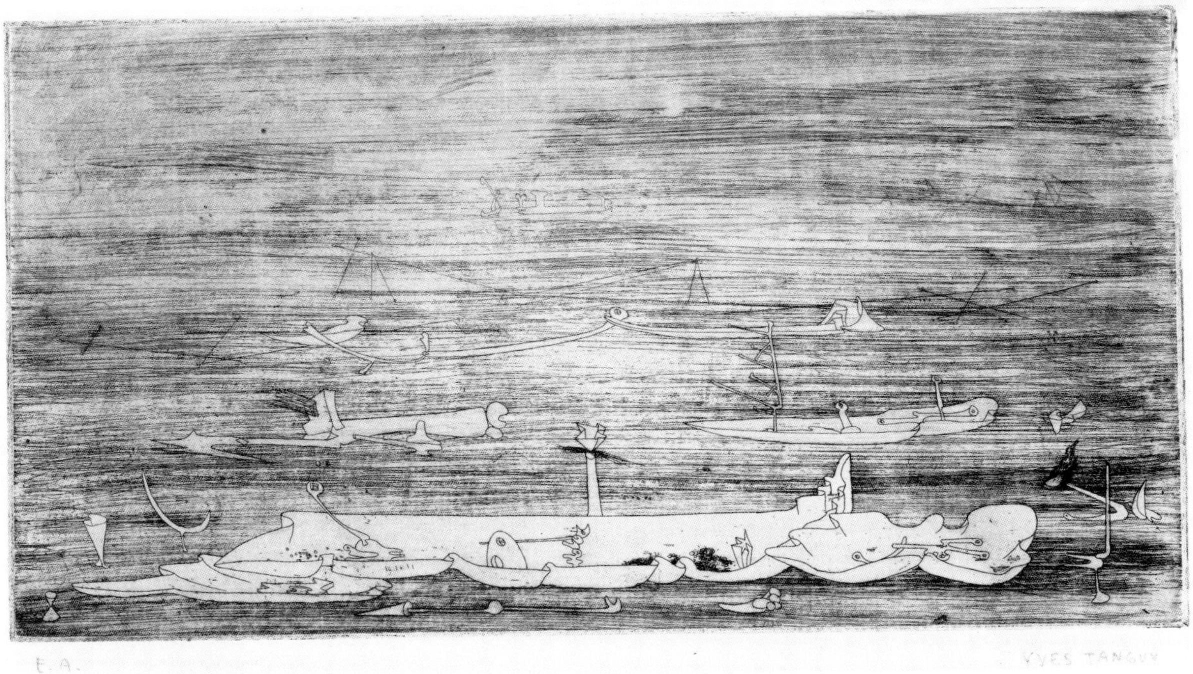

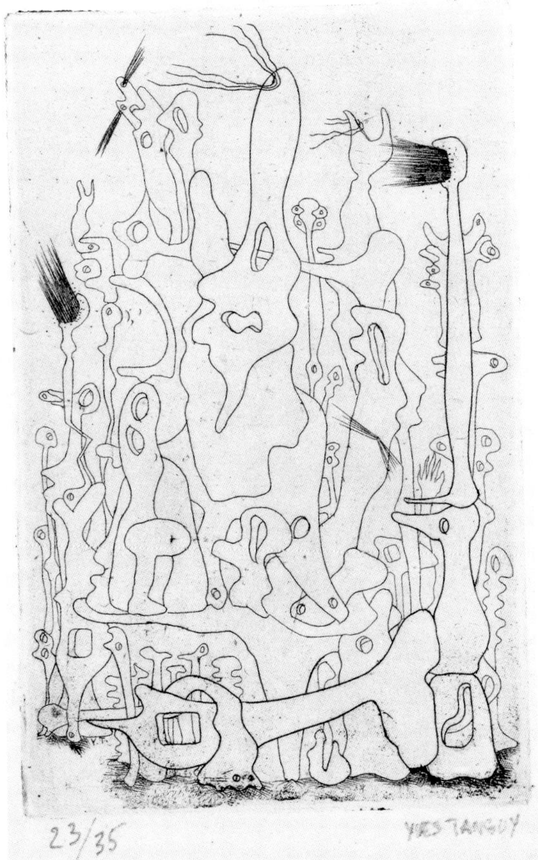

● *Fig. 127 (top)*
Yves Tanguy, Untitled, 1937 (cat. no. 118).

● *Fig. 128*
Yves Tanguy, Untitled (from *A même la terre*), 1936 (cat. no. 117).

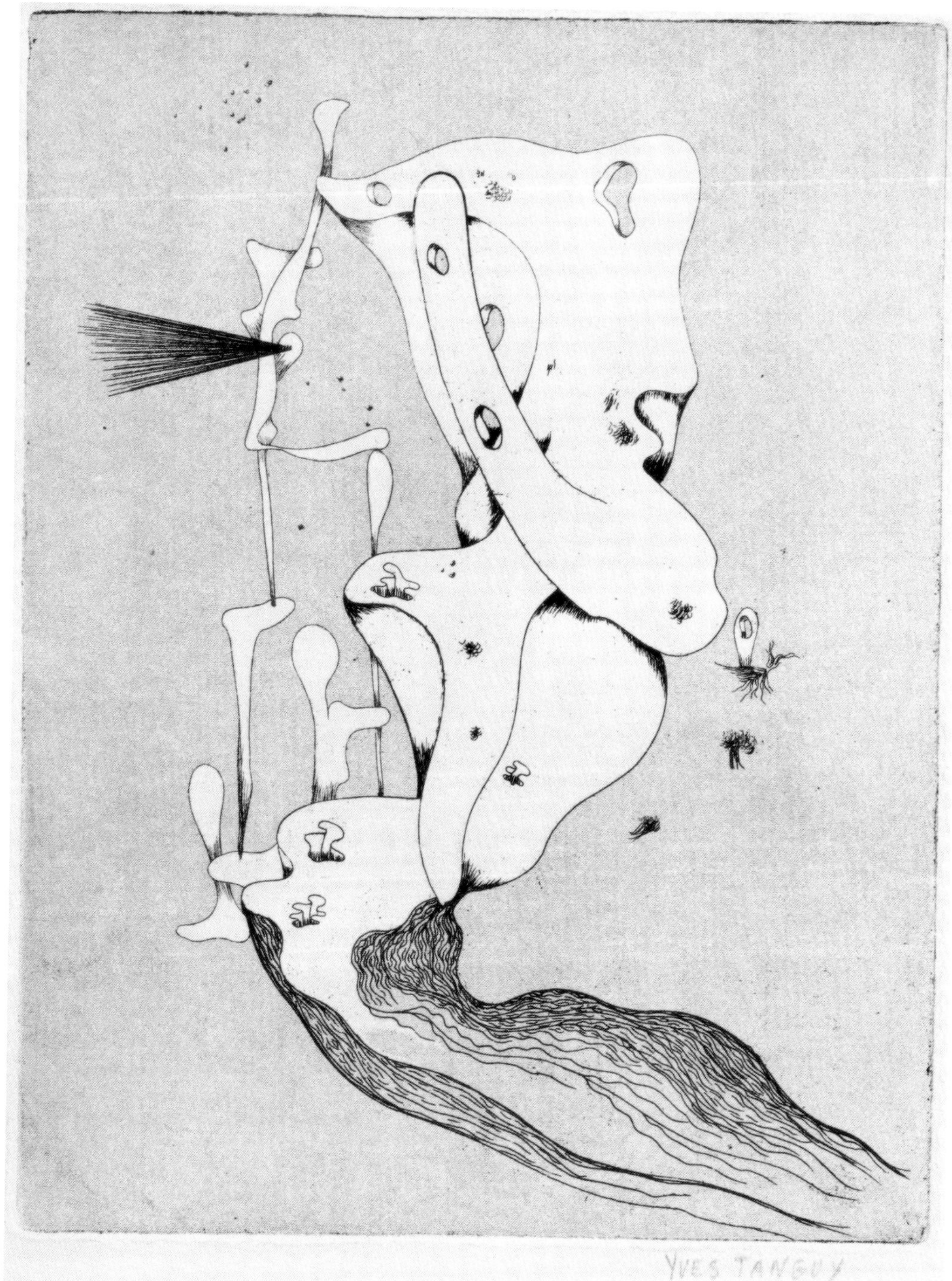

● *Fig. 129*
Yves Tanguy, Untitled (from *Primele poème*), 1934 (cat. no. 116).

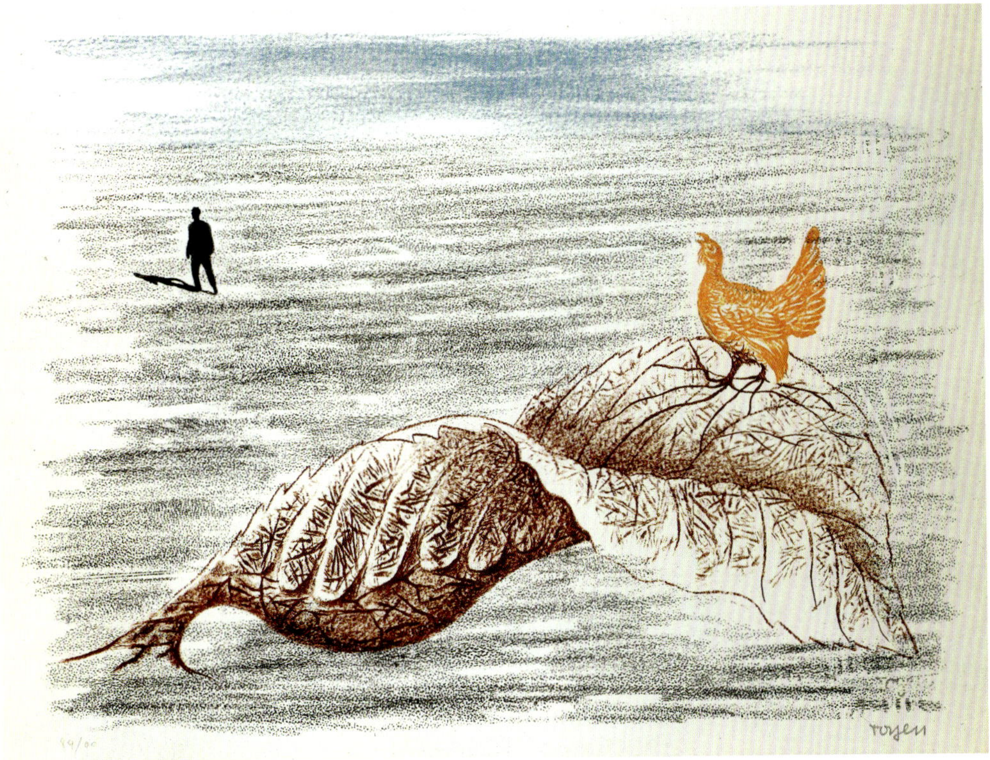

● *Fig. 130*
Toyen, *Composition*, 1950
(cat. no. 126).

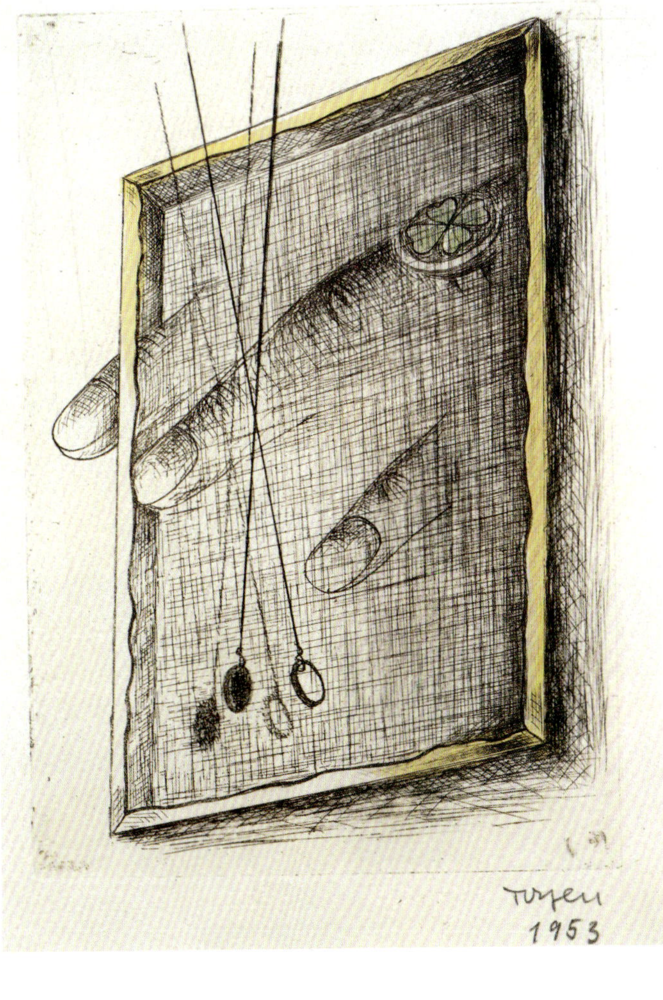

● *Fig. 131*
Toyen, Untitled, 1953
(cat. no. 127).

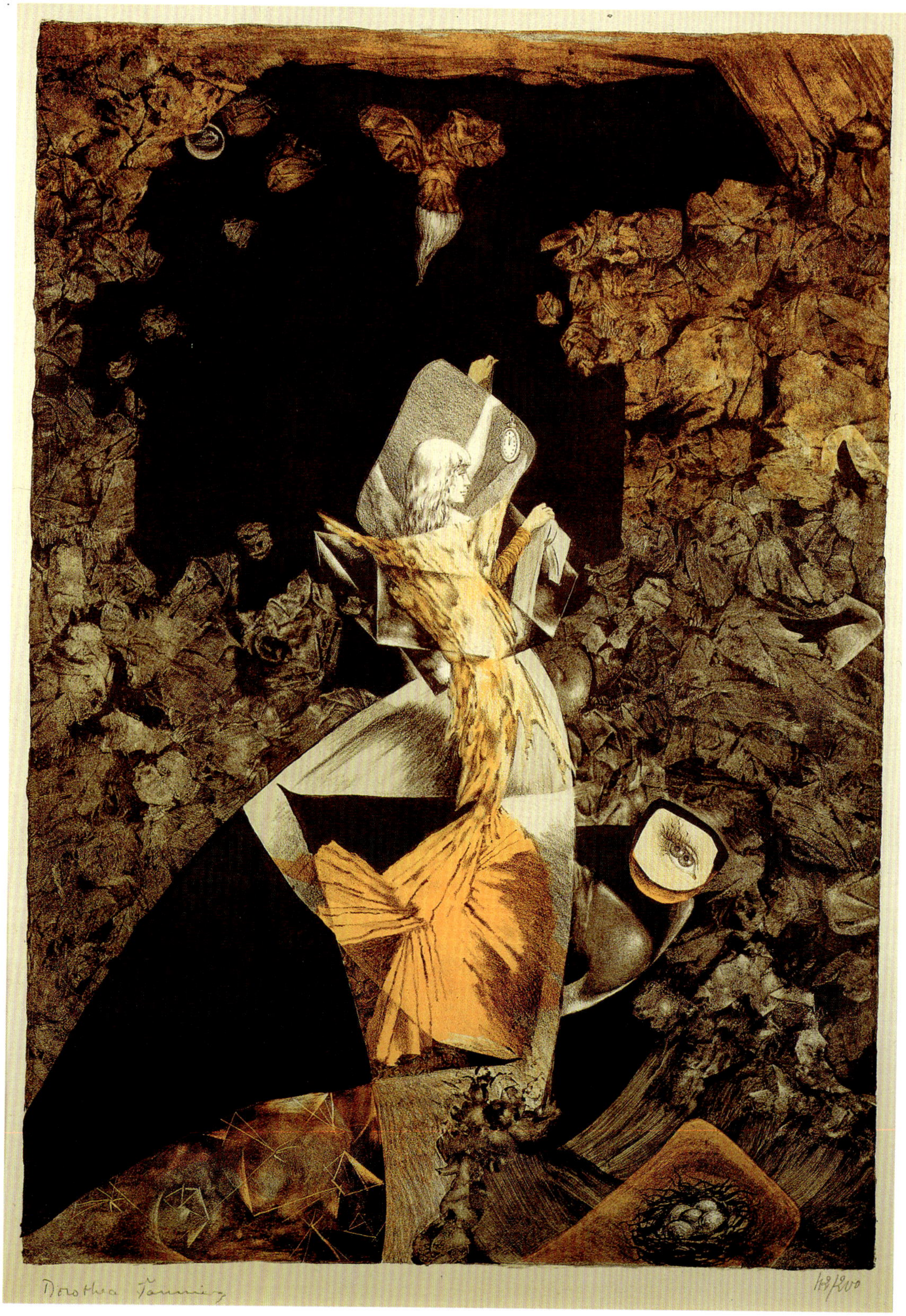

● *Fig. 132*
Dorothea Tanning, *Bateau bleu (The Grotto)*, 1950 (cat. no. 125).

Checklist

NOTE: In dimensions height precedes width. For intaglio prints the dimensions noted are those of the plate; for planographic prints sheet size is given.

Jean (Hans) Arp

(b. Strasbourg 1886; d. Basel 1966)

1. *Constellation*, 1938
Linoleum cut printed in color on tan paper
12½ x 9¾ in.
From *XXe siècle*, no. 4 (Christmas 1938)
Arntz 96(b)
(Fig. 15)

2. *Constellation*, 1951
Lithograph printed in color
22¼ x 15 in.
Arntz 328(c)
Signed l.l., numbered *LIII/LX* l.r.
(Fig. 16)

Hans Bellmer

(b. Katowice, Poland, 1902; d. Paris 1975)

3. *Céphalopode double* (Double cephalopod), 1965
Engraving on black paper
15⅞ x 17⅛ in.
Signed l.r., numbered *18/100* l.l.
Denoël 131
(Fig. 17)

4. Untitled, 1967
Etching and aquatint
11⅞ x 12¼ in.
For a poster published in conjunction with an exhibition of the Kestner-Gesellschaft, Hannover, 1967; from edition of 120 published on japan paper without text
Signed l.r., inscribed *H.C.* l.l.
Denoël 75
(Fig. 18)

Victor Brauner

(b. Piatra Neamt, Romania, 1903; d. Paris 1966)

5. Untitled (from *Frappe de l'écho*), 1940
Etching and aquatint (state i/iii)
5¼ x 3¾ in.
From Robert Rius, *Frappe de l'écho* (Paris: Editions Surréalistes, 1940); from edition of 15 on Holland van Gelder paper; the book also contains the second and third states of this print (cat. nos. 6–7)
Initialed l.r., inscribed *1er état 8/20* l.l.
(Fig. 19)

6. Untitled (from *Frappe de l'écho*), 1940
Etching and aquatint (state ii/iii)
5¼ x 3¾ in.
From Robert Rius, *Frappe de l'écho* (Paris: Editions Surréalistes, 1940); from edition of 15 on Holland van Gelder paper; the book also contains the first and third states of this print (cat. nos. 5, 7)
Initialed l.r., inscribed *2ème état 8/20* l.l.
(Fig. 20)

7. Untitled (from *Frappe de l'écho*), 1940
Etching and aquatint (state iii/iii)
5¼ x 3¾ in.
From Robert Rius, *Frappe de l'écho* (Paris: Editions Surréalistes, 1940); from the edition of 75 on vélin du marais paper; the book also contains the first and second states of this print (cat. nos. 5–6)
Signed l.r., numbered *24/70* l.l.
(Fig. 21)

8. Untitled, 1947
Etching with hand-coloring
Two prints on single sheet, 6½ x 5 in. each
From *Portfolio Number 2, 1947–1952* (New York: Brunidor Editions, 1952)
Signed, dated, and numbered *7/110* l.l.
(Fig. 79)

9. Untitled (from *Le Char triomphal de l'antimoine*), 1949
Etching and aquatint
6¼ x 4¼ in.
From Yvan Goll, *Le Char triomphal de l'antimoine* (Paris: Editions Hémisphères, 1949); from edition of 300 on Rives paper
Signed l.r., numbered *127/300* l.l.
(Fig. 22)

10. Untitled (from *Le Char triomphal de l'antimoine*), 1949
Etching and aquatint
6¼ x 4¼ in.
From Yvan Goll, *Le Char triomphal de l'antimoine* (Paris: Editions Hémisphères, 1949); from edition of 300 on Rives paper
Signed l.r., numbered *127/300* l.l.
(Fig. 23)

11. Untitled (from *Le Char triomphal de l'antimoine*), 1949
Etching and aquatint
6¼ x 4¼ in.
From Yvan Goll, *Le Char triomphal de l'antimoine* (Paris: Editions Hémisphères, 1949); from edition of 300 on Rives paper
Signed l.r., numbered *127/300* l.l.
(Fig. 24)

12. *L'Oiseau innomé* (The unnamed bird), 1958
Etching with hand-coloring
4¼ x 5⅜ in.
From Gherasim Luca, *Ce Château pressenti* (Paris: Méconnaissance, 1958)
Signed l.r., inscribed *Epreuve d'artiste* l.l.
(Fig. 25)

13. *Révulsion de la fin dans le commencement des mutations inconnues*, 1963
Etching
18½ x 14½ in.
Plate 7 from the series *Codex d'un visage* (Paris: Le Point cardinal, 1963)
Signed and dated l.r., numbered *40/60* l.l.
(Fig. 26)

Leonora Carrington
(b. Lancashire, England, 1917)

14. Untitled, 1942
Etching
8 x 9⅞ in.
From the album to support the review *VVV* (New York, 1942)
Signed l.r.
(Fig. 78)

Giorgio de Chirico
(b. Volos, Greece, 1888; d. Rome 1978)

15. *Combattimento di gladiatori* (Battle of the gladiators), 1928
Etching and drypoint
5⅜ x 7 in.
From Jean Cocteau, *Le Mystère laïc* (Paris: Editions des Quatre Chemins, 1928); from edition of 64 on Rives Amman paper
Signed l.r., numbered *66/100* l.l.
Ciranna 3
(Fig. 27)

16. *Scuola di gladiatori I* (School of the gladiators I), 1928
Etching and drypoint
7 x 5½ in.
From Jean Cocteau, *Le Mystère laïc* (Paris: Editions des Quatre Chemins, 1928); from edition of 64 on Rives Amman paper
Signed l.r., numbered *66/100* l.l.
Ciranna 4
(Fig. 28)

17. *Gli archeologi IV* (The archaeologists IV), 1929
Lithograph
15¾ x 11¾ in.
From the series *Metamorphosis* (Paris: Editions des Quatre Chemins, 1929)
Signed l.r., numbered *8/10* l.l.
Ciranna 16
(Fig. 29)

18. *Ricordo d'autunno* (Memory of autumn), 1969
Lithograph printed in color
17⅞ x 23 in.
From edition of 25 on japan paper
Signed l.r., numbered *xxi/xxv* l.l.
Ciranna 162
(Fig. 30)

Salvador Dalí
(b. Figueras, Spain, 1904; d. Figueras 1989)

19. *L'Immaculée Conception* (The Immaculate Conception), 1930
Heliogravure and etching
8¼ x 6⅜ in.
From André Breton and Paul Eluard, *L'Immaculée Conception* (Paris: Editions surréalistes, 1930)
Stamped *no. 4* on colophon page
Michler-Löpsinger 2(b)
(Fig. 31)

20. *Artine*, 1930
Heliogravure and etching on green paper
8½ x 6½ in.
From René Char, *Artine* (Paris: Editions Surréalistes, 1930)
Inscribed *no. 23* on colophon page
Michler-Löpsinger 3(c)
(Fig. 32)

21. *La Femme visible* (The visible woman), 1930
Heliogravure and engraving
9¾ x 7¾ in.
From Salvador Dalí, *La Femme visible* (Paris: Editions Surréalistes, 1930)
Stamped *no. 69* on colophon page
Michler-Löpsinger 4(d)
(Fig. 11)

22. *Le Revolver à cheveux blancs* (The white-haired revolver), 1932
Heliogravure and engraving
5⅞ x 4¾ in.
From André Breton, *Le Revolver à cheveux blancs* (Paris: Editions des Cahiers Libres, 1932)
Michler-Löpsinger 6(a)
(Fig. 33)

23. *L'Enfant-sauterelle* (Grasshopper child), 1934
Etching and engraving
14½ x 11⅝ in.
Signed l.l., numbered *50/100* l.r.
Michler-Löpsinger 7
(Fig. 34)

24. *Onan*, 1934
Heliogravure, aquatint, and drypoint
10 x 7¾ in.
From Georges Hugnet, *Onan* (Paris: Editions Surréalistes, 1934)
Signed l.l., numbered *46/72* l.r.
Michler-Löpsinger 10(d)
(Fig. 10)

25. Untitled (from *Les Chants de Maldoror*), 1934
Heliogravure and drypoint
11¾ x 7¼ in.
From the Comte de Lautréamont, *Les Chants de Maldoror* (Paris: Albert Skira, 1934)
Michler-Löpsinger 11(b)
(Fig. 9)

26. Untitled (from *Les Chants de Maldoror*), 1934
Heliogravure and drypoint
11¾ x 7¼ in.
From the Comte de Lautréamont, *Les Chants de Maldoror* (Paris: Albert Skira, 1934)
Michler-Löpsinger 19(b)
(Fig. 35)

27. Untitled (from *Les Chants de Maldoror*), 1934
Heliogravure and drypoint
11¾ x 7¼ in.
From the Comte de Lautréamont, *Les Chants de Maldoror* (Paris: Albert Skira, 1934)
Michler-Löpsinger 27(b)
(Fig. 36)

28. Untitled (from *Les Chants de Maldoror*), 1934
Heliogravure and drypoint
11¾ x 7¼ in.
From the Comte de Lautréamont, *Les Chants de Maldoror* (Paris: Albert Skira, 1934)
Michler-Löpsinger 31(b)
(Fig. 37)

29. *Grains et issues* (Grain and chaff), 1935
Etching
7½ x 5½ in.
From Tristan Tzara, *Grains et issues* (Paris: Denoël et Steele, 1935)
Signed l.l., stamped *no. 12* on colophon page
Michler-Löpsinger 55
(Fig. 70)

30. *Crânes mous et harpe crânienne* (Limp cranes and "cranian" harp), 1935
Etching and aquatint
14½ x 11⅞ in.
Inscribed *Pour Edouard son ami Salvador Dali 1935* l.l.
Michler-Löpsinger 56
(Fig. 38)

31. *Fantastic Beach Scene*, 1935
Etching in sanguine on chine collé
9½ x 11¾ in.
Inscribed *A Edward James Salvador Dali 1935* l.r.
Michler-Löpsinger 57(a)
(Fig. 39)

32. *American Trotting Horses No. 1*, 1971
Lithograph printed in color with collage
22½ x 30½ in.
From the series *Currier & Ives*
Signed l.r., numbered *2/250* l.l.
Michler-Löpsinger 1345
(Fig. 40)

Paul Delvaux

(b. Antheit-les-Huys, Belgium, 1897; d. Veurne, Belgium, 1994)

33. *Buste de femme III* (Half-length portrait of a woman III), 1960
Etching
5⅝ x 4⅝ in.
Signed and inscribed *E.A.* l.r.
Jacob 3
(Fig. 81)

34. *Les Deux Rivales* (The rivals), 1966
Lithograph printed in color
25½ x 19⅞ in.
Signed l.r., numbered *73/75* l.l.
Jacob 5 ii/ii
(Fig. 41)

35. *Anne songeuse* (Annie lost in thought), 1966
Lithograph printed in color
25½ x 20 in.
Signed l.r., inscribed *H.C.* l.l.
Jacob 7 ii/ii
(Fig. 42)

36. *La Mer est proche* (The sea is near), 1966
Lithograph
24¼ x 19⅞ in.
Signed l.r., numbered *29/75* l.l.
Jacob 8
(Fig. 43)

37. *La Dame à la bougie* (Lady with the candle), 1966
Lithograph
12⅜ x 9⅞ in.
Signed l.r., numbered *47/65* l.l.
Jacob 12 ii/ii
(Fig. 44)

38. *La Robe du dimanche* (Sunday dress), 1967
Lithograph printed in color
25 x 20 in.
Signed l.r., numbered *50/75* l.l.
Jacob 18 ii/ii
(Fig. 45)

39. *L'Eventail* (The fan), 1968
Lithograph printed in color
25⅜ x 18¾ in.
Signed l.r., numbered *70/75* l.l.
Jacob 21 ii/ii
(Fig. 46)

Oscar Dominguez
(b. Laguna, Canary Islands, 1906; d. Paris 1957)

40. *Femme à la bicyclette* (Woman with a bicycle), 1935
Etching and drypoint
10⅛ x 6⅝ in.
From Georges Hugnet, *La Hampe de l'imaginaire* (Paris: GLM, 1936)
Signed l.r., inscribed *Etat II—2/2* l.l.
(Fig. 47)

41. Untitled (from *Domaine*), 1942
Etching and aquatint
3⅞ x 5⅛ in.
From Robert Ganzo, *Domaine* (Paris: L.F.P., 1942); from edition of 60 on Rives BFK paper
Stamped *no. 9* on colophon page
(Fig. 77)

42. Untitled (from *Sombre est noir*), 1945
Etching
8½ x 6½ in.
From Amy Bakaloff, *Sombre est noir* (Paris: Privately printed, 1945); from edition of 200 on vélin du marais paper
Signed l.r., inscribed *no. 30* on colophon page
(Fig. 48)

Marcel Duchamp
(b. Blainville, France, 1887; d. Neuilly 1968)

43. *L.H.O.O.Q.*, 1964
Color reproduction with pencil additions
11⅞ x 8⅞ in.
Signed and numbered *24/35* l.l., inscribed *L.H.O.O.Q.* l.c.
Schwarz 261e
(Fig. 49)

44. *Self-Portrait in Profile*
Serigraph printed in red on black paper
24¾ x 19¾ in.
Signed and numbered *15/30* l.l., inscribed *Marcel dechiravit* l.r.
Schwarz 344
(Fig. 84)

Max Ernst
(b. Brühl, Germany, 1891; d. Paris 1976)

45. Untitled (plate 2 from *Fiat modes pereat ars*), 1919
Lithograph on light brown paper
17⅛ x 12½ in.
From the series *Fiat modes pereat ars* (Cologne: Verlag Arbeitsgemeinschaft bildender Künstler and Schlömilch Verlag, 1919)
Signed and inscribed *no. 4* l.r.
Spies-Leppien 7
(Fig. 3)

46. Untitled (plate 3 from *Fiat modes pereat ars*), 1919
Lithograph on light brown paper
17⅛ x 12½ in.
From the series *Fiat modes pereat ars* (Cologne: Verlag Arbeitsgemeinschaft bildender Künstler and Schlömilch Verlag, 1919)
Signed and inscribed *no. 4* l.r.
Spies-Leppien 7
(Fig. 50)

47. Untitled (plate 4 from *Fiat modes pereat ars*), 1919
Lithograph on light brown paper
16⅞ x 12½ in.
From the series *Fiat modes pereat ars* (Cologne: Verlag Arbeitsgemeinschaft bildender Künstler and Schlömilch Verlag, 1919)
Spies-Leppien 7
(Fig. 51)

48. Untitled (plate 5 from *Fiat modes pereat ars*), 1919
Lithograph on light brown paper
17⅛ x 12½ in.
From the series *Fiat modes pereat ars* (Cologne: Verlag Arbeitsgemeinschaft bildender Künstler and Schlömilch Verlag, 1919)
Signed and inscribed *no. 4* l.r.
Spies-Leppien 7
(Fig. 52)

49. Untitled (plate 6 from *Fiat modes pereat ars*), 1919
Lithograph on light brown paper
17 x 12⅜ in.
From the series *Fiat modes pereat ars* (Cologne: Verlag Arbeitsgemeinschaft bildender Künstler and Schlömilch Verlag, 1919)
Signed and inscribed *no. 6* l.r.
Spies-Leppien 7
(Fig. 53)

50. *Pays sage I*, 1923
Drypoint
6⅝ x 4⅞ in.
Signed l.r., inscribed *no. 6* l.l.
Spies-Leppien 10
(Fig. 5)

51. *Pays sage II*, 1923
Etching
6¾ x 4⅞ in.
Signed l.r., inscribed *no. 4 landschaft* l.l.
Spies-Leppien 11
(Fig. 54)

52. Untitled (from *Le Château étoilé*), 1936
Color frottage
12⅝ x 9¾ in.
From André Breton, *Le Château étoilé* (Paris: Editions Albert Skira, 1936)
Signed and numbered *25/50* l.r.
Spies-Leppien 17A
(Fig. 4)

53. *Correspondances dangereuses* (Dangerous harmonies), 1947
Etching and drypoint
11¾ x 8⅞ in.
From *Portfolio Number 1* (New York: Brunidor Editions, 1947)
Signed l.r., numbered *30/70* l.l.
Spies-Leppien 25A
(Fig. 55)

54. *Danseuses* (Dancers), 1950
Lithograph
22⅛ x 15¼ in.
Signed l.l., numbered *198/200* l.r.
Spies-Leppien 46D
(Fig. 56)

55. *Rhythmes* (Rhythms), 1950
Lithograph printed in color
18⅜ x 12⅛ in.
Signed l.l., numbered *12/200* l.r.
Spies-Leppien 48D
(Fig. 57)

56. *Masques* (Masks), 1950
Lithograph printed in color
15⅛ x 22⅛ in.
Signed l.l., numbered *18/200* l.r.
Spies-Leppien 49E
(Fig. 58)

Leonor Fini
(b. Buenos Aires 1908; d. Paris 1996)

57. *La Nuit vaincue* (Night conquered), 1967
Photolithograph printed in color
22⅝ x 15¼ in.
Signed l.r., numbered *69/75* l.l.
(Fig. 59)

Valentine Hugo
(b. Boulogne-sur-Mer, France, 1887; d. Paris 1968)

58. *Portrait of Rimbaud*, 1961
Lithograph
14 x 10 in.
From the album *Arthur Rimbaud vu par des peintres contemporains* (S.I. [Nice]: Privately published, 1961)
Signed l.r., numbered *37/37* l.l.
(Fig. 60)

Wifredo Lam
(b. Sagua la Grande, Cuba, 1902; d. Paris 1982)

59. Untitled, 1945
Etching
7⅞ x 6 in.
Unsigned proof; a larger version of this print was published in Pierre Loeb, *Voyages à travers la peinture* (Paris: Bordas, 1946)
Tonneau-Ryckelynck 4501
(Fig. 61)

60. *Quetzal*, 1947
Lithograph printed in color
16⅜ x 12⅞ in.
From the *Portfolio Number 1* (New York: Brunidor Editions, 1947)
Signed and inscribed *no. 31—'Quetzal'* l.r.
Tonneau-Ryckelynck 4701
(Fig. 63)

61. Untitled, 1966
Etching
5¾ x 4½ in.
A larger version of this print was published in Arturo Schwarz, *Le Surréalisme entre les deux guerres* (Milan: Galerie Schwarz, 1966)
Signed l.r., numbered *24/60* l.l.
Tonneau-Ryckelynck 6633
(Fig. 62)

René Magritte
(b. Lessines, Belgium, 1898; d. Brussels 1967)

62. *Ceci n'est pas une pipe* (This is not a pipe), 1962
Etching
4⅜ x 5¾ in.
Signed, dated, and numbered *16/60* l.l.
Kaplan-Baum 1
(Fig. 64)

63. *Les Travaux d'Alexandre* (The Labors of Alexander), 1962
Etching
4½ x 5⅞ in.
Signed and dated l.c., inscribed *e.a.* l.l.
Kaplan-Baum 2
(Fig. 65)

64. *Les Bijoux indiscrets* (The talkative jewels), 1963
Lithograph printed in color
9¼ x 11⅞ in.
Signed l.r., numbered *29/75* l.l.
Kaplan-Baum 3
(Fig. 80)

65. *Salon de mai* (The May salon), 1965
Lithograph printed in color
18⅞ x 15½ in.
Signed and dated l.l., numbered *70/107* l.r.
Kaplan-Baum 4
(Fig. 66)

66. *Paysage de Baucis* (Baucis's landscape), 1966
Etching
8⅞ x 6½ in.
Signed l.r., numbered *90/100* l.l.
Kaplan-Baum 5
(Fig. 67)

André Masson
(b. Balagny, France, 1896; d. Paris 1987)

67. Untitled (from *C'est les bottes de 7 lieues . . .*), 1926
Etching in bistre
8⅞ x 5¾ in.
From Robert Desnos, *C'est les bottes de 7 lieues cette phrase "Je me vois"* (Paris: Galerie Simon, 1926); from edition of 102 on Arches paper
Printed *no. 82* on colophon
Saphire 12; Saphire-Cramer 3
(Fig. 6)

68. Untitled (from *C'est les bottes de 7 lieues . . .*), 1926
Etching in bistre
9½ x 5¾ in.
From Robert Desnos, *C'est les bottes de 7 lieues cette phrase "Je me vois"* (Paris: Galerie Simon, 1926); from edition of 102 on Arches paper
Printed *no. 82* on colophon
Saphire 14; Saphire-Cramer 3
(Fig. 69)

69. Untitled (from *C'est les bottes de 7 lieues . . .*), 1926
Etching
9⅜ x 5¾ in.
From Robert Desnos, *C'est les bottes de 7 lieues cette phrase "Je me vois"* (Paris: Galerie Simon, 1926); from edition of 102 on Arches paper
Printed *no. 82* on colophon
Saphire 15; Saphire-Cramer 3
(Fig. 85)

70. *Ondine*, 1933
Etching
12⅞ x 10½ in.
Signed l.r., numbered *7/10* l.l.
Saphire 57
(Fig. 87)

71. *Le Crabe de terre* (Sand crab), 1942
Etching, engraving, and drypoint
11¾ x 8⅞ in.
Signed l.l.
Saphire 83
(Fig. 88)

72. *Le Génie de l'espèce* (Genius of the species), 1942
Drypoint and engraving in sanguine
14⅛ x 10⅝ in.
Signed l.l., numbered *23/30* l.r.
Saphire 84
(Fig. 76)

73. *Les Fruits de l'abîme* (Fruits of the abyss), 1942
Etching and soft-ground etching
11¾ x 7⅞ in.
From the album to support the review *VVV* (New York: Privately published, 1942)
Signed and dated l.r.
Saphire 85; Saphire-Cramer 15
(Fig. 86)

74. *Nocturne*, 1944
Etching and soft-ground etching
7⅞ x 5⅞ in.
From the deluxe edition of the *Nocturnal Notebook*
Signed l.l., numbered *7/50* l.r.
Saphire 91; Saphire-Cramer 17
(Fig. 89)

75. *Improvisation*, 1945
Etching, engraving, and aquatint
7⅞ x 5⅞ in.
Signed l.r., numbered *28/30* l.l.
Saphire 94
(Fig. 90)

Roberto Sebastián Matta Echaurren
(b. Chiloé, Chile, 1912)

76. Untitled (from *The New School*), 1943
Etching, aquatint, and soft-ground etching with silverpoint
9⅞ x 7⅞ in.
From the series *The New School*
Signed and numbered *5/11* l.l.
(Fig. 91)

77. *Par la bait naître*, 1946
Drypoint
5¼ x 4 in.
From André Breton, *Les Manifestes du surréalisme suivis des prolégomènes à un troisième manifeste du surréalisme* (Paris: Editions du Sagittaire, 1946); proof apart from the published edition
Sabatier 9
(Fig. 92)

78. *I Want to See It to Believe It*, 1947
Lithograph printed in color
16⅜ x 12⅞ in.
From the *Portfolio Number 1* (New York: Brunidor Editions, 1947)
Signed and dated l.l., numbered *23/70* l.r.
Sabatier 12
(Fig. 93)

Joan Miró

(b. Montroig, Spain, 1893; d. Palma de Majorca 1983)

79. *Daphnis et Chloé* (Daphne and Chloe), 1933
Etching and drypoint
10⅛ x 12½ in.
From edition of 10 on Japanese vellum paper
Signed and dated l.r., numbered *7/10* l.l.
Dupin 9
(Fig. 7)

80. Untitled (from *Enfances*), 1933
Etching
9⅜ x 5⅞ in.
From Georges Hugnet, *Enfances* (Paris: Editions Cahiers d'art, 1933); trial proof
Dupin 12; Cramer 2
(Fig. 95)

81. Untitled (from *Cahiers d'art*), 1934
Color pochoir
14⅞ x 11 in.
A smaller version of this print was published in *Cahiers d'art*, nos. 1–4 (1934)
Signed, dated, and numbered *2/48* l.l.
Dupin 14; Cramer 3 (hors catalogue)
(Fig. 97)

82. Untitled (from *Cahiers d'art*), 1934
Color pochoir
14⅞ x 11 in.
A smaller version of this print was published in *Cahiers d'art*, nos. 1–4 (1934)
Signed, dated, and numbered *26/48* l.l.
Dupin 15; Cramer 3 (hors catalogue)
(Fig. 98)

83. Untitled (from *24 Essais*), 1935
Etching
12¼ x 9¼ in.
From Anatole Jakovski, *24 Essais* (Paris: G. Orobitz, 1935)
Signed and numbered *24/50* l.l.
Dupin 16; Cramer 3
(Fig. 72)

84. *L'Aigle et la femme la nuit* (Eagle and woman at night), 1938
Drypoint and soft-ground etching
8⅞ x 11⅝ in.
Signed l.r., numbered *6/30* l.l.
Dupin 22
(Fig. 94)

85. *La Baigneuse* (The bather), 1938
Drypoint
6⅞ x 11⅝ in.
Signed l.r., numbered *20/30* l.l.
Dupin 23
(Fig. 96)

86. *Bijou et cadre* (Jewel and frame), 1938
Drypoint
4¾ x 3½ in.
Signed and dated (1939) l.r., inscribed *2ième état 2/2* l.l.
Dupin 24
(Fig. 99)

87. *Les Trois Soeurs* (Three sisters), 1938
Drypoint and etching
10½ x 7⅞ in.
Signed l.r., numbered *11/30* l.l.
Dupin 25
(Fig. 73)

88. *L'Eveil du géant* (Awakening of the giant), 1938
Drypoint
10⅜ x 9⅛ in.
Signed l.r., numbered *5/30* l.l.
Dupin 26
(Fig. 100)

89. *La Géante* (The giantess), 1938
Drypoint
13⅝ x 9¼ in.
Signed l.r., numbered *6/30* l.l.
Dupin 27
(Fig. 1)

90. *Femme et volcan* (Woman and volcano), 1938
Etching
8⅞ x 6¾ in.
Signed and inscribed *tirée par moi-même v/1938* l.r. and inscribed *3ième état* l.l.
Dupin 28
(Fig. 109)

91. *Portrait de Miró* (Portrait of Miró), 1938
With Louis Marcoussis
Drypoint
13 x 10⅞ in.
Signed and dated l.r., numbered *13/50* l.l.
Dupin 31
(Fig. 8)

92–99. *Série noire et rouge* (Black and red series), 1938
Eight drypoints, six printed in color

92. Untitled, 1938
10⅛ x 6⅝ in.
Signed l.r., numbered *29/30* l.l.
Dupin 32
(Fig. 101)

93. Untitled, 1938
6⅝ x 10⅛ in.
Signed l.r., numbered *29/30* l.l.
Dupin 33
(Fig. 102)

94. Untitled, 1938
Printed in color
10⅛ x 6⅝ in.
Signed l.r., numbered *29/30* l.l.
Dupin 34
(Fig. 103)

95. Untitled, 1938
Printed in color
6⅝ x 10⅛ in.
Signed l.r., numbered *29/30* l.l.
Dupin 35
(Fig. 104)

96. Untitled, 1938
Printed in color
6⅝ x 10⅛ in.
Signed l.r., numbered *29/30* l.l.
Dupin 36
(Fig. 105)

97. Untitled, 1938
Printed in color
6⅝ x 10⅛ in.
Signed l.r., numbered *20/30* l.l.
Dupin 37
(Fig. 106)

98. Untitled, 1938
Printed in color
6⅝ x 10⅛ in.
Signed l.r., numbered *29/30* l.l.
Dupin 38
(Fig. 107)

99. Untitled, 1938
Printed in color
6⅞ x 10⅛ in.
Signed l.r., numbered *29/30* l.l.
Dupin 39
(Fig. 108)

100. Untitled (from *Fraternity*), 1939
Etching
5⅞ x 3⅝ in.
From Stephen Spender, *Fraternity* (Privately printed, 1939)
Signed l.l.
Dupin 43; Cramer 8
(Fig. 110)

Pablo Picasso

(b. Malaga, Spain, 1881; d. Mougins, France, 1973)

101. *Modèle et sculpture surréaliste* (Model and surrealist sculpture), 1933
Etching
10½ x 7½ in.
Plate 74 from the Vollard suite
Signed l.r.
Bloch 187; Geiser-Baer 346
(Fig. 111)

102. Untitled (from *Contrée*), 1943
Etching
9½ x 5⅛ in.
From Robert Desnos, *Contrée* (Paris: Robert J. Godet, 1944); from edition of 200 on Lafuma pur fil paper
Numbered *30/200* l.l.
Bloch 362, 38 (book); Goeppert-Cramer 39
(Fig. 74)

Man Ray

(b. Philadelphia 1890; d. Paris 1976)

103–12. *Revolving Doors*, 1926
Ten color pochoirs
22 x 15 in. each
Published by Editions Surréalistes, Paris, 1926
Inscribed *no. 103* on colophon page

103. *Shadows*, 1926
Pilat 18A
(Fig. 112)

104. *Long Distance*, 1926
Pilat 18B
(Fig. 113)

105. *Legend*, 1926
Pilat 18C
(Fig. 114)

106. *Decanter*, 1926
Pilat 18D
(Fig. 116)

107. *The Meeting*, 1926
Pilat 18E
(Fig. 115)

108. *Mime*, 1926
Pilat 18F
(Fig. 117)

109. *Orchestra*, 1926
Pilat 18G
(Fig. 118)

110. *Dragon Fly*, 1926
Pilat 18H
(Fig. 119)

111. *Concrete Mixer*, 1926
Pilat 18I
(Fig. 120)

112. *Jeune Fille*, 1926
Pilat 18L [*sic*]
(Fig. 121)

113. *A l'heure de l'observatoire—les amoureux*
(Observatory time—the lovers), 1967
Photolithograph printed in color
23⅝ x 59 in.
Signed l.r., numbered *146/150* l.l.
Pilat 15
(Fig. 83)

Kurt Seligmann
(b. Basel 1900; d. Sugar Loaf, New York, 1962)

114. *Corsaire*, 1930
Etching
13¾ x 11¼ in.
Plate 12 from Anatole Jakovski, *Protubérances cardiaques* (Paris: Editions des Chroniques du Jour, 1933)
Signed and dated l.r., inscribed *proof, Corsaire* l.l.
Mason 31, I
(Fig. 122)

Yves Tanguy
(b. Paris 1900; d. Woodbury, Connecticut, 1955)

115. Untitled (from *La Vie immédiate*), 1932
Etching
5⅜ x 4½ in.
From Paul Eluard, *La Vie immédiate* (Paris: Editions des Cahiers Libres, 1932)
Wittrock 1 i/iii
(Fig. 12)

116. Untitled (from *Primele poème*), 1934
Etching and aquatint
6⅝ x 4⅞ in.
From Tristan Tzara, *Primele poème* (Bucharest: Editura Unu, 1934)
Signed l.r.
Wittrock 2
(Fig. 129)

117. Untitled (from *A même la terre*), 1936
Etching and drypoint
4⅛ x 2⅝ in.
From Alice Paalen, *A même la terre* (Paris: Editions Surréalistes, 1936)
Signed l.r., numbered *23/35* l.l.
Wittrock 3
(Fig. 128)

118. Untitled, 1937
Etching
4⅝ x 8¾ in.
Signed l.r., inscribed *E.A.* l.l.
Wittrock 5
(Fig. 127)

119. Untitled (from *L'Ile d'un jour*), 1938
Silverpoint etching
7½ x 3⅝ in.
From Marcelle Ferry, *L'Ile d'un jour* (Paris: Editions Surréalistes, 1938)
Signed l.r., numbered *21/30* l.l.
Wittrock 7
(Fig. 71)

120. *Rhabdomancie*, 1947
Etching and monoprint in color
11¾ x 8¾ in.
From *Portfolio Number 1* (New York: Brunidor Editions, 1947)
Signed and dated l.r., numbered *14/70* l.l.
Wittrock 13
(Fig. 13)

121. Untitled (from *Sept Microbes vus à travers un tempérament*), 1953
Etching and monoprint in color
4 x 2¾ in.
From Max Ernst, *Sept Microbes vus à travers un tempérament* (Paris: Editions Cercle des Arts, 1953)
Signed l.r., inscribed *E.A.* l.l.
Wittrock 18
(Fig. 126)

122. Untitled (from *Le Grand Passage*), 1954
Etching and monoprint in color with embossing
8⅛ x 6⅜ in.
From Jean Laude, *Le Grand Passage* (Paris: Instance, 1954)
Wittrock 19A
(Fig. 123)

123. Untitled (from *Le Grand Passage*), 1954
Etching printed in color
6¾ x 5¼ in.
From Jean Laude, *Le Grand Passage* (Paris: Instance, 1954)
Signed l.r., inscribed *épreuve d'artiste état définitif 2/3* l.l.
Wittrock 19B
(Fig. 124)

124. Untitled (from *Le Grand Passage*), 1954
Etching printed in color
6¾ x 5¼ in.
From Jean Laude, *Le Grand Passage* (Paris: Instance, 1954)
Signed l.r., inscribed *épreuve d'artiste état définitif 2/3* l.l.
Wittrock 19C
(Fig. 125)

Dorothea Tanning
(b. Galesburg, Illinois, 1910)

125. *Bateau bleu* (*The Grotto*), 1950
Lithograph printed in color
19½ x 13⅝ in.
Signed l.l., numbered *112/200* l.r.
Waddell-Ruby 5
(Fig. 132)

Toyen (Marie Cerminová)
(b. Prague 1902; d. Paris 1980)

126. *Composition*, 1950
Lithograph printed in color
12¾ x 16½ in.
From *Portfolio Number 2, 1947–1952* (New York: Brunidor Editions, 1952)
Signed l.r., numbered *44/100* l.l.
(Fig. 130)

127. Untitled, 1953
Etching with hand-coloring
5½ x 3⅝ in.
Hand-colored impression apart from edition of 36 printed in black-and-white for André Breton, Jindrich Heisler, and Benjamin Peret, *Toyen* (Paris: Editions Sokolova, 1953)
Signed and dated l.r.
(Fig. 131)

Selected Bibliography

Catalogues Raisonnés of the Artists' Prints

ARNTZ
Arntz, Wilhelm F. *Hans (Jean) Arp: Das graphische Werk, 1912–1966.* Haag, W. Germany: Arntz-Winter, 1980.

BLOCH
Bloch, Georges. *Pablo Picasso: Catalogue de l'oeuvre gravé et lithographié.* 4 vols. Bern: Kornfeld and Klipstein, 1968–79.

CIRANNA
Ciranna, Alfonso. *Giorgio de Chirico: Catalogo delle opere graphiche (incisioni e litografie), 1921–1969.* Milan: Alfonso Ciranna; Rome: Medusa, 1969.

CRAMER
Cramer, Patrick. *Joan Miró: The Illustrated Books: Catalogue Raisonné.* Translated by Gail Mangold-Vine. Geneva: Patrick Cramer, 1994.

DENOËL
Hans Bellmer: Oeuvre gravé. Preface by André Pieyre de Mandiargues. Paris: Editions Denoël, 1969.

DUPIN
Dupin, Jacques. *Miró Engraver.* 3 vols. New York: Rizzoli, 1989–92.

GEISER-BAER
Geiser, Bernhard, and Brigitte Baer. *Picasso, peintre-graveur: Catalogue raisonné de l'oeuvre gravé.* 5 vols. Bern: Editions Kornfeld, 1990–92.

GOEPPERT
Goeppert, Sebastian, Herma Goeppert-Frank, and Patrick Cramer. *Pablo Picasso: The Illustrated Books: Catalogue Raisonné.* Translated by Gail Mangold-Vine. Geneva: Patrick Cramer, 1983.

JACOB
Jacob, Mira. *Paul Delvaux: Graphic Work.* Translated by Howard Brabyn. New York: Rizzoli, 1976.

KAPLAN-BAUM
Kaplan, Gilbert E., and Timothy Baum. *The Graphic Work of René Magritte.* New York: II Editions, 1982.

MASON
Mason, Rainer Michael, Timothy Baum, and Claude Givaudan. *Kurt Seligmann: Oeuvre gravé.* Exhibition catalogue. Geneva: Cabinet des estampes, Musée d'art et d'histoire; Editions du Tricorne, 1982.

MICHLER-LÖPSINGER
Michler, Ralf, and Lutz W. Löpsinger, eds. *Salvador Dali: Catalogue Raisonné of Etchings and Mixed-Media Prints, 1924–1980.* Munich: Prestel, 1994.

———. *Salvador Dali: Catalogue Raisonné of Prints II: Lithographs and Wood Engravings, 1956–1980.* Munich and New York: Prestel, 1995.

PILAT
Pilat, Bianca Maria. *Man Ray: Opera grafica.* Milan: Studio Marconi, 1984.

SABATIER
Sabatier, Roland. *Matta: Catalogue raisonné de l'oeuvre gravé, 1943–1974.* Stockholm: Sonet; Paris: Visat, 1975.

SAPHIRE
Saphire, Lawrence. *André Masson: The Complete Graphic Work.* Vol. 1, *Surrealism, 1924–1949.* Yorktown Heights, N.Y.: Blue Moon Press, 1990.

SAPHIRE-CRAMER
Saphire, Lawrence, and Patrick Cramer. *André Masson: The Illustrated Books: Catalogue Raisonné.* Translated by Gail Mangold-Vine and Christopher Snow. Geneva: Patrick Cramer, 1994.

SCHWARZ
Schwarz, Arturo. *The Complete Works of Marcel Duchamp.* 2d rev. ed. New York: Harry N. Abrams, 1970.

SPIES-LEPPIEN
Spies, Werner, and Helmut R. Leppien. *Max Ernst: Oeuvre-Katalog: Das graphische Werk.* 4 vols. Houston: Menil Foundation; Cologne: M. Dumont Schauberg, 1975–87.

TONNEAU-RYCKELYNCK
Tonneau-Ryckelynck, Dominique. *Wifredo Lam: Oeuvre gravé et lithographié: Catalogue raisonné.* Gravelines: Edition du Musée de Gravelines, 1993.

WADDELL-RUBY
Waddell, Roberta, and Louisa Wood Ruby. *Dorothea Tanning: Hail, Delirium! A Catalogue Raisonné of the Artist's Illustrated Books and Prints, 1942–1991.* Exhibition catalogue. New York: New York Public Library, 1992.

WITTROCK
Wittrock, Wolfgang. *Yves Tanguy: Das druck-graphische Werk.* Exhibition catalogue. Düsseldorf: Wolfgang Wittrock Kunsthandel, 1976.

Books, Articles, and Exhibition Catalogues

Abadie, Daniel. *La Vie publique de Salvador Dalí*. Exhibition catalogue. Paris: Centre Georges Pompidou, 1980.

Ades, Dawn. *Dada and Surrealism*. London: Thames and Hudson, 1974.

———. *Dada and Surrealism Reviewed*. Exhibition catalogue. London: Hayward Gallery, 1978.

———. *Dalí and Surrealism*. New York: Harper and Row, 1982.

———. *André Masson*. New York: Rizzoli, 1994.

Ades, Dawn, et al. *In the Mind's Eye: Dada and Surrealism*. Exhibition catalogue for *Dada and Surrealism in Chicago Collections*. Chicago: Museum of Contemporary Art, 1984.

Adhémar, Jean, and Mariel Frèrebeau. *Max Ernst: Estampes et livres illustrés*. Exhibition catalogue. Paris: Bibliothèque nationale, 1975.

Angliviel de la Beaumelle, Agnès, and Florence Chauveau. *Yves Tanguy: Retrospective, 1925–1955*. Exhibition catalogue. Paris: Musée national d'art moderne, Centre Georges Pompidou, 1982.

Angliviel de la Beaumelle, Agnès, Isabelle Monod-Fontaine, and Claude Schweisguth. *André Breton: La Beauté convulsive*. Exhibition catalogue. Paris: Musée national d'art moderne, Centre Georges Pompidou, 1991.

Bailly, Jean-Christophe. *Dorothea Tanning*. Translated by Richard Howard. New York: George Braziller, 1995.

Barr, Alfred H., Jr., ed. *Fantastic Art, Dada, Surrealism*. Exhibition catalogue. New York: Museum of Modern Art, 1936.

Bateau Lavoir. *Paul Delvaux: Dessins et premières lithographies*. Exhibition catalogue. Paris: Bateau Lavoir, 1966.

———. *Paul Delvaux: Dessins et gravures, 1966–1969*. Cahier no. 2. Exhibition catalogue. Paris: Bateau Lavoir, 1969.

Baum, Timothy. *The Surrealist Experience*. Exhibition catalogue. Chicago: Richard Gray Gallery, 1972.

———. *Rebeccabook I*. New York: Nadada Editions, 1975.

———. *The Golden Age of Collage: Dada and Surrealist Eras, 1916–1950*. Exhibition catalogue. London: Mayor Gallery, 1987.

———. *Man Ray's Paris Portraits, 1921–39*. Washington, D.C.: Middendorf Gallery Editions, 1989.

Bernheim, Cathy. *Valentine Hugo*. Paris: Presses de la Renaissance, 1990.

Bibliothèque municipale, Tours. *Max Ernst: Ecrits et oeuvre gravé*. Exhibition catalogue. Paris: Point Cardinal, 1963.

Billeter, Erika, and José Pierre, eds. *La Femme et le surréalisme*. Exhibition catalogue. Lausanne: Musée cantonal des beaux-arts, 1987.

Blanc, Giulio V., Julia P. Herzberg, and Lowery Stokes Sims. *Wifredo Lam and His Contemporaries, 1938–52*. Exhibition catalogue. New York: Studio Museum in Harlem, 1992.

Blue Moon Gallery. *Hans Bellmer: Twenty-five Years of Graphic Works: Drawings and Prints, 1942–1967*. Exhibition catalogue. New York: Blue Moon Gallery, 1972.

Boetie Gallery. *Kurt Seligmann: His Graphic Work*. Exhibition catalogue. New York: Boetie Gallery, 1973.

Bosquet, Alain. *La Peinture de Dorothea Tanning*. Paris: Jean-Jacques Pauvert, 1966.

Bozo, Dominique. *Victor Brauner*. Exhibition catalogue. Paris: Musée national d'art moderne, 1972.

Brandani, Edoardo, ed. *Giorgio de Chirico: Catalogo dell'opera grafica, 1969–1977*. Bologna: Bora, 1990.

Butor, Michel, Jean Clair, and Suzanne Houbart-Wilkin. *Paul Delvaux: Catalogue raisonné de l'oeuvre peint*. Brussels: Cosmos Monographies, 1975.

Camfield, William A. *Max Ernst: Dada and the Dawn of Surrealism*. Exhibition catalogue. Munich: Prestel-Verlag; Houston: Menil Collection, 1993.

Castleman, Riva. *Modern Art in Prints*. New York: Museum of Modern Art, 1973.

———. *Prints of the Twentieth Century: A History*. New York: Museum of Modern Art, 1976.

———. *A Century of Artists Books*. Exhibition catalogue. New York: Museum of Modern Art, 1994.

Castro, Fernando. *Oscar Domínguez y el surrealismo*. Madrid: Edicions Catedra, 1978.

Caws, Mary Ann, Rudolf E. Kuenzli, and Gwen Raaberg, eds. *Surrealism and Women*. Cambridge: MIT Press, 1991.

Center for Inter-American Relations. *Leonora Carrington: A Retrospective Exhibition*. Exhibition catalogue. New York: Center for Inter-American Relations, 1976.

Centre culturel Thibaud de Champagne. *Valentine Hugo: Peintures, gravures, dessins*. Exhibition catalogue. Troyes: Centre culturel Thibaud de Champagne, 1977.

Centre national d'art moderne. *Dorothea Tanning*. Exhibition catalogue. Paris: Centre national d'art moderne, 1974.

Chadwick, Whitney. *Women Artists and the Surrealist Movement*. New York: New York Graphic Society, 1985.

———. *Leonora Carrington: La realidad de la imaginacion*. Exhibition catalogue. Mexico City: Consejo Nacional para la Cultura y las Artes, Ediciones Eras, 1994.

Contensou, Bernadette, and Danielle Molinari. *L'Atelier Lacourière-Frelaut; ou, 50 ans de gravure et d'imprimerie en taille-douce, 1929–79*. Exhibition catalogue. Paris: Musée d'art moderne de la ville de Paris, 1979.

Dachy, Marc, et al. *René Magritte et le surréalisme en Belgique*. Exhibition catalogue. Brussels: Musées royaux des beaux-arts en Belgique, 1982.

De Bock, Paul-Aloïse. *Paul Delvaux: L'Homme, le peintre, psychologie d'un art*. Brussels: Laconti, 1967.

Dedieu, Jean-Claude. *Leonor Fini*. Exhibition catalogue. Ferrara: Galleria civica d'arte moderna, Palazzo dei diamanti; Casalecchio di Reno: Edizioni d'Arte, 1983.

Descharnes, Robert. *Salvador Dalí*. Translated by Eleanor R. Morse. New York: Harry N. Abrams, 1985.

———. *Salvador Dalí*. Exhibition catalogue. Montreal: Montreal Museum of Fine Arts, 1990.

Emerson, Barbara. *Delvaux*. Antwerp: Fonds Mercator, 1985.

Fagiolo Dell'Arco, Maurizio. *Giorgio de Chirico: Vita e opere di De Chirico attraverso incisioni e litografie*. Exhibition catalogue. Milan: Galleria d'arte moderna; Interarte, 1980.

Ferrari, Germana. *Matta: Index dell'opera grafica dal 1969 al 1980*. Catalogue published in conjunction with the exhibition *Il cuore e un occhio*. Viterbo: Palazzo degli Alessandri; Amministrazione provinciale di Viterbo, 1980.

Fini, Leonor, and José Alvarez. *Le Livre de Leonor Fini: Peintures, dessins, ecrits, notes de Leonor Fini*. 2d ed. Lausanne: Editions Mermoud-Clairefontaine; Paris: Vilo, 1979.

Foresta, Merry, et al. *Perpetual Motif: The Art of Man Ray*. Exhibition catalogue. Washington, D.C.: National Museum of American Art, Smithsonian Institution; New York: Abbeville Press, 1988.

Fornés, Edouard. *Dalí et les livres*. Exhibition catalogue. Nîmes: Musée d'art de la ville de Nîmes. Translation of catalogue for exhibition held at the Royal Chapel of Barcelona, 1982, and published by the Generalitat de Catalunya.

Fort Worth Art Museum. *Surrealist Prints from the Collection of the Museum of Modern Art*. Exhibition catalogue. Fort Worth: Fort Worth Art Museum, 1985.

Foucault, Michel. *This Is Not a Pipe: Illustrations and Letters by René Magritte*. Translated by James Harkness. Berkeley: University of California Press, 1983.

Fouchet, Max-Pol. *Wifredo Lam*. New York: Rizzoli, 1976.

Freeman, Judi. *The Dada and Surrealist Word-Image*. Exhibition catalogue. Los Angeles: Los Angeles County Museum of Art; Cambridge: MIT Press, 1989.

Galerie Levy. *Victor Brauner: Peintures, dessins, gouaches et l'oeuvre graphique*. Exhibition catalogue. Paris: Galerie Levy, 1978.

Galerie Louise Leiris. *André Masson: 90 oeuvres sur papier*. Exhibition catalogue. Paris: Galerie Louise Leiris, 1986.

Garvey, Eleanor M. *The Artist and the Book, 1860–1960, in Western Europe and the United States*. Exhibition catalogue. Boston: Museum of Fine Arts; Cambridge: Harvard College Library, 1961.

Garvey, Eleanor M., and Peter A. Wick. *The Arts of the French Book, 1900–1965*. Dallas: Southern Methodist University Press, 1967.

Gauthier, Xavière. *Leonor Fini*. Paris: Musée de Poche, 1973.

Giedion-Welcker, Carola. *Jean Arp*. Documentation by Marguerite Hagenbach. Translated by Norbert Guterman. New York: Harry N. Abrams, 1958.

Guibbert, Jean Paul. *Leonor Fini Graphique*. Lausanne: Editions Clairefontaine, 1971.

Hammacher-van den Brande, Renilde, ed. *Paul Delvaux*. Exhibition catalogue. Munich: Kunsthalle der Hypo-Kulturstiftung; Hirmer Verlag, 1989.

d'Harnoncourt, Anne, and Kynaston McShine, eds. *Marcel Duchamp*. Exhibition catalogue. Philadelphia: Philadelphia Museum of Art, 1973.

Hubert, Renée Riese. *Surrealism and the Book*. Berkeley and Los Angeles: University of California Press, 1988.

———. *Magnifying Mirrors: Women, Surrealism, and Partnership*. Lincoln: University of Nebraska Press, 1994.

Hunter, Sam. *Joan Miró: His Graphic Work*. New York: Harry N. Abrams, 1962.

Jean, Marcel, ed. *The History of Surrealist Painting*. Translated by Simon Watson Taylor. New York: Grove Press, 1960.

———. *The Autobiography of Surrealism*. Documents of Twentieth-Century Art. New York: Viking Press, 1980.

Kent Fine Arts. *Dorothea Tanning: On Paper, 1948–1986*. Exhibition catalogue. New York: Kent Fine Arts, 1987.

Krauss, Rosalind E., Jane Livingston, and Dawn Ades. *L'Amour fou: Photography and Surrealism*. Exhibition catalogue. Washington, D.C.: Corcoran Gallery of Art; New York: Abbeville Press, 1985.

Langsner, Jules. *Man Ray*. Exhibition catalogue. Los Angeles: Los Angeles County Museum of Art, 1966.

Levy, Julien. *Surrealism*. New York: Black Sun Press, 1936.

Lippard, Lucy R., ed. *Surrealists on Art*. Englewood Cliffs, N.J.: Prentice-Hall, 1970.

Lust, Herbert. *Hans Bellmer*. New York: Isidore Ducasse Fine Arts, 1990.

de Margerie, Anne. *Valentine Hugo, 1887–1968*. Paris: J. Damase, 1983.

Mason, Rainer Michael. *Vrai Dali, fausse gravure: L'Oeuvre imprimé, 1930–1934*. Exhibition catalogue. Geneva: Cabinet des estampes, Musée d'art et d'histoire, 1992.

Mayor Gallery. *Victor Brauner, 1903–1966*. Exhibition catalogue. London: Mayor Gallery, 1987.

Melly, George. *Paris and the Surrealists*. New York: Thames and Hudson, 1991.

Merewether, Charles, Catherine David, and Lowery Stokes Sims. *Wifredo Lam: A Retrospective of Works on Paper*. Exhibition catalogue. New York: Americas Society Art Gallery, 1992.

Meuris, Jacques. *Paul Delvaux*. Exhibition catalogue. Tokyo: Musée national d'art moderne, 1975.

———. *Magritte*. Translated by J. A. Underwood. New York: Overlook Press, 1990.

Minneapolis Institute of Arts. *Arp, 1886–1966*. Translated by John Gabriel et al. Exhibition catalogue. Cambridge: Cambridge University Press, 1987.

Morris, Cyril Brian. *Surrealism and Spain, 1920–1936*. Cambridge: Cambridge University Press, 1972.

Mourlot, Fernand, et al. *Joan Miró: Lithographs*. 6 vols. New York: Tudor Publishing, 1972–92.

Musée d'art moderne de la ville de Paris. *Miró: L'Oeuvre graphique*. Exhibition catalogue. Paris: Musée d'art moderne de la ville de Paris, 1974.

———. *Wifredo Lam: 1902–1982*. Exhibition catalogue. Paris: Musée d'art moderne de la ville de Paris, 1983.

Musée national d'art moderne, Centre Georges Pompidou. *Styrsky, Toyen, Heisler*. Exhibition catalogue. Paris: Musée national d'art moderne, Centre Georges Pompidou, 1982.

Nadeau, Maurice. *Les Dessins de Paul Delvaux*. Paris: Denoël, 1967.

Naumann, Francis M. *New York Dada, 1915–23*. New York: Harry N. Abrams, 1994.

Palais des beaux-arts, Brussels, and Centre national d'art et de culture Georges Pompidou, Paris. *Retrospective Magritte*. Exhibition catalogue. Paris: Centre national d'art et de culture Georges Pompidou, 1978.

Passeron, Roger. *André Masson: Gravures, 1924–1972*. Fribourg: Office du Livre, 1973.

Peterson, Donald E., et al. *Joan Miró: A Retrospective*. Exhibition catalogue. New York: Solomon R. Guggenheim Museum; New Haven: Yale University Press, 1987.

Philadelphia Museum of Art. *Joan Miró: Prints and Books*. Exhibition catalogue. Philadelphia: Philadelphia Museum of Art, 1966.

Pieyre de Mandiargues, André. *Le Trésor cruel de Hans Bellmer*. Paris: Editions le Sphinx, 1979.

Plazy, Gilles. *Dorothea Tanning*. Paris: Filipacchi Books, 1979.

Poling, Clark V. *Surrealist Vision and Technique: Drawings and Collages from the Pompidou Center and the Picasso Museum, Paris*. Atlanta: Michael C. Carlos Museum, Emory University, 1996.

Raeburn, Michael, ed. *Salvador Dalí: The Early Years*. Exhibition catalogue. London: Hayward Gallery; Thames and Hudson, 1994.

Rainwater, Robert, ed. *Max Ernst: Beyond Surrealism: A Retrospective of the Artist's Books and Prints*. Exhibition catalogue. New York: New York Public Library; Oxford: Oxford University Press, 1986.

Read, Herbert, ed. *Surrealism*. London: Faber and Faber, 1936.

———. *Dada and Surrealist Art*. New York: Harry N. Abrams, 1968.

———. *Miró in the Collection of the Museum of Modern Art*. New York: Museum of Modern Art, 1973.

Robert Elkon Gallery. *Paul Delvaux, René Magritte*. Exhibition catalogue. New York, 1988.

Rossier, Elisabeth, and Charles Goerg. *Max Ernst: Oeuvre gravé: Dessins, frottages et collages*. Exhibition catalogue. Geneva: Cabinet des estampes, Musée d'art et d'histoire, 1970.

Rubin, William S. *Dada, Surrealism, and Their Heritage*. Exhibition catalogue. New York: Museum of Modern Art, 1968.

Rubin, William S., et al. *Matta*. Exhibition catalogue. New York: Museum of Modern Art, 1957.

———. *Giorgio de Chirico*. Exhibition catalogue. Munich: Haus der Kunst; Paris: Musée national d'art moderne, Centre Georges Pompidou, 1982.

Rubin, William S., and Carolyn Lanchner. *André Masson*. Exhibition catalogue. New York: Museum of Modern Art, 1976.

Sayag, Alain. *Hans Bellmer, photographe*. Exhibition catalogue. Paris: Musée national d'art moderne, Centre Georges Pompidou; Filipacchi, 1983.

Sayag, Alain, and Claude Schweisguth. *Matta*. Exhibition catalogue. Paris: Musée national d'art moderne, Centre Georges Pompidou, 1985.

Schmitt, Ursula. *Matta: Kataloget over en nasten komplet samling af Mattas grafiske arbejder*. Exhibition catalogue. Silkeborg, Sweden: Silkeborg Museum, 1968.

Scott, David H. T. *Paul Delvaux: Surrealizing the Nude*. Essays in Art and Culture. London: Reaktion, 1992.

Serger, Helen. *Hans Bellmer: Graphic Work*. Exhibition catalogue. New York: Helen Serger-La Boetie and Janice Banks, 1973.

Soby, James Thrall. *The Early Chirico*. New York: Dodd, Mead, and Company, 1941. Rev. ed., published under the title *Giorgio de Chirico*. New York: Museum of Modern Art, 1955.

———. *Salvador Dalí: Paintings, Drawings, Prints*. Exhibition catalogue. New York: Museum of Modern Art, 1941.

———. *Yves Tanguy*. Exhibition catalogue. New York: Museum of Modern Art, 1955.

———. *Arp*. Exhibition catalogue. New York: Museum of Modern Art, 1958.

———. *René Magritte*. Exhibition catalogue. New York: Museum of Modern Art, 1965.

———, ed. *Joan Miró*. Exhibition catalogue. New York: Museum of Modern Art, 1959.

Solomon R. Guggenheim Museum. *Max Ernst: A Retrospective*. Exhibition catalogue. New York: Solomon R. Guggenheim Museum, 1975.

Spies, Werner. *Loplop: The Artist in the Third Person*. New York: George Braziller, 1983.

———. *Max Ernst: Frottages*. Translated by Joseph M. Bernstein. Rev. ed. New York: Thames and Hudson, 1986.

———, ed. *Max Ernst: A Retrospective*. Exhibition catalogue. London: Tate Gallery; Munich: Prestel, 1991.

Stella, Dominique. *Victor Brauner, 1903–1966*. Exhibition catalogue. Milan: Galleria Credito Valtellinese; Mazzotta, 1995.

Stich, Sidra. *Anxious Visions: Surrealist Art*. Exhibition catalogue. Berkeley: University Art Museum; New York: Abbeville Press, 1990.

Stubbe, Wolf. *Graphic Arts in the Twentieth Century*. New York and London: Praeger, 1963.

Tanning, Dorothea. *Birthday*. Santa Monica, Calif.: Lapis Press, 1986.

Waldberg, Patrick. *Totems and Tabous: Lam, Matta, Penalba*. Exhibition catalogue. Paris: Musée d'art moderne de la ville de Paris, 1968.

Webb, Peter, and Robert Short. *Hans Bellmer*. London and New York: Quartet Books, 1985.

Westerdahl, Eduardo. *Oscar Dominguez*. Madrid: Servicio de Publicaciones del Ministerio de Educacion y Ciencia, 1971.

Wilson, Sarah. *Dorothea Tanning between Lives: Works on Paper*. Exhibition catalogue. London: Runkel-Hue-Williams, 1989.

Yves Tanguy: Un Recueil de ses oeuvres / A Summary of His Works. New York: Pierre Matisse, 1963.

Zuckerman, Neil P. *Leonor Fini, the Artist as Designer: An Exhibition of Ballet, Theater, Film, Book, and Commercial Designs*. Exhibition catalogue. New York: 112 Greene Street; CFM, 1992.

Index

Numbers in **BOLDFACE** refer to illustrations.

Photography Credits

Photographers and/or sources of illustrations, whose courtesy is gratefully acknowledged, are listed below.

Giraudon/Art Resource, NY: Fig. 2
Photograph ©The Museum of Modern Art, New York: Fig. 14

CATALOGUE DESIGN
SoS, Los Angeles

EDITOR
Karen Jacobson

INDEXER
Kathleen Preciado

Composed on a Quadra 840AV with Quark Xpress using Typewriter Elite, Typewriter Gothic, and Fournier typefaces. Printed in an edition of 2,500 softcover and 3,500 casebound on Moistrite Matte by the Stinehour Press, Lunenburg, Vermont.